THE HOME-FRONT WAR

Recent Titles in
Contributions in American History

THE HOME-FRONT WAR

World War II and American Society

Edited by
Kenneth Paul O'Brien and
Lynn Hudson Parsons

Prepared under the auspices of
the Research Foundation of the State University
of New York and the National Endowment for
the Humanities

Contributions in American History, Number 161
David E. Kyvig, Series Adviser

GREENWOOD PRESS
Westport, Connecticut • London

Library of Congress Cataloging-in-Publication Data

The home-front war : World War II and American society / edited by
Kenneth Paul O'Brien and Lynn Hudson Parsons.
        p.   cm.—(Contributions in American history, ISSN 0084–9219
; no. 161)
     "Prepared under the auspices of the Research Foundation of the State
University of New York and the National Endowment for the Humanities."
     Includes bibliographical references (p.   ) and index.
     Contents: World War II and the Bill of Rights / Richard Polenberg
—Hollywood and the politics of representation : women, workers,
and African Americans in World War II movies / Clayton R. Koppes—
Creating "Common Ground" on the home front : race, class, and
ethnicity in a 1940s quarterly magazine / William C. Beyer—"My
children are my jewels" : Italian-American generations during World
War II / George E. Pozzetta—Remembering Rosie : advertising
images of women in World War II / Maureen Honey—Women defense
workers in World War II : views on gender equality in Indiana /
Nancy Felice Gabin—"The vice admiral" : Margaret Chase Smith and the
investigation of congested areas in wartime / Janann Sherman—Did
the "good war" make good workers? / John Modell—Bad news from the
good war : democracy at home during World War II / Roger Daniels.
    ISBN 0–313–29211–6
    1. World War, 1939–1945—United States. 2. United States—Social
conditions—1933–1945. 3. United States—History—1933–1945.
4. United States—Politics and government—1933–1945. I. O'Brien,
Kenneth Paul. II. Parsons, Lynn H. III. Series.
D769.H66 1995
973.91—dc20   95–3803

British Library Cataloguing in Publication Data is available.

Library of Congress Catalog Card Number: 95–3803
ISBN: 0–313–29211–6
ISSN: 0084–9219

First published in 1995

Greenwood Press, 88 Post Road West, Westport, CT 06881
An imprint of Greenwood Publishing Group, Inc.

Printed in the United States of America

The paper used in this book complies with the
Permanent Paper Standard issued by the National
Information Standards Organization (Z39.48–1984).

10 9 8 7 6 5 4 3 2 1

This book is dedicated to Patrick C. O'Brien and to the memory of Arthur H. Parsons, Jr., the first a soldier and the second a civilian during World War II. Pat left the mean streets of Manhattan in 1940 at the age of 19 to join the army. He later saw combat in Europe and, like so many others, was discharged in 1946. But he quickly decided to make the army his career and reenlisted. In 1948 Officers' Candidate School officially termed him an "officer and a gentleman;" he was the latter in any case.

Art devoted considerable time away from his municipal librarian's job, sallying forth as an air raid warden in a coastal Massachusetts town, organizing war bond drives, raising money for the American Red Cross, and, most important, quietly filing away the extra war posters that came into his office from the Office of War Information. Nearly half a century later, they were discovered by his eldest son. They provided the inspiration for "Lest We Forget." We haven't, and we won't.

K. P. O'B.

L. H. P.

Contents

Acknowledgments

This book is a product of "*Lest We Forget*," a Public Humanities Project commemorating the 50th anniversary of America's entry into World War II, held in the Rochester (New York) area between October 1991 and December 1992. It was funded by a $250,000 grant from the National Endowment for the Humanities (NEH) and sponsored by the State University of New York (SUNY) College at Brockport. It included a public lecture series hosted by Rochester's Strong Museum, a combined museum exhibit involving the Strong and several other cooperating institutions, a film festival hosted by the International Museum of Photography at the George Eastman House, and a series of three academic symposia hosted by the College at Brockport. The chapters presented herein represent the editors' choice of the more compelling of those papers, consistent with the theme of the volume.

"*Lest We Forget*" was made possible through the collaboration of several dozen individuals and institutions. We are indebted first and foremost to the NEH, which provided both support for the project itself and for a critical planning conference in early 1990, without which the rest of the project might never have taken off. We—and the readers of this volume—have a debt of gratitude to Wilsonia Cherry, Senior Program Officer at the NEH, who provided help and counsel throughout the entire three-year period of planning and implementation.

Four nationally known scholars—D'Ann Campbell, Walter LaFeber, Leo Ribuffo, and Melvin Small—took time off from their crowded academic schedules to act as consultants, advisers, and contributors to the entire project. Rollie Adams, President and chief executive officer of the Strong Museum, was involved with the planning virtually from the start and was most generous in his encouragement and overall support. So too was John Van de Wetering, President of the SUNY College at Brockport, who offered encouragement when the project was but a gleam in our eyes. Our colleague Joan Shelley Rubin did a superb job in coordinating the combined museum exhibits, as did Carolyn Vacca, the Deputy County Historian, who shared in every step of the planning and writing of the award-wining exhibit, "The War Comes Home: Monroe County and the Second World War."

We are grateful to Richard Black, Richard Incardona, Nick Mascari, and Karla Merrifield of the SUNY College at Brockport's Community Relations Office for their prize-winning promotional efforts on behalf of "*Lest We Forget*." Susan Nurse, the assistant project director, took on the challenge of handling the schedules and lodging accommodations of the dozens of participants, acting at times as hostess, travel guide, gofer, correspondent, and diplomat. She played all the roles exceedingly well. Barbara Thompson and John Butz assisted with the compilation and editing of the bibliography. Jeanne Saraceni, of the college's Documents Preparation Center, typed the final manuscript. As always, Brenda Peake, our departmental secretary, was there whenever we needed her, which was often.

To our wives, Diane and Anne, who faithfully attended nearly all the events connected to "*Lest We Forget*" whether they wanted to or not—and who at times threatened to give a new meaning to the term "war widow"—we reaffirm our love and affection. We promise we won't try anything like this again, at least for a while.

K. P. O'B.

L. H. P.

THE HOME-FRONT WAR

1

Introduction: The Home-Front War

Kenneth Paul O'Brien and Lynn Hudson Parsons

Timuel Black, an African American from Chicago, returned to the United States at the end of World War II with deeply mixed feelings about his country. "We're coming up the Hudson River," he told Studs Terkel:

You could see the shore. The white soldiers upon deck said, "There she is!" They're talking about the Statue of Liberty. There's a great outburst. I'm down below and I'm sayin', Hell, I'm not goin' up there. Damn that. All of a sudden, I found myself with tears, cryin' and saying the same thing they were saying. Glad to be home, proud of my country, as irregular as it is. Determined that it could be better. Just happy that I had survived and buoyed up by the enthusiasm of the moment. I could no longer push my loyalty back, even with all the bitterness that I had.[1]

His tears, begrudging "loyalty," and "bitterness" were the products of the gulf between the egalitarian rhetoric of what some call the American creed and the reality of living in a multi-racial society that systematically denied opportunities, even rights, to vast numbers of its citizens.

Paradoxically, this gulf had been both exposed and papered over by the American government's need to mobilize all groups behind a war effort that generated millions of posters, words, and images, all aimed at including as many Americans as possible in what came to be called the war effort.[2] This campaign sought to engage the energies of all Americans in the work of war, whether on the battlefield or on the home front. Even those who traditionally had been refused economic opportunities and rights were the subjects of specific appeals, but the unity campaign was waged within parameters set by the traditions of sexism, racism, and segregation. In the organization for total war there were limits to calls for inclusion.

Like all wars, World War II became both a series of discrete events that people had experienced and a collection of memories assigning meaning to those experiences. In time, the remembered terrors, problems, and pains of the war years receded, leaving a collective residue of good feeling, one that Studs Terkel captured in 1984 with his ironically entitled book, "*The Good War*." Many of Terkel's colleagues, as he liked to call those he interviewed, remembered the war era as years of great difficulty, both personal and national, but for others—and for millions of their fellow Americans—the title held no irony. It was understood as a literal truth. As the authors of *The Homefront: America During World War II* concluded in 1984: "Many of the wartime generation . . . still consider those years our country's finest hour. This nostalgic view . . . becomes, in its own way, a legacy of World War II."[3]

How do we explain this phenomenon, that the most destructive war of the century could become transmuted in memory into a golden age? First, framed by the stark deprivation of the depression on one side and the ambiguities of the cold war on the other, the war years became a haven of certainty, a clear demonstration of national power and purpose. Second, the violence that occurred was often abroad, out of sight of the overwhelming majority of Americans. Given the domestic violence of the 1930s and the internecine warfare of the McCarthyite 1950s, the war years themselves appeared oddly peaceful, at least when the focus is confined to domestic tranquility. The temptation to see World War II in these terms was, and remains, great. Even so well informed and generally caustic a historian as William L. O'Neill concluded his recent history of these years with a paean to his father's generation:

This country proved that ethnic diversity enriched rather than weakened. Its fighting men met every test. Its leaders may have faltered, but did not fail. The people overcame their enemies, surmounting as well the difficulties presented by allies, a chaotic and divided government . . . to gain . . . "the inevitable triumph." "Sweet land of liberty," the children sang, and so it was, and so it would remain—thanks to a great generation.[4]

In looking back at these years, memory has proven to be misleading. Our collective memory, for example, has created a misunderstanding about the nation's war aims. The horror of the Holocaust has recast the struggle into a moral conflict that the American combatants themselves rarely, if ever, felt.[5] There is irony here in the notion that the war was primarily a struggle against racial bigotry. The obscenity of the Nazis' organized mass murders made it ever more difficult in the post-war years to sustain the traditional arguments that had fostered American patterns of exclusion, whether based on religious, ethnic, or racial distinctions. In the end, there was little question that the official national government position followed, albeit reluctantly, American wartime ideological statements, tilting away from a separatist past and toward a more inclusive future. This proved to be the case, despite the continuation of deep-seated patterns of racial discrimination that often resulted in violence in post-war America.

That was not the only misleading American memory of the war. One of the most striking—yet least-remembered characteristics of this war—was its utter disregard for human life. World War II unleashed powers of destruction previously unimagined, devastating much of the Eurasian land mass before it was finally over. Tarawa, Iwo Jima, Hiroshima, Dresden, Dachau--all are part of the heritage of this war, a conflict that touched almost every corner of the planet, killing over 50 million human beings, the majority of whom were civilians. Dropping atomic bombs on two Japanese cities in August 1945, then, was the final legacy. In modern parlance, this war took few prisoners.

For the overwhelming majority of Americans, particularly those who had remained on the home front, their direct experience of the war was quite different. They had little opportunity to witness its destructive power, other than that provided by the newsreel images that flickered weekly across America's theater screens. As numerous historians have remarked, the United States alone among the major belligerents emerged from the war with almost no physical damage to its cities and towns. Of the more than 50 million humans who were killed by the war, fewer than 1 percent were Americans. American skies, unlike those in Europe and Asia, were often filled with fireworks, which celebrated one or another of the seven successful bond drives, each an occasion for fondly remembered public celebrations of national unity.

Bond drives were more than a necessary means for financing the war; they were intended as constant reminders for those at home that there was, in fact, a war being fought an ocean away. Home-front sacrifices, all were reminded, were necessary for battlefield success. People at home had a range of sponsored activities that linked them to both those on the battlefields that ranged across the globe and to one another in common cause. Rationing programs that began with rubber and gasoline soon spread to greatly desired foods, including meats, coffee, and butter. When interviewed about rationing, wartime survivors often respond with stories of "oleo," that white vegetable fat that had to be laced with yellow food coloring to give it the appearance, certainly not the texture or taste, of butter.[6] Scrap drives, milkweed pod collections, air raids, blackouts, and numerous Red Cross activities were also part of the day-to-day wartime life of most American communities, providing constant reminders of war needs.

Changes in the normal rhythms of life were everywhere apparent, but nowhere more evident than in the newly expanded factories. The war increased the productive power of the society. Americans, young and old, male and female, of every hue and religious persuasion, were asked to put aside their traditional competition for jobs and stream into factories that now, for the first time in a generation, employed almost everyone. Between 1940 and 1944, unemployment fell from the still depressed level of nearly 10 percent to 1.3 percent, necessitating the creation of the War Manpower Commission in 1942 to keep the factories supplied with workers. With millions of employable young men in uniform, home-front workers were more representative of the general population than ever before. Beginning in 1943, as the manpower pool dwindled, women were brought into manufacturing positions in record numbers, increasing their share of such jobs from 22 to 32 percent in the four years of wartime expansion. African-Americans also shared in the newly created job pool, as they came to hold 8 percent of all war jobs by 1945. For many others who had been excluded from the prewar labor markets, including the young and the handicapped, the war also dramatically changed their employment prospects in industry.

Government-sponsored hoopla and economic expansion provided the seeds for what Michael C. C. Adams calls the "myth" about the war. As he describes the myth: "Everyone was united: there were no racial or gender tensions, no class conflicts. Things were better, from kitchen gadgets to public schools. Families were well adjusted; kids read a lot and respected their elders."[7] To help Americans believe in this version of the war years, Hollywood created film after film reinforcing the view. Few in the movie capital wished to challenge the prevailing mythology being orchestrated by government propagandists who made unity in the war one of their major themes.[8]

In reality, of course, America was hardly united, at least not to the extent remembered. Beneath the veneer of national compliance, a black market flourished in rationed goods. When African Americans and women were employed in jobs that had been the traditional preserve of white males, hostility often resulted, sometimes even violence. The same boom that brought endless jobs also brought widespread distress. Small manufacturers found themselves without the raw materials to make goods. Appliance and auto dealers discovered they had no products to sell. If the bureaucracy grew dramatically in Washington, services often suffered on other levels, as many civil servants were enticed into factory work by the higher wages paid by contracts for war production. The same was true for teachers. Local medical care became a problem as nurses and doctors, desperately needed by the armed forces, left their home communities. Family life changed. Fewer men were home to gather around holiday tables. Even those families fortunate enough to have adult men at home often had to adjust to midnight shifts and 52-hour workweeks. Leisure itself became a problem as well. The traditional twentieth-century American pressure valve, the privately owned and operated automobile, was effectively put to rest by gasoline and tire rationing, the 35 mile-per-hour speed limit, and the ban on pleasure driving.   Then there were those young teenagers, many of whom left schools for either the service or war work in 1944 and 1945. Others were thought to be seen running wild in the streets, leading to a chorus of complaints about rising rates of juvenile delinquency.

This war, which disrupted American lives, resulted in an astonishing geographical mobility. In addition to the 12 million men and women who left their homes for military service, 15 million other Americans changed their resident counties by war's end. Millions of southerners, black and white, left their native farm areas for urban centers, following the national highway system to the jobs in the North and West. Among the consequences were overcrowded schools, overburdened housing stock, and underfunded public transportation systems. In 1943, the attendant dislocations had erupted in violence—race riots—in both Los Angeles and Detroit, two cities where the boom economy was at its greatest.

In April 1989, the Organization of American Historians brought together a disparate group of scholars at the annual meeting for a round-table discussion of their wartime experiences. Other than their standing as American historians, their only common bond was age; they had all been young adults during World War II. To commemorate the 50th anniversary of the war, the panel organizers had asked its members to tie their own experiences to the historiography about the war years, combining both the immediacy of personal narrative and the dispassionate reflection of scholarship. That panel, composed of both men and women, people of color and descendants of European immigrants, presented a series of snapshots, each deeply personal, that in sum challenged the prevailing myths about the war. The pervasive racism of the time provided the most vivid memories for several members of the panel, but such memories, as Richard Wightman Fox has noted, are never pure. They "are filtered and patterned; there is no unmediated, unmodified recollection." [9] The scholars' memories were certainly different from those of the "myth," but are they any more true? Had not these historians lived in a particular community, one that reinforced certain of their recollections of years past?

To begin sorting out some of the differences between memory and history as they applied to World War II, members of the history department at SUNY, College at Brockport proposed an extensive project to the National Endowment for the Humanities. The goal was to engage scholars and interested members of our community—Monroe County, New York—in a year-long dialogue that would clarify the issues of personal and collective memory and the written record, looking most closely at the issues framed by the pervasive memory of national unity and the less attractive evidence of divisions based on group diversity. This book, taken from that project, is composed of nine pieces united by several common concerns. First, many of the authors focus on issues raised by ethnicity and gender, comparing particular groups' wartime experiences with those of the broader culture. Second, the history of these groups was lived and understood within the context provided by the government's war propaganda machine, which, through posters, pictures and publicity releases, sought to engender a common sense of purpose. If the first concern—distinct group experiences—forms the frame for diversity, the second—the need for public persuasions—speaks to the limits of the war-induced unity.

The collection opens with Richard Polenberg's "World War II and the Bill of Rights," a consideration of the extent to which civil liberties were curtailed by the war. Since the publication of his *War and Society* (1972), Polenberg has been regarded as one of the leading historians of the domestic American experience during the war. In this chapter, he looks at several civil-liberty issues, particularly those that came before the Supreme Court. Despite a number of landmark decisions that appeared to strengthen civil liberties during the war, the nation's (and the Court's) record was, on balance, much more modest. According to Polenberg, the decisions were infused with a "virulent racism" that had found its way from the broader culture into the Court's chambers. Racism lay at the root of the decisions on the Japanese-American cases. These cases and other misuses of power by the executive branch ultimately curtailed, but did not destroy, the range of expression during the war.

The cultural values that framed specific governmental actions are the subject of the next two chapters. Clayton R. Koppes' "Hollywood and the Politics of Representation: Women, Workers and African Americans in World War II Movies" concentrates on two of the most important creative centers of images during the war: Hollywood and the Office of War Information. Using a selection of films, Koppes examines the definitions that evolved for acceptable representations of gender, race, and the working class. Although loath to allow anyone outside their community to determine the specific content of their films, Hollywood producers were willing to support the war effort by employing less offensive images than those that they had frequently used in the prewar era. But, as Koppes finds, not all imagery was equally susceptible to government manipulation. It proved far easier for government functionaries to alter the representations of women and workers than those of African Americans. This variation underscores the depth of American racial prejudice.

William Beyer's "Creating 'Common Ground' on the Home Front: Race, Class, and Ethnicity in a 1940s Quarterly Magazine" shifts the focus from film, the most popular cultural form, to print, with the story of *Common Ground*, a magazine that began publication in September 1940. Originally dedicated to examining the thorny issues raised by America's European ethnic communities, the periodical later became a vehicle for airing the broadest concerns about American ethnicity and race. In fact, the editors specifically sought African-American writers, while at that same time encouraging Japanese Americans to detail their lives behind barbed wire. During wartime, when "unity" was fostered above all, the magazine survived, indeed, prospered. With victory, however, came different, ultimately more intractable, problems. Beyer's chapter, concentrating on an unabashedly liberal community of writers and illustrators, is an important addition to our understanding of the fragility of wartime "unity" as it faced cultural and ethnic diversity in cold war America.

While Beyer's focus is on the ways in which European ethnics were treated by the intellectual community during the war, the next chapter looks at the impact of war on one of those groups: the Italian Americans, who, it should be remembered, had been defined as "enemy aliens" at the war's beginning. George Pozzetta's "'My Children Are My Jewels': Italian-American Generations during World War II" finds deep intergenerational conflict within the Italian American communities. The war, according to Pozzetta, unleashed conflicts both within the community and between the community and the broader society. This chapter, using Italian language newspapers and records of local social and cultural institutions, looks at these issues for the first time and provides a clearer understanding of the "complex, multipart process of negotiation" that resulted from war-induced pressures.

In part, Pozzetta's chapter illuminates the peculiar problems that the war raised for women—particularly young working women—in the Italian-American communities, who, as they left for war work, found themselves criticized by their more traditional elders. Many women in the broader culture faced similar problems. Maureen Honey was among the first of the scholars whose research a decade ago began to redefine our understanding of women in wartime. At that time, she examined the literary images of working women during wartime, and her contribution to this volume, "Remembering Rosie: Advertising Images of Women in World War II," is an extension of that work. In this piece, she analyzes advertising images from the war period, looking closely at the extent to which appeals for labor participation relied on older ideas of women as both homemaking nurturers and objects of male desire. These cultural continuities underlay the pervasive biases that often pushed working women out of factory gates, returning them to their homes, after the war.

What happened to the millions of Rosies once they passed through the factory gates? Until the 1980s, the experience of working-class women who entered the industrial labor force remained largely unexamined. Nancy Gabin's "Women Defense Workers in World War II: Views on Gender Equality in Indiana" is a corrective. Indiana had a disproportionately large increase in war contracts. As women were actively recruited into the expanding wage labor force, the "boundaries separating women's and men's work were redrawn, rather than erased." Gabin follows this thread of working women's experience during wartime, making clear the complexities that they encountered, particularly in those industries that had been unionized and had traditionally employed males exclusively. Without question, the war provided women with unprecedented opportunities to work, especially in basic industries that were converted to wartime production. What remains in dispute is the meaning assigned to this influx of women workers. Gabin focuses her chapter on the issue of gender equality and concludes that the middle third of the century was indeed "a critical period in the history of women and work."

As historians of American women have documented, the war brought many changes to women's lives, offering opportunities for employment where none had existed before, as well as loneliness, even isolation. Both single and married women contended with innumerable problems that they were ill equipped to face, yet the nation needed their labor in offices, factories, and shipyards. Janann Sherman's study of Margaret Chase Smith's early years in the Congress, "'The Vice Admiral': Margaret Chase Smith and the Investigation of Congested Areas in Wartime," documents how Smith carefully nudged the men who sat with her on the House Naval Affairs Subcommittee for Congested Areas toward a clear, even fair, understanding of the problems they were studying. The subcommittee held hearings in the boomtowns and cities along both coasts, looking at the impact of war industries on these rapidly growing areas. Its attention was often focused on "vice," (by which the members meant prostitution), and on worker absenteeism, a particular sin of newly employed women workers. In each case, Smith helped frame the issues for her male colleagues, deflecting their criticism of the women in the impacted areas toward a greater appreciation of the complexity of choices faced by working women. Her efforts were reflected in the subcommittee's final reports, which proved to be an important achievement for the women who lived in the boomtowns.

As the war provided new opportunities for women, it did the same for men, particularly those who were not in the prewar privileged classes. Patrick C. O'Brien was one of these. He entered the army in 1940 with no more than a 10th grade education from New York City schools. But by making the army his career, he obtained both a formal education and a middle-class lifestyle for his family that seemed most unattainable in 1940.[10] Such anecdotal evidence has been a crucial part of the myth of the "good war": the assumption that it led to extensive social mobility. John Modell continues his recent studies of the impact of the war on the lives of the surviving soldiers with the question, "Did the 'Good War' Make Good Workers?" To provide an answer, he follows a complex trail, beginning with the proposition that military experience would be of great value to postwar business, a position that was given currency during the war. By careful analysis, however, Modell discovers that few employers were willing to grant specific advantages to veterans simply because of their military experience, even when it had involved leadership. They saw little direct application of leadership in war to leadership in business. Formal education, however, was a "coin with which employers were already familiar," according to Modell. In the end, this chapter is especially compelling as it works in uncharted territory: the intersection of military experience, class, and postwar occupational mobility.

The book closes with Roger Daniels' "Bad News from the 'Good War': Democracy at Home during World War II," an examination of some of the less glorious aspects of the war experience. Well known as a pioneer scholar of the government's wholesale incarceration of more than 120,000 people of Japanese descent, Daniels uses Terkel's title as his point of departure for a discussion of Executive Orders 8802 (which established the Fair Employment Practices Commission) and 9066 (which authorized the internment of the Japanese Americans and Aleuts). He places the discussion of the orders in a historical continuum, recognizing that they were influenced by a long history. The war experience, asserts Daniels, was a paradox, a battle waged across the globe in the name of the "Four Freedoms," the very freedoms that were often denied at home. In Daniels's judgment, the government's actions during the war directly set the stage for the excesses of McCarthyism that followed.

What emerges from these chapters (and the recent scholarship of which they are a part) is a complex series of pictures of a modern, liberal society at war. If, as William L. O'Neill's *Democracy at War* reminds us, it was not a "total" war mobilization, it was nevertheless one that dramatically altered the patterns by which Americans lived their lives. Great efforts were made to include almost every ethnic community in the war effort. Women were actively recruited into a labor force that needed them for efficient war production. Unlike the experience of World War I, constitutional rights to free expression were ultimately sustained. Men's life chances were changed by their war experience. But in each case, there was another side to the story. The ethnic communities were never included on an equal basis, a fact that was clearly evident to African Americans at the time. Women were in the factories for the duration only, and even that was not on an equal footing with the men who often worked by their side. While rights to free expression were protected, 120,000 men, women, and children (two-thirds of whom were American citizens) were put behind barbed-wire fences in remote areas with little protection from heat or cold. Finally, prewar socioeconomic class remained a crucial determinant in the race for material goods in the postwar world.

The war's varying impacts on American society and culture, then, were neither easily defined nor understood. Rather than a single garment of one color, they formed, instead, a patchwork quilt composed of different pieces that gave the appearance of unity, a fragile unity often achieved only by maintaining, rather than challenging, many of the long-term bases upon which group distinctions— inequalities— had been built. This complex story commands our closest attention today. Much of the subsequent domestic American political debate has focused on precisely these issues: who is to be included in the operating definition of American society and on what basis? Now, a half century after this cataclysm, many of the veterans of World War II, both those who went to battle and those who fought the home-front war, are passing away. Their memories have provided the rich details that inform our understanding of their struggles, and whether the material was gathered from distinguished historians, Studs Terkel's "colleagues," or Sherna Gluck's "Rosies," it has been essential to our histories. But the memories, whether privately held or publicly proclaimed, are not enough. As this book demonstrates, World War II was the time when the nation had to face its divided and divisive past. Today, we still grapple with these issues, trying to craft a national history that speaks to two intertwined realities: our common national heritage and the distinctly different experiences of a variety of groups. The difficulty of this task was made apparent in 1994, with the uproar that greeted the Smithsonian Institution's announcement of a planned exhibit that would focus on the atomic bombs that were dropped in August 1945, using the Enola Gay itself as the centerpiece of the exhibit. As further evidenced by these chapters race, class, and age were critically important lines of demarcation for the American wartime landscape. That might well be one of the most important legacies of the home-front war, for they remain so today.

NOTES

1. Studs Terkel, *"The Good War": An Oral History of World War II.* (New York: Pantheon, 1984), 282.

2. George H. Roeder Jr., *The Censored War: American Visual Experience during World War Two.* (New Haven, CT: Yale University Press, 1993), 82-83.

3. Mark Harris, Franklin Mitchell, and Steven Schechter, *The Homefront: America during World War II.* (New York: G. P. Putnam, 1984), 239-40.

4. William O'Neill, *A Democracy at War: America's Fight at Home and Abroad in World War II.* (New York: Free Press, 1993), 434. See also Allan Winkler, *The Politics of Propaganda: The Office of War Information, 1942-1945* (New Haven, CT: Yale University Press, 1978), 38-72.

5. See O'Neill's *A Democracy at War*, but the book that explores this aspect of the war years most fully is Paul Fussell's *Wartime: Understanding and Behavior in the Second World War* (New York: Oxford University Press, 1989).

6. See "Monroe County Remembers the War," Monroe County Historian's Office, SUNY College at Brockport, Brockport, NY. The interviews with 83 county residents were conducted by a group of graduate students in the summer of 1992 as part of an oral history seminar. The funding for transcription of the tapes was provided by grants from the New York Council for the Humanities and the Daisy Marquis Jones Foundation.

7. Michael C. C. Adams, *The Best War Ever: America and World War II* (Baltimore: Johns Hopkins University Press, 1994), xiii-xiv.

8. That World War II sparked an outpouring of Hollywood films is beyond doubt, and this story has been told most carefully in Clayton Koppes and Gregory Black's *Hollywood Goes to War: How Politics, Profits, and Propaganda Shaped World War II Movies.* (New York: Free Press, 1987). But this is a story of many facets, one of the most provocative of which appears in George Roeder's *The Censored War.* Roeder opens his second chapter, "A Cast of Millions," with the claim that "World War II was the first movie every American could be in." (p. 43).

9. For the transcriptions of those extraordinary presentations, see "A Round Table: The Living and Reliving of World War II," *Journal of American History* 77 (1990):553-93. Richard Wightman Fox's thoughtful commentary introduces the six recollections.

10. Patrick C. O'Brien is the father of Kenneth P. O'Brien. The son was told a tale, perhaps apocryphal, that his name, his initials really, were an indication of his father's work on the evening of his birth in October 1943. This is just one very small measure of the many ways that the war entered American lives.

2

World War II and the Bill of Rights

Richard Polenberg

THE TWO FACES OF WAR

In December 1941, just a week after the Japanese attack on Pearl Harbor, the United States celebrated the 150th anniversary of the adoption of the Bill of Rights. Marking the occasion, President Franklin D. Roosevelt said "We will not, under any threat, or in the face of any danger, surrender the guarantees of liberty our forefathers framed for us in our Bill of Rights."[1] But a day earlier Roosevelt had declared just as firmly that "some degree of censorship is essential in war time, and we are at war."[2] The president's remarks foreshadowed the disparate way in which World War II affected the rights added to the Constitution in 1791. During the years 1941–1945, certain fundamental liberties received unprecedented protection, and were, in fact, dramatically expanded. Others were abridged in frightening, unpredictable ways. How this came about, and why, is the subject of this chapter.

The course of civil liberties during the war was shaped largely by the nature of the conflict and the absence of opposition to it. Since virtually all Americans believed the war was both just and necessary, fought for honorable purposes against a radically evil enemy, there was very little dissent. What criticism there was, moreover, came not from the political Left, as in World War I, but rather from a minuscule number of right-wing extremists. Consequently, there was little or no public hysteria about internal threats to the nation's safety. The key decisions concerning civil liberties, moreover, were made by President Roosevelt and members of his administration, most of whom considered themselves liberals, all of whom were haunted by the specter of the suppression that had occurred during World War I, but few of whom had qualms about curbing criticism if it could be done quietly and deftly. Many of those decisions were reviewed by the Supreme Court, a bitterly divided body, rarely able to speak in a unified voice.

FREEDOM IN WARTIME

Those divisions were clearly evident in three crucial areas in which the Court affirmed First Amendment freedoms of religion and speech. The first set of cases, involving the Jehovah's Witnesses, saw the justices do a full about-face within the space of three years. A proselytizing group, the Jehovah's Witnesses employed many techniques—parades, door-to-door canvassing, street-corner rallies, and sound trucks—to spread their version of religious truth. The Witnesses were also unwilling to exhibit typical forms of obeisance either to the state or to its symbols. They did not believe they had to obtain licenses or permits to spread the word of God. They refused to salute the American flag, citing the injunction in Exodus 20:4-5 that "thou shalt not bow down thyself" to any "graven image."

By 1940, however, 18 states and many school districts in other states required that children who attended public school salute the flag each day as part of a patriotic exercise. In Minersville, Pennsylvania, a largely Catholic community of about 10,000 in the anthracite region of the state, two children— Lillian and William Gobitis—were expelled from school in 1935 after they refused to salute the flag. The Gobitis family appealed the school board's decision and was victorious first in federal district court and then in the Court of Appeals. But Pennsylvania carried the case to the U. S. Supreme Court. In June 1940, by a vote of eight to one, the justices overturned the lower court rulings and upheld the compulsory flag salute.

Writing for the majority, Justice Felix Frankfurter argued that "national unity is the basis of national security."[3] He added that the Court must defer in this matter to the expressed wishes of the state legislatures. The First Amendment, Frankfurter thought, while it protected freedom of religion, did not relieve citizens from discharging their civic or political responsibilities. Justice Harlan Fiske Stone dissented, much to Frankfurter's chagrin, claiming that the flag-salute requirement forced schoolchildren to violate their deepest religious convictions. In the weeks following the Court's decision, hundreds of attacks on Witnesses occurred, some quite brutal and violent. The persecution continued on a lesser scale after the United States entered the war, and by 1942, three Justices indicated that they thought *Gobitis* had been "wrongly decided."[4] There were also two new appointees to the Court, one of whom, Robert Jackson, would write the opinion in June 1943 that reversed *Gobitis*.

The facts in *West Virginia State Board of Education v. Barnette* were similar to those in *Gobitis*. Three children, whose parents were Jehovah's Witnesses, had been expelled from school when they refused to salute the flag. What had changed in the course of three years was the attitude of the Justices. Only one had sided with the Witnesses in 1940; now, six did. Relegated to the minority, Frankfurter wrote a bitter dissent (his opinion was endorsed but not signed by Justices Stanley Reed and Owen Roberts) that maintained that while the school district's requirement might be unwise, the Court should refrain from overturning the will of the legislature. Judicial restraint, Frankfurter asserted, prohibited members of the Court from writing their "personal notions of policy into the Constitution."

Justice Robert Jackson's majority opinion eloquently stated a different conception of the Court's responsibility. "The very purpose of the Bill of Rights was to withdraw certain subjects from the vicissitudes of political controversy, to place them beyond the reach of majorities and officials," Jackson declared "One's right to life, liberty, and property, to free speech, a free press, freedom of worship and assembly, and other fundamental rights may not be submitted to vote; they depend on the outcome of no elections." Jackson went on to say, "If there is any fixed star in our constitutional constellation, it is that no official, high or petty, can prescribe what shall be orthodox in politics, nationalism, religion, or other matters of opinion, or force citizens to confess by word or act their faith therein." To sustain the salute, Jackson held, the Court would, in effect, have to say that the Bill of Rights, which "guards the individual's right to speak his own mind, left it open to public authorities to compel him to utter what is not in his mind." However important it was to inculcate national unity, he concluded, "compulsory unification of opinion achieves only the unanimity of the graveyard."[5]

Frankfurter was understandably angry that the Court had turned against his formulation. When he learned that Hugo Black, who had voted to uphold the flag salute in *Gobitis*, would vote against it in *Barnette*, Frankfurter snapped, "Why, has he re-read the Constitution?"[6] If anything, however, Frankfurter was even more upset when the Court blocked the government's attempt to denaturalize citizens who had expressed extreme views. Two such cases reached the Supreme Court during the war. The first involved William Schneiderman, who had emigrated to the United States from Russia as a child and had become a member of the Communist Party, to which he belonged in 1927, the year he was naturalized. In 1939, the government moved to strip him of his citizenship on the grounds that, as a member of the Communist Party, he could not have honestly been "attached" to the principles of the Constitution when he took the oath of loyalty.

In June 1943, the Court ruled, by a vote of five to three, that to revoke citizenship on account of a person's ideas would jeopardize the status of all naturalized citizens who had ever entertained unpopular opinions. Writing for the majority, Justice Frank Murphy was primarily concerned "to protect freedom of speech." Murphy did not want any infringement on what, in an early draft of his opinion, he termed "freedom of political thought." In his opinion, Murphy discounted Schneiderman's belief in revolution, noting that both Thomas Jefferson and Abraham Lincoln had defended the right of revolution. The only basis for denaturalization, Murphy said, was the committing of overt acts, not the expression of ideas or mere membership in an organization. The Court's proper duty, he concluded, was to decide the issue on the basis of "the spirit of freedom and tolerance in which our nation was founded."[7]

Murphy privately told Frankfurter, who voted with the minority, that the "faith" of his "whole life" was "wrapped up in support of Liberty." This failed to appease Frankfurter, who replied, "I think it only fair to state, in view of your general argument, that Uncle Joe Stalin was at least a spiritual co-author with Jefferson of the Virginia Statute for Religious freedom."[8] Frankfurter joined the dissenting opinion by Harlan Fiske Stone, which argued that Congress had decided that aliens who advocated forcible overthrow of the government or who were affiliated with groups that advocated it, were disqualified from holding citizenship. Were the Communists to gain power, Stone said, they would establish a regime in which "the freedoms guaranteed by the Bill of Rights" would be abolished. Frankfurter also believed that the Court's majority was acting out of political considerations, since the Soviet Union was our wartime ally. He predicted that when it came to deciding whether a fascist sympathizer could be denaturalized, "there will be some fine somersaulting."[9]

In fact, however, the Justices avoided such acrobatics. In 1944, a second case, involving Carl Wilhelm Baumgartner, came before the Court. Born in Germany, he had emigrated to the United States, had been naturalized in 1932, and the following year had begun making pro-Nazi statements. He joined the German-American Bund and preached the merits of Nazism to a Sunday school class. His diary showed him to be viciously anti-Semitic. The government claimed he had taken the oath of allegiance "with mental reservations" since he favored Germany, and so had committed fraud. Frankfurter now wrote for a unanimous Court. Noting that Baumgartner had expressed his controversial views after he was naturalized and that no inference could properly be made as to his outlook in 1932, Frankfurter added, "The expression of views which may collide with cherished American ideals does not necessarily prove want of devotion to the nation." In his concurring opinion, Frank Murphy maintained that a naturalized citizen enjoys the same rights of free speech and press as any other citizen: "Without 'clear, unequivocal and convincing' proof that he did not bear or swear true allegiance to the United States at the time of his naturalization he cannot be denaturalized." The naturalized citizen, Murphy asserted, "is not required to imprison himself in an intellectual or spiritual straitjacket."[10]

Even more than the decisions rejecting the compulsory flag salute and defending the rights of naturalized citizens, the Court's opinion in the case of Elmer Hartzel afforded protection to First Amendment freedoms in wartime. In 1942, Hartzel, who had worked as a financial analyst for banks and investment companies in Chicago, wrote and distributed three pamphlets. In one, "The British: An Inferior Breed," he claimed that England was a degenerate and parasitic nation. In another, "The Jew Makes a Sacrifice," he held that Jews had helped push the United States into the war and were working to establish a communist system. A typical sentence read, "The slimy blood lust of the 'holy people' now stands revealed." The third screed was entitled, "The Diseased Spinal Cord." Hartzel said that president "Rosenfeld" had been stricken by polio, a disease usually contracted by children. "As with syphilis his paralysis is indicative of severe maladjustments within the nation," Hartzel wrote, "he is in fact a degenerate," and his program contains the "germs of infantilism, paralysis and death."[11] Hartzel mailed copies to about 600 individuals, including several members of the U. S. Senate and House of Representatives and a number of men in the armed services, including the commanding general of the army air forces.

Hartzel was indicted under the 1917 Espionage Act, which made it unlawful to willfully attempt to cause insubordination, disloyalty, mutiny, and refusal of duty in the armed forces or to willfully obstruct the government's recruitment and enlistment services. He was tried in federal district court and found guilty. In October 1943, his conviction was upheld by the Circuit Court of Appeals, which noted that the vicious attack on President Roosevelt could "seriously affect, if not destroy, the morale of the nation, both the civilian and the military." With morale destroyed, "insubordination, disloyalty and mutiny would be the inevitable result."[12] The case then worked its way to the Supreme Court. In June 1944, by a narrow five to four margin, the Justices overturned Hartzel's conviction and set him free. To say the margin was narrow hardly does justice to the Court's deliberations. As Sidney Fine's biography of Frank Murphy demonstrates, the case might very well have been decided the other way.

During the oral argument, Murphy turned to Frankfurter and whispered that Hartzel "was doing Hitler's work in our midst." When the justices met in conference, Murphy sided with a five-member majority that was prepared to affirm the conviction. Given his reputation as a liberal, he was assigned the task of writing the majority opinion. But after a month of "research and reflection," he changed his mind. He still believed that Hartzel was "a very subtle promoter of Hitler's cause" and was trying to "undermine the war effort," but his belief in free speech would not permit him to uphold the conviction. Murphy was now in a quandary: he wanted to change his vote, but in so doing he would create a majority for reversal. He wanted the majority to uphold Hartzel's conviction; he just did not want to be part of that majority! If Frankfurter is to be believed, Murphy then tried to talk one of the other four justices in the new "majority" to vote the other way, thereby permitting him, Murphy, to issue his opinion as a dissent. Finding no takers, Murphy had no choice but to have his opinion become the Court's. That is how Elmer Hartzel's conviction was overturned.[13]

Murphy's opinion, which focused narrowly on the issue of intent, concluded that Hartzel had not intended to cause insubordination or disloyalty. However "vicious and unreasoning" his attacks, Murphy said, "an American citizen has the right to discuss these matters either by temperate reasoning or by immoderate and vicious invective."[14] In view of this ruling, as well as *Barnette*, *Schneiderman*, and *Baumgartner*, it is not surprising that civil libertarians congratulated themselves on the wartime record and breathed a collective sigh of relief that there were no infringements of First Amendment freedoms such as had occurred during World War I. In 1943, the American Civil Liberties Union (ACLU) declared that the nation "is almost wholly free of those pressures" that had brought about repression in the earlier conflict. The watchdog organization detected no pressure "for suppressing dissent"; it found not only that rights were being maintained but also that there were "vigorous campaigns to strengthen and extend them." Two years later the ACLU commented with some satisfaction on "the almost complete absence of repression."[15]

REPRESSION IN WARTIME

These reassuring pronouncements, however, told only half the story. Repression was not almost completely absent; it merely took subtler and more unexpected forms. Indeed, liberals themselves sometimes took positions and backed measures that undermined the protections presumably guaranteed by the Bill of Rights.

Franklin D. Roosevelt had a highly restrictive view of freedom of the press in wartime. Even during the 1930s, the president had thought that the press had treated his administration unfairly; he regarded the declaration of war as an opportunity to impose certain restrictions. In January 1942, he sent a memorandum to J. Edgar Hoover, Director of the Federal Bureau of Investigation, calling his attention to a pro-fascist sheet edited by William Dudley Pelley and commenting, "Now that we are in the war, it looks like a good chance to clean up a number of these vile publications."[16] In May, he suggested to Attorney General Francis Biddle that editorials in the Chicago *Tribune* and *New York Daily News* that were critical of the Allies might warrant action under the 1918 Sedition Act. "The tie-in between the attitude of these papers and the Rome–Berlin broadcasts is something far greater than mere coincidence," Roosevelt said.[17] Again, in October, the president noted, "I would raise the question as to whether freedom of the press is not essentially freedom to print correct news," and he added that freedom meant freedom to criticize on the basis of "factual truth. I think there is a big distinction between this and freedom to print untrue news."[18]

Thin-skinned about criticism, FDR was capable of acting vindictively when reporters or publishers crossed him. "I am all in favor of chloroforming for certain newspapermen," he told a friend, perhaps only half-facetiously, naming people like Drew Pearson, and "some of the more subtle murderers like Arthur Krock."[19] When Henry Luce, the publisher of *Time* and *Life*, applied for credentials as a war correspondent in order to visit China, Roosevelt personally saw to it that the request was denied. On another occasion, John O'Donnell, a reporter for the *New York Daily News*, brought a libel suit against J. David Stern, the pro-administration publisher of the *Philadelphia Record*, for an editorial attacking O'Donnell for having written a story about the convoying of Lend-Lease material to England. In December 1942, as the trial was about to get under way, Roosevelt interrupted a press conference to present O'Donnell with a mock Iron Cross, for services rendered to Adolf Hitler.

Throughout the first year of the war, the president urged Biddle and his aides in the Justice Department, most of whom considered themselves liberals, to take action against far-right critics on the grounds that their speech was seditious. It did not take very much urging, for most liberals shared the president's outlook. Writing in the *Columbia Law Review* in 1942, David Riesman, a Harvard Law School graduate who had recently served as a clerk for Supreme Court Justice Louis D. Brandeis, justified liberal support for wartime restrictiveness. Riesman presented a wide-ranging defense of the use of group libel laws to prosecute antidemocratic forces, and explained the need to "resolutely re-examine the liberal preconceptions, and discard them where they may be invalid." Those liberal preconceptions held that the chief danger to freedom came from a powerful state, when, in fact, it now came from "'private' fascist groups." Riesman concluded that "the Constitution is not a final bar" to such a reexamination, especially in wartime, when "it has become necessary to consider the possibility of repression."[20]

Riesman offered a more scholarly and perhaps a more nuanced way of saying what other liberals stated more bluntly. Aubrey Williams, a veteran of many New Deal battles, told Roosevelt in February 1942: "The *right* of free speech carries with it the *obligation* not to use it to aid the enemy. The Russians have set a damn good example there," he added, without the least trace of irony.[21] Freda Kirchwey, editor of *The Nation*, wrote a month later: "The treason press in the United States . . . is an integral part of the fascist offensive." "They should be exterminated exactly as if they were enemy machine-gun nests in the Bataan jungle. . . . Tolerance, democratic safeguards, trust in public enlightenment—these happy peace-time techniques have demonstrated their inadequacy."[22] One of the obligations a democracy did not have, she said, was to commit suicide.

Not only did many liberals fear subversion and accept the need for controls, but many of them felt at one, socially and politically, with the government officials who were implementing restrictive policies. This sense of personal identification helps explain the reaction of the ACLU to the government's decision to relocate Japanese Americans from the West Coast. In February 1942, when President Roosevelt issued the executive order banishing all Japanese Americans from the West Coast, prominent civil libertarians, including most members of the ACLU executive board, failed to condemn the step. Faced with a choice between two resolutions, one supporting legal challenges to relocation orders not based on "immediate military necessity" and the other supporting evacuation if it had "a reasonable relationship to the danger intended to be met," the ACLU opted for the latter by a margin of two to one, thereby producing what one scholar has termed "a clear victory for those who would subordinate civil liberties to wartime considerations and political loyalties."[23]

Those who condemned relocation were in a distinct minority. The majority view was expressed by Alexander Meikeljohn: "For us to say that they are taking away civil rights, would have as much sense as protesting because a 'measles' house is isolated. The Japanese citizens, as a group, are dangerous both to themselves and to their fellow–citizens."[24] Meikeljohn and other ACLU leaders, such as Roger Baldwin, sympathized with the government officials in charge of relocation, in part, because they were friends of those officials. Dillon S. Myer, who headed the War Relocation Authority, maintained an "extraordinary alliance with leading civil libertarians." Calling Baldwin and Meikeljohn into his office, Myer related, he "indicated that we needed their sympathetic understanding . . . and both men showed a fine understanding."[25] Baldwin, who was "enjoying again the status of Washington insider," met regularly with top Washington officials and then returned to New York City to give the ACLU board confidential briefings, once reporting that the officials are about as much troubled as we ourselves." Baldwin even wrote to General John L. DeWitt, who, as head of the Western Defense Command, supervised the process of putting 80,000 American citizens in concentration camps, to congratulate him on carrying out evacuation "with a minimum of hardship" and with "comparatively few complaints of injustice and mismanagement."[26]

If liberals wished to support their friends in high places, liberals who themselves held government positions wanted to make sure they did not develop a reputation for "softness." Nothing more clearly illustrated this than the decision to prosecute a group of pro–fascist extremists. In July 1942, egged on by President Roosevelt, Attorney General Biddle moved to indict 28 "native fascists" for violating the 1917 Espionage Act. Their attacks on government policy, the Department of Justice maintained, amounted to a conspiracy to cause insubordination in the armed forces. Later, at their trial, the prosecutor asserted that the defendants had tried to induce soldiers to desert. An unsavory lot, to be sure, the defendants represented no danger to the United States, as was evident even to members of the Department of Justice. Yet, liberals in the department favored the prosecution, partly to project an image of toughness. One of Biddle's assistants, James H. Rowe, Jr., informed his chief that the public had begun to regard them as "civil liberties boys" and "softies." "We had better get moving fast," Rowe said, in order to "jack up our public relations."[27]

The trial hardly succeeded in accomplishing that goal. Legal proceedings, marked by disruptive courtroom shenanigans, dragged on through much of 1944 but a mistrial was finally declared late in the year when the judge died. The defendants had legal counsel, of course, but not courtesy of the ACLU. The organization refused to provide assistance, deciding that unless due process issues were involved, it would not participate "in cases where, after investigation, there are grounds for a belief that the defendant is cooperating with or acting on behalf of the enemy, even though the particular charge. . . might otherwise be appropriate for intervention."[28]

The difficulty in gaining a conviction of the "native fascists" suggested that there might be a more efficient way of silencing critics of administration policy. Quiet, informal pressure, backed up, if necessary, by the threat of legal action, could also accomplish the government's purpose, as in fact it did in the case of Father Charles E. Coughlin. Although he no longer had a weekly radio program (which had once reached millions of listeners), Coughlin still published the monthly *Social Justice*, with 200,000 subscribers. "The Jew should retire from the field of politics and government," a typical article declared. "He has no more business in that sphere than has a pig in a china shop."[29] After December 7, 1941, Coughlin, in effect, charged that Jews and Communists had tricked Americans into entering the war.

The outcry against him by liberals was predictable. Dr. Seuss, the future author of *The Cat in the Hat* and *Horton Hatches the Egg*, drew a cartoon that depicted Hitler reading *Social Justice* and saying, "Not bad, Coughlin. . . but when are you going to start printing it in German?"[30] In April 1942, Biddle asked the Postmaster General to suspend the second-class mailing privileges of Coughlin's journal on the grounds that it echoed the enemy's line and could damage troop morale. The same "themes" found in Axis propaganda, Biddle said, could be found in *Social Justice*. Coughlin was quite willing to testify before a grand jury, but Biddle was afraid to do anything that might allow the priest to pose as a martyr. Instead, he asked Leo T. Crowley, a prominent lay Catholic, to explain the problem to Archbishop Edward Mooney of Detroit. Within three days, Mooney ordered Coughlin to remain silent (or be defrocked), and he complied. *Social Justice* ceased publication.

Additional examples of the use of informal pressure to silence critics of government policy may be found in Patrick Washburn's *A Question of Sedition*, a study of African–American newspapers. Early in the war, Washburn notes, these newspapers adopted the so–called "Double V" campaign, demanding victory at home over discrimination as well as victory abroad over fascism. This necessarily involved sharp criticism of some domestic policies and annoyed the Roosevelt administration. Just as the president pushed for action against fascist sympathizers, so he urged Biddle to talk to black editors "to see what could be done about preventing their subversive language."[31] Subversive, in this case, meant language condemning racial injustice, segregation, and discrimination. Biddle, however, proved instrumental in blocking any attempt to indict black newspapers for sedition.

Nevertheless, the government accomplished its purpose more subtly, by the use of pleas, veiled threats, and hints that a failure to tone down criticism might result in the withholding of newsprint from the papers or even in criminal indictments. FBI agents routinely visited black editors in their offices to complain about reporters who, for example, wrote about discrimination against black soldiers in the South. Unnerved by the visits, the black press retreated and became less outspoken as the war progressed. From April to August 1942, Washburn points out, the space devoted to the Double V campaign declined by half, and it was virtually dead a few months later.

One instance illustrated the larger pattern. In January 1943, a black soldier was court–martialed, convicted of sedition, and given a 20–year sentence. At his trial, he claimed that he was influenced by articles in two black papers, the *Baltimore Afro-American*, and the *Pittsburgh Courier*. Rather than publicize his statement, military officials arranged a meeting with the executive editor of the *Courier* and reported what the convicted solder had said. The next day, the newspaper's president, Ira F. Lewis, wrote to thank the army for its "liberal attitude" in not releasing the testimony. Lewis added further assurances that his paper stood squarely behind the government, noting proudly that every employee had purchased war bonds. He realized, Lewis said, parroting the official military line, that "the War Department cannot become a laboratory for an analysis of social ills."[32]

RACISM AND THE BILL OF RIGHTS

The most egregious example of how the war could undermine the guarantees of the Bill of Rights is provided by the relocation and internment of 110,000 West Coast Japanese Americans. Two–thirds of those who were thus uprooted were American citizens. When government officials were considering their options with respect to Japanese Americans, Secretary of War Henry L. Stimson wrote in his diary, "We can not discriminate among our citizens on the ground of racial origin," for to do so would "make a tremendous hole in our constitutional system."[33] The reason Stimson and others eventually decided to dig that hole, and the reason why the Supreme Court refused to recognize that it had been dug, was that most Americans accepted odious racist stereotypes of the Japanese, and, by extension, of Japanese Americans.

As John Dower demonstrates in *War without Mercy*, unadulterated race hatred shaped the behavior of the Americans as well as of the Japanese. The Japanese emphasized what they assumed was their own racial and cultural superiority, regarding Americans as "the demonic other"—immoral, decadent, and barbarous.[34] For their part, Americans regarded Japanese as subhuman and inherently inferior—primitive, childish, and mad. The wartime image of the Japanese was, most commonly, the image of an animal, a reptile, or an insect: they were depicted as monkeys, baboons, gorillas, dogs, rats, rattlesnakes, cockroaches, and vermin. It was often said that they hissed, like snakes. In motion pictures, Japanese were called "monkeypeople" and "ringtails" or "slant-eyed rats." In *Flying Tigers* (1944), an American soldier says, "I hear those Japs glow in the night like bugs."[35]

When the government decided to relocate Japanese Americans, Dower points out, "they were not merely driven from their homes and communities on the

West Coast and rounded up like cattle, but actually forced to live in facilities meant for animals for weeks and even months before being moved to their final quarters."[36] Confined in stockyards, racetracks, cattle stalls at fairgrounds, they were even housed for a time in converted pigpens. When they finally got to the concentration camps, they might find that state medical authorities tried to prevent them from receiving medical care or, as in Arkansas, refused to permit doctors to issue state birth certificates to children born in the camps, as if to deny the infants' legal existence, not to mention their humanity. Later, when the time came to begin releasing them from the camps, racist attitudes often blocked their resettlement.

The decision to intern Japanese Americans was based largely on the argument, made at the time by Earl Warren, then Attorney General of California, that it was impossible to tell the loyal Japanese Americans from the disloyal: when dealing with "the Caucasian race we have methods that will test the loyalty of them. . . . But when we deal with the Japanese we . . . cannot form any opinion that we believe to be sound."[37] The decision to keep the internees in the camps when no possible justification any longer existed was also based on racism. In the winter of 1943–44, Biddle said the practice of keeping "loyal American citizens in concentration camps on the basis of race" for any longer than was militarily necessary is "repugnant to the principles of our government."[38] But at a cabinet meeting in May, 1944, Stimson convinced Biddle that terminating the program would make a "row" on the West Coast. Secretary of the Interior Harold Ickes urged Roosevelt to open the gates, for keeping innocent people in camps "would be a blot upon the history of this country."[39] In June 1944, however, the president decided against any sudden action. "The whole problem, for the sake of internal quiet, should be handled gradually," he said.[40]

In weighing the constitutionality of the relocation and internment program, the Supreme Court fell victim to the prevailing racist mood. In 1943, in the Hirabayashi case, the Court ruled that a curfew affecting only Japanese-American citizens was constitutional. Chief Justice Harlan Fiske Stone said in conference that "it is jarring to me that U.S. citizens were subjected to this treatment," but he added that the constitutionality of the curfew depended on whether a reasonable basis for imposing it existed at the time.[41] Writing for a unanimous Court, he conceded that racial distinctions in law were "odious to a free people" but maintained that the "racial attachments" of Japanese Americans to "the Japanese enemy" provided a reasonable basis for the government's action.[42] Frank Murphy was prepared to dissent but reluctantly concurred when Felix Frankfurter and others begged him to "maintain and enhance the *corporate* reputation of the Court."[43]

The Court did not take up the issue of exclusion until December 1944 in the Korematsu case. Fred Korematsu had been picked up by the police in San Leandro, California, after refusing to observe the relocation order. This time, Chief Justice Stone only could muster a six to three majority in favor of

upholding the government's policy. Seeking to win, or hold on to, Justice
Wiley Rutledge's vote, Stone said to him, "If you can do it for curfew you can
do it for exclusion."[44] Although Stone did not say so, "it" could only have
referred to making what Stimson had called a tremendous hole in our
constitutional system—or, given the review functions of the Court, making
believe the hole was not there. This time Murphy did dissent, and he was
joined by Owen Roberts and Robert Jackson. Murphy explained that the
exclusion order fell into "the ugly abyss of racism." His opinion contained
pointed references to "obvious racial discrimination," an "erroneous assumption
of racial guilt," a "legalization of racism," and "racial restriction which is one
of the most sweeping and complete deprivations of constitutional rights in the
history of this nation." In view of these bold assertions, Hugo Black's majority
opinion, which lamely asserted that "Korematsu was not excluded from the
Military Area because of hostility to him or his race" had about it an air of
unreality.[45]

"THE GOOD WAR"?

This evaluation of how World War II affected the Bill of Rights is consistent
with an ongoing historiographical reconsideration of the concept of a "good
war."[46] To be sure, the war did not produce the inroads on freedom of speech
that many had expected and did not lead either to widespread hysteria or to mob
violence. Moreover, the Supreme Court protected the First Amendment rights
of religious dissenters, naturalized citizens, and political extremists and often did
so in language that ringingly affirmed fundamental liberties.

But there was another side to the war, equally important if not as widely
recognized at the time: a president anxious to restrict newspapers that were
critical of his policies; liberals who justified those restrictions and who either
failed to maintain a critical perspective on policy makers or sought to bolster a
reputation for toughness; the use of subtle, informal pressures to silence critics;
and a virulent racism, so contagious that it spread even to the chambers of the
Supreme Court. As Alexis de Tocqueville noted long before in *Democracy in
America*, if a protracted war "does not lead to despotism by sudden violence,
it prepares men for it more gently by their habits."[47]

NOTES

1. Cited in Samuel Walker, *In Defense of American Liberties: A History of the
ACLU* (New York, 1990), 135.

2. Cited in Patrick S. Washburn, *A Question of Sedition: The Federal Government's
Investigation of the Black Press during World War II* (New York, 1986), 41.

3. 310 U.S. 586 (1940).

4. *Jones* v. *Opelika*, 316 U.S. 584 (1942).

5. 319 U.S. 624 (1943).

6. Joseph P. Lash, ed., *From the Diaries of Felix Frankfurter* (New York, 1974), 209.

7. *Schneiderman* v. *United States*, 320 U.S. 118 (1943).

8. Cited in J. Woodford Howard, *Mr. Justice Murphy: A Political Biography* (Princeton, 1968), 311-15.

9. Lash, ed., *From the Diaries of Frankfurter*, 259.

10. *Baumgartner* v. *United States*, 322 U.S. 665 (1944).

11. *Hartzel* v. *United States*, 322 U.S. 680 (1944).

12. Ibid.

13. Sidney Fine, *Frank Murphy: The Washington Years* (Ann Arbor, MI, 1984), 424-26.

14. *Hartzel* v. *United States*, 322 U.S. 680 (1944).

15. American Civil Liberties Union, *Freedom in Wartime* (New York, 1943), 3-4; American Civil Liberties Union, *Liberty on the Home Front* (New York, 1945), 5.

16. Cited in Washburn, *Question of Sedition*, 48-49.

17. Cited in Richard Polenberg, *War and Society: The United States, 1941-1945* (Philadelphia, 1972), 45.

18. Ibid.

19. Cited in Ted Morgan, *FDR: A Biography* (New York, 1985), 561.

20. David Riesman, "Democracy and Defamation: Control of Group Libel," *Columbia Law Review* 42 (1942): 727-80.

21. Cited in Polenberg, *War and Society*, 46.

22. Freda Kirchwey, "Curb the Fascist Press!" *The Nation*, 154 (March 28, 1942), 357-58.

23. Peter Irons, *Justice at War* (New York, 1983), 129.

24. Cited in Walker, *In Defense of American Liberties*, 139.

25. Cited in Richard Drinnon, *Keeper of Concentration Camps: Dillon S. Myer and American Racism* (Berkeley, CA, 1987), 116-17.

26. Cited in Walker, *In Defense of American Liberties*, 143.

27. Cited in Washburn, *Question of Sedition*, 75.

28. Cited in Walker, *In Defense of American Liberties*, 157.

29. Cited in Polenberg, *War and Society*, 47.

30. Sheldon Marcus, *Father Coughlin* (Boston, 1973), 207.

31. Cited in Washburn, *Question of Sedition*, 81.

32. Ibid., 151-52.

33. Cited in Polenberg, *War and Society*, 62.

34. John W. Dower, *War without Mercy: Race and Power in the Pacific War* (New York, 1986), 180.

35. Bernard F. Dick, *The Star-Spangled Screen: The American World War II Film* (Lexington, KY, 1985), 181, 230-231.

36. Dower, *War without Mercy*, 86.

37. Cited in Polenberg, *War and Society*, 62-63.

38. Cited in Irons, *Justice at War*, 271.

39. Cited in ibid., 273.

40. Ibid.

41. Cited in ibid., 232.

42. *Hirabayashi* v. *United States*, 320 U.S. 81 (1943).

43. Cited in Irons, *Justice at War*, 244.

44. Cited in ibid., 322.

45. *Korematsu* v. *United States*, 323 U.S. 214 (1944).

46. See Richard Polenberg, "The Good War? A Reappraisal of How World War II Affected American Society," *Virginia Magazine of History and Biography*, 100 (July 1992): 295-324.

47. Alexis de Tocqueville, *Democracy in America*, ed. Phillips Bradley, 2 vols. (New York, 1945), Vol. 1, 269-80.

3

Hollywood and the Politics of Representation: Women, Workers, and African Americans in World War II Movies

Clayton R. Koppes

In 1941, the United States went to war under the banner of "the people's war."[1] The Roosevelt government's rhetoric and imagery invoked a democratic inclusiveness in contrast to the Axis' exclusivity and domination. The byword for the war effort became "unity"—a cohesive country evolving toward equality for all. In the construction of unity, however, propaganda officials faced a difficult contradiction—the persistent inequalities suffered by women, workers, and African Americans. Crafting representations of these unequal groups that were credible and yet managed to project a vision of unity and equality became one of the principal challenges. In the sometimes contentious, sometimes collaborative relationship between the arbiters of propaganda and popular culture, the representations of unity reflected the political battle lines of wartime America.

Government propaganda efforts focused on the movies, the era's most important medium of popular culture. Hollywood studios were eager to make movies about the war. The moguls seconded the government's view that films had a major role to play in maintaining morale and promoting patriotism. They also rang up record profits as audiences, flush with good-paying war jobs, crowded the theaters. Unlike some industries that were virtually commandeered for the war, Hollywood continued to enjoy relative freedom—so long as it cooperated with the government on sensitive political issues.

Throughout the war the studios' output was monitored and negotiated with the Office of War Information (OWI), the government propaganda agency. Franklin D. Roosevelt, the "great communicator" of his era, created OWI by executive order in June 1942. Heading OWI was the popular radio commentator Elmer Davis, who insisted that his agency's only goal was to "tell the truth."[2] But he also believed, as he confided to his staff, that "the easiest way to propagandize people is to let a propaganda theme go in through an entertainment picture when people do not realize they are being propagandized." OWI's Bureau of Motion Pictures (BMP) was run from Washington by Lowell Mellett, a former Scripps-Howard editor and ardent New Dealer. His deputy in Hollywood was Nelson Poynter, the 39-year-old liberal publisher of the *St. Petersburg Times*. While Mellett and Poynter had the right political credentials for OWI, their inexperience with film—Poynter seldom went to the movies—proved to be a serious handicap in dealing with Hollywood.

OWI insisted its job was to advise, not censor. Poynter maintained that the studios could distribute any film they wanted in the United States, but this ostensibly generous statement masked OWI's considerable power. The agency wielded the moral suasion of a wartime bureau and, moreover, gradually won economic muscle to back up its demands. By early 1943, the Office of Censorship, which controlled export licenses for films, followed OWI's recommendations in almost all cases. Export was critical since domestic exhibition usually covered production costs while foreign bookings provided the profit. If they ignored OWI, studios risked not only their patriotism but their profits. Never before or since has a U. S. government agency exercised so much control over a medium of mass culture.

The BMP's reviewing staff embraced the liberal sentiments reflected in Vice President Henry A. Wallace's "century of the common man." The staff codified its view of the war in a 42-page *Manual for the Motion Picture Industry*, first issued in July 1942 and periodically updated. The manual became required reading on studio lots. The first question to ask, said the bureau, was "Will this picture help win the war?" Emphasizing the decency inherent in common people everywhere, the BMP argued the war was against the Axis ruling clique and the doctrine of fascism. An Allied victory promised everyone a world New Deal—a regulated capitalism with an extension of social welfare programs.[3]

OWI reviewers embraced a protofeminist outlook, progressive racial views, and pro-labor sentiments. BMP's largely female reviewing staff was sharply attuned to what women meant to the war effort and what the war meant to women. They urged the studios to show women taking the place of men on the job, enjoying equal opportunity and equal pay, and putting their children in day-care centers. Drawing perhaps on their own experience, these analysts argued that "American women are finding new expression in jobs they have assumed" and would not "return 'en masse' to the kitchen" at war's end. Hollywood could place a woman in a welder's mask easily enough—it was a new form of costume drama—but women's "new expression" strained movie conventions.[4]

Blacks posed a still bigger challenge. The propagandists recognized that second-class citizenship undermined black morale and called America's sincerity about the Four Freedoms into question. "Any form of racial discrimination or religious intolerance, special privileges of any citizen are manifestations of Fascism," the agency insisted in 1942. But wartime racial realities were a propagandist's nightmare. The Jim Crow system was entrenched, and, as Walter White of the National Association for the Advancement of Colored

People (NAACP) pointed out, African Americans had to "fight for the right to fight." OWI argued that, although American minorities had "not entered utopia," progress toward racial equality was possible only in a democracy. However plausible that argument was for the long haul, it was painful for blacks as they watched the government temporize during the war. White and other African-American spokesmen were disillusioned when the buoyant hopes they had entertained for the movies in the war's early days were repeatedly undercut.

Unlike blacks, labor unions had shouldered their way to a place at the political table under the New Deal. OWI analysts believed that unions had a central place in democracy. They applauded labor's gains during the war, during which, with Roosevelt's support, union membership roughly doubled. Though union issues were not so bloody in Hollywood as in the steel and auto industries, the Hollywood moguls accepted craft unions only after bitter struggles in the 1930s. Most studio chieftains recoiled at OWI's notion that their cameras should be turned to endorse labor organizing.

OWI's protofeminism, nascent racial equality, and pro-union views plunged it into the political turmoil that pervaded the movie colony. Writers (and, to a lesser extent, directors) generally welcomed OWI's approach. The ranks of the Hollywood Left were drawn from these quarters, plus some actors and actresses, where prewar organizing against fascism had been centered. As one moved up the production hierarchy, however, the producers and studio heads looked askance at OWI, both for its liberalism and for its external threat to their production autonomy. (The major exception among the studio chieftains were Jack and Harry Warner, who adored FDR.) Hollywood's political turmoil intensified during the war. To counter the perceived leftism in Lotus Land, movie colony conservatives such as Sam Wood, Walt Disney, Gary Cooper, and Victor Fleming organized the Motion Picture Alliance for the Preservation of American Ideals in 1944. The infamous postwar era of "naming names" and blacklisting was but a continuation of the political tensions roiling the film colony since the 1930s.

OWI's intervention added an explicitly political judgment to movie content control. Since 1934, all Hollywood productions had to run the gauntlet of the Production Code Administration (PCA), the industry's in-house censorship agency crafted in negotiations between the industry and the Roman Catholic hierarchy to preserve the movies' profits by bending to the Church's moral concerns. The PCA's chief enforcer was Joseph Breen, a deeply conservative and anti-Semitic Roman Catholic, who faithfully represented the Church's conservative line on gender roles and political issues. In his hands, the production code, written in 1930 by Daniel A. Lord, a Jesuit dramatics professor at St. Louis University, became a juridical text against which all screenplays and finished pictures were measured. Breen reversed the tide of pictures from the early 1930s that featured strong, assertive women who challenged conventional gender roles. In the late 1930s, the PCA tried to divert and dilute antifascist and interventionist pictures until overtaken by world events.

The PCA's effects were captured by the playwright, screenwriter, and journalist extraordinaire Ben Hecht, who wrote in 1954:

Two generations of Americans have been informed nightly that a woman who betrayed her husband (or a husband his wife) could never find happiness; that sex was no fun without a mother-in-law and a rubber plant around; that women who fornicated just for pleasure ended up as harlots or washer-women; that any man who was sexually active in his youth later lost the one girl he truly loved; that a man who indulged in sharp practices to get ahead in the world ended in poverty and with even his own children turning on him . . . that injustice could cause a heap of trouble but it must always slink out of town in Reel Nine; that there are no problems of labor, politics, domestic life or sexual abnormality but can be solved happily by a simple Christian phrase or a fine American motto.[5]

Not that OWI planned to deviate markedly from Hecht's index of Hollywood masterplots. The "propagandacrats" intended to work within the studio system. They achieved a tacit agreement with the PCA: so long as the PCA did not interfere with political questions, OWI would not tread on the PCA's moral turf. While each agency disagreed occasionally with the other's judgments, they kept their dissents private. The PCA was appalled at *Mission to Moscow*, Warner Brothers' valentine to Stalin in 1943, but contented itself with a subdued warning to the studio. OWI rarely dissented from the PCA's morality and, indeed, sometimes found it too lax. The propagandists worried that a five-time divorcee in *Palm Beach Story* (Paramount, 1942), Preston Sturges's spoof of the idle rich, made American morals seem "incredibly cheap" to foreign audiences. With some modification to incorporate propaganda themes, the propagandacrats found American cinema congenial to the message of reassurance they sought. They readily adopted Hollywood's individualized treatment of social problems. As Robert A. Rosenstone has pointed out, "Dramatic features put individuals in the forefront of the historical process, which means that the solution of their personal problems or their individual redemption substitutes itself for the solution of historical problems."[6]

For OWI and many reviewers, the ultimate mythic portrait of the home front was David O. Selznick's three-hour-long *Since You Went Away*, released in the summer of 1944. The film cost $2.4 million to produce, about the same per minute as his 1939 blockbuster, *Gone With the Wind*. Selznick worked closely with OWI and sounded many of its themes. Saluting what he termed "the Unconquerable Fortress: The American Home," Selznick crafted a message of unity in the face of wartime tensions about women, blacks, and workers.

Since You Went Away is a virtual compendium of OWI-approved vignettes of American unity in the face of wartime dislocations. Over the protests of his wife, Anne (played by Claudette Colbert), advertising executive Tim Hilton has gone to war, leaving her to care for their home and children, Jane (Jennifer Jones) and Brig (Shirley Temple). Anne pulls herself together and assumes the role of wartime mother. She rents out a spare room to the irascible Colonel Smollett (Monte Woolley). She goes to work as a welder—and welds all day without mussing a hair or smearing a line of lipstick. The factory and the war offer her a lesson in democracy. She befriends a Czechoslovak emigré, whose name was "like nothing we ever heard at the country club," and learns firsthand about Nazi tyranny. The immigrant's travail leads Anne to break with Mrs. Hawkins, a snobbish friend from the country club who is more concerned with social status than the war effort.

When Anne and her daughters make a tiring train trip for a brief rendezvous with Tim, they see firsthand the dichotomy between individual selfishness and patriotic sacrifice. Their train lingers in a siding as seemingly endless troop trains thunder by. A businessman grouses in the diner, "If we're late, I'll miss the biggest deal of my life." A navy man who has lost an arm retorts, "I've got plenty of time from now on." European refugees tell how the Germans cut off meat and milk when they moved in. Oblivious to what she has heard, a plump society woman, devouring corn on the cob, spits out that being limited to two meals a day in the diner is "simply outrageous." A more patriotic woman avers, "I swear I can't tell any difference between it and butter." A sailor ponies up five months' pay for war bonds. A wealthy man insists it "suits me if they tax me 100 percent!" Judging from the howl that went up—from Hollywood executives, among others—when the government proposed a 100 percent tax on income above $25,000, his war spirit was as rare as rationed rubber.

Even the film's love interest—the high-speed romance between Jane and Colonel Smollett's grandson, Bill (Robert Walker)—affords a lesson in how to understand the war. Bill makes one of the classic transitions of war films, from a sensitive young man worried about the morality of killing and doubting his courage to a brave soldier convinced of his cause. As facilitator and redeemer, Jane helps him summon his strength to be a warrior. On their last afternoon together Bill and Jane become engaged. When he leaves on the midnight train, she dashes breathlessly alongside as it gathers speed and cries that she'll meet him in New York the next day so they can get married and have a baby! Bill, the rational male, says no: wait until the day after the war. A few months later he is, inevitably, killed in action. With help from a kindly male psychiatrist, Jane converts her grief into war work, postponing college to serve as a nurse's assistant in a veterans' hospital. The scene carries OWI's message that programs were in place to assist veterans in resuming normal lives. *Since You Went Away* instructs Americans in how to submerge personal grief in geopolitical necessity.

As he had in *Gone with the Wind*, Selznick also tried to reassure white audiences about racial tensions, while reducing blacks' complaints. He dropped the stale racial stereotypes a screenwriter proposed to stash in the black maid's luggage: a half-drunk bottle of gin, a dog-eared book on winning the lottery, and a pistol. Selznick sprinkled some crowd scenes with blacks and even replaced a demeaning scene of giggling black recruits when African-American WACs protested after a sneak preview. The main black character, portentously named Fidelia, was played with some dignity by the scene-stealing Hattie McDaniel. But no matter how much Selznick prettied up the picture with heartwarming flourishes, McDaniel remained trapped in the maid's role with its inherent limitations and historical baggage. Miss Scarlett's devoted slave-turned-servant in one war, she is still Mrs. Hilton's live-in maid in another conflict. When Mrs. Hilton can no longer afford Fidelia's services, the housekeeper trundles off to get a factory job—but then returns every evening to cook and clean for Mrs. Hilton, for free. As critic James Agee said sardonically, Fidelia "satisfied all that anyone could possibly desire of a Negro in restive times."[7] In the face of ongoing discrimination and race riots, Selznick promised that African Americans would remain docile people who knew their place and that race relations could be cured by personal sensitivity.

For an anxious public, *Since You Went Away* promised a happy ending for the war through the Hiltons' personal drama. The film closes with the Hilton family circle drawn up around the hearth on Christmas Eve. Pan to father's empty chair. The phone rings: he is safe and coming home! From outside the snow-covered house, we see Anne hugging her daughters in the dormer window as "Adeste Fideles" plays, and a caption appears: "Be of good courage, and He shall strengthen your heart, all ye that hope in the Lord."

Selznick's story of personal sacrifice and growth, family solidarity, and political awareness made *Since You Went Away* the definitive cinematic statement about the home front for OWI and for many reviewers. Ulric Bell, head of the BMP's Overseas Branch, praised the "corking story." His successor, William Cunningham, thanked Selznick for his "splendid cooperation with this office." Most critics saluted the picture, though with reservations. *Life* thought it captured "ordinary American thinking" in a "genuinely heart-warming" way. *Commonweal*'s Philip Hartung wished Selznick had cut the "theatrical corn" and avoided the happy ending of Tim's return. He nonetheless rated *Since You Went Away* "the definitive home-front movie . . . until a realist comes along to show us what life is really like in America during World War II."[8] Selznick's wartime appeal lay, however, precisely in his reassurance—realistic or not—that the war's terrors would work out all right.

What Selznick attempted for the home front generally, *Tender Comrade* essayed for the specific issue of women. OWI was delighted. Ulric Bell gave it "all cheers and hosannas," and the agency's women reviewers termed it "the most effective and moving screen portrayal" of the role of women in the war. The director was Edward Dmytryk, and the screenwriter was Dalton Trumbo, both of whom were members of the Hollywood Ten who subsequently defied the House Un-American Activities Committee (HUAC) in 1947 and were sent to prison. (The picture achieved a certain notoriety when Mrs. Leila Rogers, mother of the film's star Ginger Rogers, testified before HUAC that her daughter's line "share and share alike—that's democracy" was Communist propaganda. Her strained interpretation of that innocent line indicated, in reality, how scarce communist sentiments were in Hollywood films.) Yet, despite a production team that seemingly was attuned to women's issues, *Tender Comrade* subverted women's "new expression" by staying within Hollywood conventions of domesticity.[9]

The story is a simple one. Chris Jones (Robert Ryan) goes to war. His new wife, Jo (Ginger Rogers), gets a job in an aircraft factory. She and three other women pool their earnings and rent a big old house, which is miraculously available, instead of "rathole" apartments. Bolstered by the addition of a German emigré as housekeeper, they devote great swatches of screen time to lectures on democracy and how little, everyday things, from blackmarketeers to hoarding, relate to the war effort. Just after Jo gives birth to a son, Chris is killed, which triggers her soliloquy on the meaning of Chris's death.

To be sure, *Tender Comrade* featured women perhaps more prominently than any other wartime film. Yet it subverted positive images of women at almost every turn. Although the film saluted women war workers, it strongly implied, despite the OWI manual, that they would return to the kitchen "en masse" after the war. The jobs would be there for the men. From time to time women got the politically aware speeches—which were usually reserved for men—about the war issues. They understood how daily activities that might seem trivial fitted into the larger geopolitical picture, as when Jo unmasks an erring housemate as a hoarder in a virtual show trial in their living room.

Tender Comrade undermines its positive appeal with trite movie conventions about women. Jo is a petulant, emotional young bride who needs Chris's strong, rational guidance. The women often appear silly, flighty, and stereotypically bitchy. Jo is "a possessive, dominating shrew," erupted Manny Farber in *New Republic*, "whose cruel, selfish and over-indulgent love and concept of marriage should cure a lot of soldier-home-sickness."[10] Farber's fear of the castrating female—an invocation of another set of gender stereotypes—suggested how tricky this terrain could be.

Tender Comrade offered reassurance that the war's temptations would not disrupt traditional patriarchal order. Life revolves around your man, the kitchen, and children. When Jo flirts with getting a job before the war, Chris puts his foot down, and she yields. "I don't want money," she says. "I only want you." When one husband returns on furlough, all the housemates flock around him and cook their specialties for him. The hard-bitten Barbara, who had resolved never to "knuckle down to any man," decides to date other men while her husband is overseas. But just as she prepares to leave with her date, she hears on the radio that her husband is missing on the sunken *Yorktown*. Appalled at what she was about to do, she cancels the date and blurts out: "I'm just a big no-good dame! . . . If I ever get that guy in my arms again, I'll knuckle down to that man, Jo."

Tender Comrade also implicitly reassures an anxious society that women would not succumb to a danger so great it could scarcely be acknowledged—lesbianism, encouraged by a same-sex environment. Under the code's prohibition of "sex perversion," homosexuality could not be breathed, much less discussed. But *Tender Comrade* goes out of its way to cast the homosocial household in a heterosexual framework. Almost every scene emphasizes that these women are participating in an extraordinary, temporary departure from heterosexual normality. The lesbian temptation presents itself in the all-female "family" the women forge in their new house and in their assumption of male roles at work. But "manly" work does not intrude on femininity *bona fide* of heterosexual purity; the women troop to work in smartly cut work clothes and weld all day without mussing a hair. At home they betray no hint of "aberrant" attraction for each other; they sublimate their passions by thinking of *his* return.[11]

But not all men will return. OWI was eager to instruct Americans in how to experience the death of loved ones in war. Dmytryk and Trumbo obliged with a more tragic—and melodramatic—ending than Selznick contemplated. The film concludes with Jo's soliloquy on why ordinary people have to die to make the world a better place. When she gets the telegram telling her Chris has been killed, she explains to their infant son, Chris, Jr., that his father "went out and died so you could have a better break when you grow up." He didn't leave him any money—no million dollars or country clubs. "He only left you the best world a boy could ever grow up in." As tears glisten in Jo's eyes, Chris says in a voice-over: "Free to live with you, enough food and our own home. That's what the war's about, I guess." She closes the bedroom door and starts downstairs. She begins to break down. She hears her housemates' voices. "Come on, Jo. Head up. Take it on the chin like a good guy, like a soldier's wife should." She pulls herself together, straightens up, walks resolutely downstairs and out of the picture. Dissolve to clouds and then Chris and Jo, walking hand in hand beneath a vast sky, as music swells in triumph.

For many this mawkish ending to a didactic picture was the last straw. James Agee called it "one of the most nauseating things I ever sat through." Preview audiences concurred. "Ending was *awful!* Too much propaganda!" exclaimed a viewer from a preview in Glendale. Another patron felt as if she had attended a lecture on "why we are fighting this war."[12] These audiences were scarcely being propagandized without knowing it, as Elmer Davis had hoped. For one of life's most personal moments *Tender Comrade* provides a political meaning, coupled with the promise of regeneration through sons. We are all soldiers now, says the male production hierarchy. Jo internalizes the warrior code of death without tears.

Whatever the shortcomings of the Hollywood/OWI approach to women's issues, they received a more extensive and nuanced airing than did those affecting African Americans. OWI set out with ambitious goals to improve racial representations, only to settle for occasional gestures in the turmoil of wartime racial politics.

OWI dared not acknowledge that reality. When the propagandists saw that Roosevelt was unwilling to take even minimal steps to secure black rights, they fell back on the catchword of "unity." OWI deputy director George A. Barnes decided to employ "in effect a direct and powerful Negro propaganda effort as distinct from a crusade for Negro rights." OWI set out to "discreetly promote" recognition of minorities' achievements. As an OWI official conceded later, the goal was to "keep us out of trouble, keep pressure groups off our necks." Despite its strong words on behalf of black rights in 1942, OWI found itself backpedaling quickly. In the context of wartime racial politics, the propagandists contented themselves with "discreetly promot[ing]" recognition of minorities' achievements and averting the extremes of stereotyping. A forthright stance on behalf of civil rights had to wait until after the war.[13]

A key test case occurred in the summer of 1942 over MGM's "The Man on America's Conscience." Of the many candidates for that title MGM bestowed it on president Andrew Johnson. Screenwriter John L. Balderston crafted a script reflecting Hollywood's usual sympathy with the Old South. Slavery evaporated. Much of the dramatic tension turned on the personal conflict between Andrew Johnson (Van Heflin) and Thaddeus Stevens, the Pennsylvania champion of the freed people (played by Lionel Barrymore). Johnson embodied compassion for the former slave owners, who returned in glory to their plantations and to the Union. Balderston, who had written the screenplay for the 1931 classic *Frankenstein*, employed his considerable talents with monsters to twist Stevens into a crippled, demonic figure who exploited the helpless Johnson's alcoholism and even consorted at cards with John Wilkes Booth.

Word of this travesty touched off a furor with the NAACP and its liberal and leftist supporters. OWI through Lowell Mellett asked MGM to withhold the picture for a time or at least tone down the offensive parts. That was strong medicine—or so it seemed. MGM protested bitterly, demanding whether "a minority in the country shall dictate what shall or shall not be on the screen through the Mellett office."[14] Perhaps the studio forgot that Hollywood kowtowed to the Legion of Decency and the southern censors and blue-penciled material likely to be offensive to a variety of economic pressure groups.

Both OWI and MGM wanted to put the embarrassing controversy to bed quickly and quietly. Neither party wanted a protracted row over governmental and studio prerogatives early in the war. For its part OWI signaled that improving representations of blacks took second place to the perceived larger war issues. Nelson Poynter told the disappointed Walter White that it would be "a mistake to make a major issue of this film." Poynter explained: "We have . . . to be willing to lose a battle and win a war."[15]

MGM reluctantly agreed to reshoot parts of the nearly finished film—an expensive operation—to "take most of the curse off." The title was changed to the less emotional *Tennessee Johnson*. Stevens' personal villainy was reduced. The film became another variation on a favorite Hollywood theme: the success story. Johnson rises from apprentice to small-town tailor to political grandee.

Tennessee Johnson becomes a paean to American opportunity. At a climactic moment Johnson and his dutiful wife, who represents his better nature, embrace on the word *equal*. As president he applies a putative equality. When he grants amnesty to white southerners, he declares, "Here at this desk where Lincoln freed the slaves, I now free their masters." Johnson shrewdly fends off Stevens' proposal to give blacks "forty acres and a mule"—a measure that is made to seem purely vindictive class politics.

OWI celebrated the resulting film as, in Mellett's words, "a forceful dramatic exposition of the development of democratic government in our country." Agency reviewers also applauded this latest version of the log cabin to White House myth. Democracy and upward mobility were ideal propaganda tools. But the film's message, however satisfying to the majority, was achieved more at the expense of black representations than on their behalf. MGM eliminated the worst racial stereotypes and made Stevens, the freedpeople's champion, less odious. As historian Thomas Cripps points out, these cuts showed that an alliance of blacks, liberals, and leftists could wring some changes from the studios.[16]

But *Tennessee Johnson* also clearly inscribed the limits of the politics of wartime representations. OWI and the studios found tacit agreement under the banner of unity: if an issue was troublesome, write it out. *Tennessee Johnson* contains just four blacks, all of them docile servants in Washington, D.C., and only two lines even hint of slavery. Andrew Johnson applies a formal equality, ignoring the vast gulf in power and wealth between the old slaveholders and their former subjects. The celebration of democracy overlooked the fact that slavery was ended with bullets, not ballots. Until blacks mustered the political clout of southern censors or the Roman Catholic Church, they had to settle for modest elisions and occasional nods of recognition. OWI's formulaic unity, while it was a step beyond Hollywood's worst moments, became its own cage for containment of racial representations.

The temptation to revert to the most odious stereotypes, even minstrelsy, remained strong. When Warner Brothers, often considered the most liberal studio, filmed the Irving Berlin musical revue *This Is the Army* in 1943, it retained the demeaning images of blacks as gin-swilling Saturday-night strutters. In their main sequence the zoot-suited black soldiers, made up as for a minstrel show, strut through a stereotypical Harlem set with their girlfriends on their arms. As they swing past "Dixie's" beauty shop and the "Orchid Club" gin mill, they sing "That's What the Well-Dressed Man in Harlem Will Wear." Saturday-night strutting has given way to wartime seriousness. Gone is "Mr. Dude," with his "flashy tie . . . top hat, white tie, and tails. . . ." He has been replaced by "Brown Bomber Joe": heavyweight champion Joe Louis, who was used in OWI posters as a symbol of African-American support for the war. But the limits to racial inclusion were maintained. When the men in this all-male revue dress in drag, white GIs don the garb of Little Bo Peep and southern belles, while black soldiers are costumed as whores and tramps. As in the real army, this cinematic army remains strictly segregated.

The image of a people apart persisted in other musicals, even when African Americans won recognition for their starring roles. *Cabin in the Sky* showcased leading black entertainers—Lena Horne, Eddie (Rochester) Anderson, and Louis Armstrong. The BMP objected to the portrayal of African Americans as "simple, ignorant, superstitious folk, incapable of anything but the most menial labor," but OWI's Washington headquarters did not want to take up the issue. The picture dismayed liberal reviewers, such as James Agee, who criticized the "Sambo-style entertainers," and Manny Farber, who found the strong performances "well turned decorations on something which is a stale insult."[17]

In *Stormy Weather* Lena Horne broke through to stardom, but in a compromised way. She avoided the jungle and maid roles foisted on many black actresses but remained, as she put it, "a butterfly pinned to a column singing away in Movieland." The film's musical supervisor, William Grant Still, a distinguished black composer trained at the Oberlin College Conservatory of Music, encountered repeated frustrations in trying to upgrade the music and musicians. Twentieth Century Fox producer Alfred Newman threw out his arrangements because they were too sophisticated and chose black musicians who, Still said, "clowned" their way through the audition. The composer noted angrily, "In Hollywood if it's Negro music it has to be crude to be authentic."[18]

In the spring of 1943, OWI abandoned even these modest efforts to change the portrayal of blacks. Southern racists in Congress sharply attacked the agency, in part over its stand on race relations. Anti-Roosevelt legislators hacked the budget of OWI's domestic branch to a mere 10 percent of its former level. The OWI movie liaison continued unabated through its Overseas Branch, but chastened BMP reviewers shifted from concern for black opinion to how the portrayal of blacks would affect the image of America abroad. George Barnes counseled the OWI staff that the most they should attempt was occasionally to have a "Negro speak intelligently" and a "sprinkling of average looking Negro people" in crowd scenes.[19]

Some wartime films contained strong black characters, to be sure. But they were rare, usually appeared only in extraordinary circumstances, and were largely incidental to the main story. In *Casablanca* (1943) Humphrey Bogart's musical sidekick, Sam, though still in the cinematic ghetto of the entertainer, assumes a relatively equal role by wartime standards. OWI applauded. *The Ox-Bow Incident* (1943) was a hit with the propagandists on all counts. Leigh Whipper played a man who courageously held out against the lynching of an innocent man. In Alfred Hitchcock's *Lifeboat* (1943), Joe (played by Canada Lee) is offered a vote when the storm-tossed denizens of a lifeboat ponder whether to kill the Nazi submarine captain they have rescued. His chance to vote is treated as a magnanimous gesture, however, not a right. Implying he cannot exercise such responsibility, Joe abstains. *Lifeboat* meanwhile perpetuates old stereotypes: Joe's nickname is Charcoal, he is an adept (if reformed) pickpocket, he is treated patronizingly, and he logs less time on camera than the white characters, including the U-boat captain.

African-American figures' best chance to bend the bars of the cage of unity occurred in combat pictures, where Hollywood gave blacks more equality than the war or navy departments were prepared to consider. In *Crash Dive* (1943) and *Sahara* (1943), blacks played heroic combat roles, although *Crash Dive*, like the navy, limited African Americans to menial tasks. Perhaps the greatest departure was *Bataan* (1943), in which Kenneth Spencer added a black face to the baker's dozen of ethnically diverse GIs. Though he spends much of his screen time humming the "St. Louis Blues," Spencer approaches equality. He sits in the circle discussing strategy but speaks only once, and then to voice his faith in the United States, not to argue tactics. When he sets an explosive charge, he follows instructions from his white partner, who pushes the plunger. The Spencer character dies as heroically as the others.[20] *Bataan*'s symbolism, however compromised, conveyed a world that was still an aspiration, not a reality.

Although OWI often yielded to cinematic evasions and falsifications on gender and race issues, OWI took a firmer stand on behalf of a key component of the New Deal coalition: labor unions. The agency pressured a reluctant Hollywood occasionally to portray unions as constructive democratic forces.

The movies seldom dealt with the world of work; play was more fun. As critic Dwight Macdonald observed, for the movies "work was the dark side of the moon."[21] If work made moviemakers uneasy, unions were still more troublesome. When Warner Brothers tried to break the taboo on union subjects with *Black Fury* (1936), the Production Code Administration insisted the studio treat coal company management more favorably. *How Green Was My Valley* (1942) treated unions sympathetically, but in the geographically and historically distant setting of industrializing Wales.

Labor emerged as a central—and controversial—theme when conservative producer King Vidor, a founder of the Motion Picture Alliance for the Preservation of American Ideals, undertook his epic of wartime steelmaking, *An American Romance*. Though OWI eagerly encouraged a picture on the wartime production "miracle," the agency was appalled when Vidor followed a Hollywood tradition by lauding management and traducing unions. *An American Romance* exemplified the waste and megalomania a powerful filmmaker could employ. Produced at a cost of $3 million, the three-hour technicolor saga was one of the most expensive films of the era; Vidor wrote his own screenplay, which was revised by no fewer than 12 writers. The story tracked a penniless immigrant from Ellis Island to triumph as a union-busting motor car magnate. The screenplay appalled OWI. "This story is a deluxe automobile edition of Horatio Alger," complained a BMP reviewer, "and if Henry Ford had written it, it could scarcely express the Ford philosophy more clearly." American industrialists were the heroes; unions were sinister. Vidor intended to show work on the assembly line as fulfilling and exciting. Believing the picture could become "one of the most useful of 1943," OWI mustered its political capital to realign the film's labor politics.[22]

BMP's chief reviewer, Marjorie Thorson, compiled a catalog of desired changes. The glorification of management and demonization of unions had to change. Steve Dangos, the immigrant hero, should not work as a scab. When workers staged a sit-down strike at his auto plant, Dangos dispersed them with armed guards and tear gas—"a fascist tactic pure and simple," Thorson said. OWI's suggestions did not go down easily at Metro, the maker of *Tennessee Johnson*. Production chief E. J. Mannix "yelled and screamed," Poynter said, and charged that OWI was trying to force him to make a "'new deal picture.'" Vidor and Mannix eventually agreed, however, to incorporate enough OWI suggestions to make the treatment of unions compatible with the New Deal labor settlement.[23]

An American Romance, released in October 1943, continued Hollywood's love affair with the American dream. Even if OWI reviewers thought its immigrant's progress was idealized, they deemed this message to be good propaganda. Dangos walks (yes, walks) from New York to Minnesota, gets a job in the iron mines, and marries Anna, the proverbial goddess schoolteacher. To their great disappointment, their firstborn is a girl. But this setback is more than overcome when four sons appear, whom they name George Washington Dangos, Thomas Jefferson Dangos, Abraham Lincoln Dangos, and Theodore Roosevelt Dangos—a living Mount Rushmore. Just as Steve is about to leave for his naturalization ceremony, word comes that George has been killed in World War I. Steve and Anna convert their grief into a patriotic ritual, reciting the pledge of allegiance together in their bedroom, then going on to the ceremony. Like *Tender Comrade*, *An American Romance* instructs the audience that war deaths are to be borne stoically and with the comfort that they are meaningful.

Vidor manipulates the imagery of unity to show management, labor, and country—like the Dangos family—sharing a common goal. When Steve's fledgling automobile factory is about to be snuffed out, a working-class cousin appears almost as a genie from a lamp and offers his savings. "Let's all be partners," cries an inspired worker. Forgoing wages, employees pitch in to build a model car, which captures the popular imagination and propels the firm to success. A labor spokesman called it "our dream come true—a wonderful magic dream." In keeping with OWI's teaching, labor and management share the same dream.

Despite the workers' sacrifice for his success, Steve cannot accept the union. His intransigence leads to corporate peril and personal tragedy. The company suffers through a three-month strike, until the entire board, including son Thomas Jefferson, presses Steve to meet the union halfway. The union president points out, "Efficient production demands cooperation between labor and management." Isolated and embittered, Steve rejects the board and his son and goes into retirement, nurtured by his devoted wife, who, like Andrew Johnson's, represents the better side of his nature.

Familial and corporate skies brighten as people put aside parochial quarrels in behalf of something greater than themselves: the war. A labor-management committee induces Steve to return to the shop to iron out production kinks. Steve is reconciled with son Thomas. As the sound track weaves variations on "America," bombers flow from the Dangos plant and soar skyward, as father and son, labor and management, bask in a common purpose.

An American Romance was transformed from a paean to rugged individualism into a celebration of management-labor cooperation. Wartime realities belied this rosy view: the production miracle was achieved in the face of heavy worker casualties and persistent management-labor conflict. But in *An American Romance* OWI liberals and Hollywood conservatives achieved an uneasy truce under the flag of wartime unity.

OWI's monitoring of movies' political content necessitated changes in Hollywood's conventional treatment of unequal groups. The degree of change depended, however, on where each group fitted in a rough calculation of the political and cultural consensus of the era. Although workers and their unions remained controversial, they boasted enough political clout for OWI to fight for them against MGM conservatives on *An American Romance*. The propagandists wanted a "New Deal picture" that showed orderly, responsible unions working for the war effort in tandem with enlightened, union-friendly management. By contrast, African Americans found that OWI bureaucrats, for all their impassioned interoffice memoranda on *Tennessee Johnson*, dared go no further than the New Deal's hesitant, largely symbolic racial politics. Women did not yet form a coherent political bloc, and the unsettling social trends of women's "new expression" challenged patriarchically organized politics. OWI-approved movies, such as *Tender Comrade*, saluted women as war workers, but only if they were contained within a conventional maternal framework. For women and African Americans the democratic inclusion promised by "the people's war" had to await the postwar reconstruction of politics and popular culture.

NOTES

1. The phrase is from "Government Information Manual for the Motion Picture Industry," summer 1942, box 15, Office of War Information files, Record Group 208, Washington National Records Center, Suitland, MD. This chapter is based in part on Clayton R. Koppes and Gregory D. Black, *Hollywood Goes to War: How Politics, Profits, and Propaganda Shaped World War II Movies* (New York, 1987), which contains more detailed citations on OWI, Hollywood, and specific films under discussion. I wish to acknowledge the assistance of my coauthor on the book.

2. Elmer Davis to Byron Price, January 27, 1943, box 3, OWI files.

3. "Government Information Manual for the Motion Picture Industry." (Summer, 1942).

4. Ibid.

5. Ben Hecht, *A Child of the Century* (New York, 1954), 437-38.

6. Robert A. Rosenstone, "Like Writing History with Lightning: Historical Films/Historical Truth," *Contention* 2 (Summer 1993): 195.

7. James Agee, *Agee on Film* (Boston, 1958), 63. See also Thomas Cripps, *Making Movies Black: The Hollywood Message Movie from World War II to the Civil Rights Era* (New York, 1993), 86-88.

8. Ulric Bell to David O. Selznick, September 28, 1943, William Cunningham to Selznick, July 21, 1944, feature review, *Since You Went Away*, July 20, 1944, box 3525, OWI files; *Life* (July 24, 1944), 53; *Commonweal* 40 (1944), 374-75. See also the perceptive reading in Jeanine Basinger, *A Woman's View: How Hollywood Spoke to Women 1930-1960* (New York, 1993), 194-97.

9. Bell to William Gordon, December 30, 1943, feature review, *Tender Comrade*, Dec. 28, 1943, box 3515, OWI files.

10. *New Republic* (June 26, 1944): 850.

11. On fears of homosexuality during World War II see Allan Bérubé, *Coming Out Under Fire: The History of Gay Men and Women in World War II* (New York, 1990); John Costello, *Virtue under Fire* (Boston, 1985), 69-72.

12. Comment cards from preview audiences in Pasadena, December 14, 1943, and Glendale, December 16, 1943, RKO headquarters, Los Angeles.

13. "OWI Recommendations for Negroes," 1943, George A. Barnes to Bell, May 17, 1943, box 3509, OWI files; Philleo Nash, "A Minorities Program for OWI, Domestic Branch," n.d., ca. August 1942, box 18, Philleo Nash Papers, Harry S. Truman Library, Independence, MO. See also Clayton R. Koppes and Gregory D. Black, "Blacks, Loyalty, and Motion Picture Propaganda in World War II," *Journal of American History* 73 (1986): 383-406.

14. Maurice Revnes to Mellett, August 28, 1942, box 1433E, OWI files. See also Thomas Cripps, "Movies, Race, and World War II: *Tennessee Johnson* as an Anticipation of the Strategies of the Civil Rights Movement," *Prologue*, 14 (1982): 49, 54.

15. Poynter to Walter White, August 28, 1942, box 3510, OWI files.

16. Feature review, *Tennessee Johnson*, December 1, 1942, box 3510, OWI files. See Cripps, *Making Movies Black*, 72.

17. Feature review, *Cabin in the Sky*, January 14, 1943, box 3524, OWI files; *New Republic* (July 5, 1943), 20; *Time* (April 12, 1943), 96.

18. William Grant Still to Walter White, January 25, 1945, White to Edwin R. Embree, February 13, 1943, box II A285, National Association for the Advancement of Colored People files, Manuscript Division, Library of Congress, Washington, DC; feature review, *Stormy Weather*, May 5, 1943, box 3518, OWI files; Lena Horne and Richard Schickel, *Lena* (Garden City, NY), 1965), 135.

19. Barnes to Bell, May 17, 1943, box 3509, OWI files.

20. Daniel Leab, *From Sambo to Superspade: The Black Experience in Motion Pictures* (Boston, 1975), 126.

21. Macdonald, quoted in Peter Stead, *Film and the Working Class: The Feature Film in British and American Society* (New York, 1989), 243.

22. Script review "America," November 5, 1942, box 3525, OWI files.

23. Ibid.; Poynter to Mellett, November 12, 1942, box 3525, OWI files.

4

Creating "Common Ground" on the Home Front: Race, Class, and Ethnicity in a 1940s Quarterly Magazine

William C. Beyer

We begin in difficult times. Never has it been more important that we become intelligently aware of the ground which Americans of various strains have in common; that we sink our tap roots deep into its rich and varied cultural past and attain rational stability in place of emotional hysteria; that we reawaken the old American Dream, the dream which, in its powerful emphasis on the fundamental worth and dignity of every human being, can be a bond of unity no totalitarian attack can break.[1]

With this urgent statement of purpose, *Common Ground*, a new quarterly journal of literature, education, and politics, appeared in mailboxes and on newsstands across the country in September 1940. With the United States edging ever closer to open involvement in World War II, the quarterly was, in the words of one of its principal backers, "addressed to the foreign born and to Americans who ought to know more about them."[2] The magazine was the creation of three idealists: Read Lewis, a genteel, cautious, Columbia University-trained lawyer with roots in New England and close ties to the settlement house movement; Louis Adamic, an expansive, intense, best-selling author who had immigrated from Slovenia; and M. Margaret Anderson, a capable, likable, second-generation Swedish-American high school English teacher from upstate New York with an interest in immigration history. Its funding came from the Carnegie Corporation of New York, a foundation that saw itself strengthening the home front during wartime.

Aimed at fostering national unity and forestalling divisions stemming from American class differences and nationality backgrounds, *Common Ground* was published by the Common Council for American Unity, based in New York City.[3] Americans, the quarterly's editors believed, could be unified in the present because they shared fundamental experiences in the past: their apparent diversity masked essential unity. But as the hot war against the Axis became the cold war against Communism, the fault lines within U.S. society shifted from nationality to race. To bridge the chasms among groups of Americans, *Common Ground*'s contributors first looked to persuasive intercultural educational

techniques developed in the 1930s but then increasingly turned to more direct
legal means, which would be used more widely in the 1950s and 1960s. By the
time the magazine folded after the autumn 1949 issue, war—hot and
cold—heightened the tensions that made voluntary national unity increasingly
elusive.

Common Ground's name seems to have been Louis Adamic's idea, although
both Read Lewis and Margaret Anderson later remembered "common" and
"comon ground" as concepts "in the air" at the time.[4] In each instance,
"common" meant "shared" or "united" rather than "proletarian," as it often had
in the 1930s. With the Carnegie grant in hand, Adamic drove relentlessly to
create the magazine during May and June 1940. His urgency was born of fears
that immigration restrictionists were about to fan smoldering public fears of
subversive Nazi and Communist sympathizers into a roaring antialien campaign.
Such a campaign, Adamic judged, would cause recent immigrants to set
backfires of their own, and the spiraling confrontation would deprive all
Americans—new and old stock alike—of a sense of genuine solidarity.[5] Responding to the hysteria in June, Adamic pushed publication up from October to
early September. Throughout the hot summer, he exhorted executive director
Lewis to attend instantly to administrative details and managing editor Anderson
to ready text ever more quickly. By August 10, 1940, copy for the first issue
went to the printers at Princeton University Press.[6]

The editors offered the contents of that first issue as "a fairly inclusive hint"
to its readers of who and what would be subsequently welcomed.[7] Over half the
bylined articles in the issue were reprints, three published as far back as the
1920s. Readers were offered essays by America's foremost literary critic Van
Wyck Brooks, the well-known Maine novelist Mary Ellen Chase, University of
Chicago president Robert M. Hutchins, Harvard immigration historian Arthur
M. Schlesinger, and Adamic himself. Regardless of how new any of the articles
were, all bore on the central theme of diversity: European Americans, African
Americans, Jewish Americans—all were represented. Chase's lead article on
Puritan principles was subtitled "Old-Stock American Traditions." A previously
unpublished prison inmate named William Reilly wrote of second-generation
immigrant disorientation. Polish-American Lola Kinel wrote seriously, and
Armenian immigrant Leon Surmelian wrote humorously, of their Americanization. African-American journalist George S. Schuyler argued against Americans' superstitions about "race," and *Jewish Frontier* editor Marie Syrkin
sketched the appeal of a secure young Zionist for a high school Jewish club.
Besides a bibliography of recommended children's books, the first issue
promised four permanent departments: "Organizations and Their Work" (news
items on local efforts to further "unity within diversity"), "Schools and
Teachers" (news about useful educational techniques or materials), "From the
Immigrant Press" (quotations from editorials and articles in foreign-language
papers), and "The Bookshelf" (book reviews).

The quarterly was unique, but its concerns were not. The threat of war and the need for unity hung in the air. As Adamic, in the first issue, was defending America's diversity in the face of a war-imposed uniformity, other writers were making the same point elsewhere. In the *Southwest Review*, for example, Howard Mumford Jones surveyed the whole of American literary history to counter German propaganda intended to heighten racial and ethnic tensions. Alfred Kazin closed *On Native Grounds: An Interpretation of Modern American Prose Literature* with warnings against aping the Axis's "half-men, the death's heads grinning over the spoil of our time" and imposing a false, external unity upon the cultural diversity discovered and celebrated in the 1930s.[8]

Common Ground fitted prevailing concerns so neatly that it caught on immediately. Prepublication announcements brought enthusiastic endorsement and offers of assistance from, among others, Sherwood Anderson, Van Wyck Brooks, and Oswald Garrison Villard, and during the next six months, reviews hailing *Common Ground* appeared in the major New York papers and in periodicals across the country: the *Cleveland Press*, the *Chicago Times*, the *San Francisco Chronicle*, *Commonweal*, and many foreign-language newspapers. When the first printing of 5,000 copies went quickly, Lewis and the editors ordered a second run of 2,500 more from Princeton.[9]

Exactly who the magazine's readers were, or could be, nobody knew. Who they *should* be the editors knew precisely:

It [*Common Ground*] should be in every public library, on the desk of at least a half-dozen teachers in every secondary school and college in the U.S., in the hands of ministers, priests, rabbis, editorial writers, social workers, and other key persons.[10]

Adamic even dreamed of a large, popular audience eventually among the people who had made his books best-sellers.

Subscriptions came at a heartening rate. By the end of six months, paid circulation had rocketed to 4,000, a strong showing for a new publication with only two issues behind it, especially one operating on "a fairly intellectual basis," as Anderson put it. Besides, $2 for a quarterly was expensive. Subscriptions to monthlies such as *American Mercury* and *Survey Graphic* went for $3 and to weeklies such as *The Nation* and *The New Republic* for $4.75 and $4.50 respectively.[11]

Writers responded along with readers. Each day's mail brought a stack of submissions. During January 1941, 500 poured in, and the magazine averaged 200 per month during the first six months. Educators responded with special eagerness to the editors' obvious interest in their concerns. An article entitled "Schools and Teachers" in the Winter 1941 issue reported on a survey of 300 colleges regarding racial and cultural curricula. In response, at least three colleges in New York, South Dakota, and New Jersey offered new courses. In fact, educators at all levels soon came with "numberless requests" and an increasing flow of scripts telling of experiments at cultivating "common ground" in the schools.[12]

A mimeographed appeal "To American Writers and Literary Agents" struck notes Adamic had been sounding for some time. American insecurity—"the feeling that the 'American Dream' was only a notion, that democracy is washed up, a failure"—fostered disunity. The resulting nostalgia for "earlier Anglo-Saxon America or the Old Country as it is remembered" took on added urgency amid the "crash of civilization abroad." To counter this, *Common Ground* proposed to enlist the "strength, the intelligence, the imagination, the color of the diverse peoples who have chosen this continent for theirs, as the place where free men may still build a good world of their own making."[13]

Pointing to exemplary pieces published in the first three issues, the appeal to writers and agents invited other kinds of articles as well: "Explorations in self-criticism on the part of different national, racial, and religious groups; personal analyses of what it means to be a Catholic, a Swede, an Armenian, Jew, etc. in America now"; "stories of places founded or settled by national or religious groups"; "discussions of the culture conflicts existing within individuals of the second and third generation"; and fiction, poetry, and humor—"everything that will help light up this vast, important subject"—in fewer than 5,000, and preferably within 2,500 words.

As for taboos—we don't want generalities, mere editorializing. We are out for vivid, graphic detail, specific incident that makes its point by implication rather than by editorializing, moralizing, preaching, or too much exposition. We don't want defensiveness or mere anger and exposes. We don't want a negative approach that leaves us hopeless, raging but helpless. Pieces should have a sense of direction, give us some inkling of a place where we can take hold and do something positive about the situation.[14]

These constructive pieces would evoke America in the making and demonstrate how individuals and communities were developing out of America's different nationalities, races, religions, and, as the editors soon acknowledged, regions. Class differences that preoccupied the United States in the 1930s were, tellingly, never salient in *Common Ground*.

The quarterly's early issues bear clear evidence of Louis Adamic's influence. His reputation drew talent. The texts exhibit his willingness to brave controversy. Most important, he coined and collected a vocabulary for envisioning America, and he urged it on all who would share his vision and work to implement it. People still refer to *Common Ground* as "Adamic's magazine," even though Read Lewis co-founded it, and Margaret Anderson edited it in name for 31 issues and in fact for all 37.[15]

The early euphoria was short-lived. In the spring of 1941, Hitler raced into Yugoslavia, the consequences of which soon consumed the attention of Adamic, after all, a Yugoslav immigrant. The preoccupation fueled his growing doubt that Read Lewis was bold enough to make *Common Ground* big enough to become a force ensuring unity within diversity on the home front. By December

1941, just days before Pearl Harbor, Lewis resigned himself to Adamic's departure as editor.[16] Anderson brought out the first issue without Adamic in the troubled wake of Pearl Harbor.

Working as usual at least four months in advance of publication, she had most of the spring 1942 issue lined up by the previous December. The declaration of war meant hurriedly reorganizing some material and scurrying after other material more closely tied to mobilization. Eleanor Roosevelt and Adamic's friend Blair Bolles, diplomatic correspondent for the *Washington Star*, led off with articles praising America's immigrants and resident aliens whose contributions would help with the war and whose fair treatment would provide democratic hope to the world's oppressed. "The Japanese American Creed" by the national secretary of the Japanese American Citizens League and three complicated but loyal reactions to Pearl Harbor by "Americans with Japanese faces" made *Common Ground* one of the first national magazines to publish material by Japanese Americans after Pearl Harbor. Roi Ottley's "A White Folks' War?" asked the frank question that blacks would pose skeptically and persistently throughout the war. Sigrid Undset, the Norwegian Nobel laureate, invited Norwegian Americans to reassess their isolationism in the context of their responsibilities after the Japanese surprise attack. The war also was touched on by several other contributors.[17]

The longest work in the post–Pearl Harbor issue was a long reminiscence by a young folksinger from Oklahoma. Woody Guthrie's "Ear Players" was not about war but about growing up "Okie," about work, the lack of it, and music. While Guthrie's articles in *Common Ground* sound notes of regional affirmation and proletarian protest familiar from the 1930s, he hit hardest the chords of unity: America's cultural diversity provides a rich folk music tradition; folk music attests to the shared experiences of ordinary Americans; music is a source of national unity.[18]

The war quickly shifted the realities on which *Common Ground* was focused. In the previous June, for example, African Americans had forced President Franklin D. Roosevelt to promise federal action against job discrimination. Moreover, they pressed throughout that year for integrated units in the armed forces while enduring humiliating, even murderous, Jim Crow measures on base and off. The shift was confirmed by the pressures leading to the white mob that barred black families from Detroit's federally funded Sojourner Truth Homes in February 1942, the March 1942 internment of 120,000 Japanese and Japanese Americans in concentration camps, and the dragnet that indiscriminately swept up 600 young Mexican Americans in Los Angeles' Sleepy Lagoon case in August 1942.[19]

During 1942, articles in *Common Ground* dealt with 37 different groups, concerned as it was with all the peoples of the United States.[20] At the same time, Margaret Anderson moved its focus toward those at the edges of wartime America. The shift reflected a national trend. Both major short story annuals for 1942, Martha Foley's *The Best American Short Stories* and the *O. Henry*

Memorial Award Prize Stories, noted what Foley called the "amazing" increase in stories about the foreign-born and underprivileged, especially about African Americans. Rather than the agitprop packed into many stories from the early 1930s or tales motivated by pity from an earlier sentimental tradition, Foley found that the stories published in 1942 were "told for the human values in them."[21]

For the three nationality groups described as "enemy aliens"—Germans, Japanese, and Italians—the war heightened tensions markedly. *Common Ground* quickly backed ameliorative measures such as the Alien Registration Act, Justice Department publicity against antialien vigilantes, and Office of Production Management jawboning with employers. All these efforts were designed to mitigate more draconian attempts to deport, discriminate against, and otherwise burden aliens.[22]

Among these three groups, the Japanese stood out. Pearl Harbor released hysteria against both resident Japanese and Japanese Americans on the West Coast. The internment of all 120,000 between the West Coast and the Mississippi River immediately made their situation more grave than that of those of German and Italian birth or descent. While continuing to publish articles by and about German and Italian Americans, Margaret Anderson hastened in the spring of 1942 to open *Common Ground* further to Japanese Americans. Before the Japanese Americans even left the assembly centers for the internment camps, Anderson was writing to the newspaper at the Santa Anita center, explaining that "*Common Ground* is a magazine for all Americans and we'll welcome contributions from Santa Anita as well as the other assembly centers."[23]

Not surprisingly, the internees were soon speaking for themselves in *Common Ground*. Voices coming out of the camp were reassuringly loyal and positive. There were, however, disagreements, and Anderson did nothing to mask them. Mary Oyama could joke about life at the hastily arranged assembly center in the stables at the Santa Anita racetrack, but her hints at the generational strains, the bitterness, and the fear told of life in the camps more honestly than did Robert L. Brown, public relations director at the Manzanar center. His facile account made Manzanar sound like a summer camp where internees, "stomachs full of good substantial food," sacked out on cots and became irritated only on the odd occasion when a "playful" soldier awakened someone by shining a searchlight from his sentry tower through the sleeper's window. As time went on, commentary about the camps in *Common Ground* grew more pointed. In the meantime, Oyama's chin-up description struck a sympathetic chord in many readers.[24]

Although certainly not "enemy aliens," African Americans likewise found that war had heightened tensions for them. Blacks had grown increasingly impatient with segregation in the armed forces, job discrimination by federal agencies, employment barriers in defense work, and the Roosevelt administration's unwillingness to challenge southern resistance to change any of it. The armed forces and most federal housing remained segregated throughout World

War II. Black GIs and their spouses regularly suffered indignities, and worse, at southern military bases and towns while African-American workers in northern and western war industries found housing inadequate and overpriced.[25]

The resulting discontent found its way into *Common Ground*. Anderson published the protest despite the magazine's general commitment to being positive and avoiding exposés. Among the very first authors from whom Adamic had solicited material after *Common Ground*'s inception, Langston Hughes personified the good-mannered protest of its African-American contributors. He also became the most helpful member of the magazine's editorial advisory board: directing other authors to the magazine, signing promotional letters, speaking at New York area high schools, and participating regularly in the organization's discussion forum, "American Common." He also published a total of 16 works in *Common Ground*, more than any other contributor and almost certainly more than he published in any other magazine during the 1940s. *Common Ground* provided Hughes his most dependable access to the national reading public of the time.[26]

Other voices called on *Common Ground* from different directions. In March 1943, Margaret Anderson moderated a discussion of New York contributors and readers that ultimately altered *Common Ground*'s coverage of the U.S. concentration camps for Japanese and Japanese Americans. Influenced by what she heard, especially from those recently released, she solicited several articles for the next issue.[27] Anderson herself wrote the lead article, unequivocally titled "Get the Evacuees Out!" It differed in tone from everything about Japanese and Japanese Americans previously published in *Common Ground*:

It seems crystal clear that against our Japanese Americans democracy has done a deep wrong. . . . over 100,000 people . . . have been detained now over a year in government camps, euphemistically known as relocation centers but uncomfortably close to concentration camps, . . . because they happen to have been born with Japanese faces and names, and because the rest of us . . . forgot for a moment the story of transplantation that lies behind all American citizenship.[28]

An article by Eddie Shimano, "Blueprint for a Slum," went sharply beyond the gradualist position found in earlier issues of *Common Ground*. Shimano presented compelling details on the physical discomforts and psychological damage of camp life that demoralized individuals and disintegrated families. He criticized sending Christmas presents to the camps—a scheme that Margaret Anderson had promoted to *Common Ground* readers the year before. Gift-giving by itself, he argued, avoided the basic problems of the 35,000 children under 15 in the camps and "implied an unconscious willingness to accept these government created slums and utilize them as convenient charity cases by which gift-givers could take a short-cut to Heaven." Instead, concerned citizens should pressure government officials to provide psychologists for camp schools, to give the immigrant-generation Issei greater formal responsibility, to dismantle the barbed wire and guard towers, "and, above all, get the evacuees out!"[29]

"So many sticks of dynamite." That is how the lead article in the spring 1943 issue of *Common Ground* described "the thirty million persons of foreign birth or parentage in the United States."[30] Two years before, a New York judge testifying before the Senate Foreign Relations Committee predicted imminent civil war between America's old stock and foreign-born. The social dynamite was out there all right, but the explosions were going off along lines of race, not foreign birth. America seemed to face the prospect of civil war, one different from that which Louis Adamic had feared, yet potentially just as devastating. By 1944, Clifton Fadiman would describe the War Writers' Board as deciding "'to enlist as many as possible of the media of communication on the side of American unity which will prevent the [interracial] civil war now threatening.'"[31]

In June 1943 racial tensions exploded seemingly everywhere along the home front. On June 3, in Los Angeles, white servicemen began 10 days of rioting against alleged provocations by Mexican-American juveniles. On June 15, coverage swung to Beaumont, Texas, where a day of violence between white and black war plant workers left 2 dead and 50 injured. On June 21, attention locked on interracial battles in Detroit, which in two days saw 25 blacks and 9 whites killed, hundreds injured, and property damage into the millions of dollars—the worst domestic confrontation in 25 years.[32]

Amid the brutality of the rioting and the despair it bred, Margaret Anderson saw larger implications and set about putting them before *Common Ground*'s readers. Just over a week after Detroit, for example, she turned to one of her editorial advisers, Lin Yu Tang:

Could you do something for us on racism which seems at the moment to engulf us all? I am convinced it is the central social issue of our time and that it requires constant illumination to steer sound action and preventive measures. Terribly too few people realize that racism is fascism and that we're well on the way to both in this country. The WRA [War Relocation Authority] tells me it has on file great quantities of resolutions, letters, etc. protesting the release of Japanese Americans. . . . The race riots throughout the country against the Negro and the Mexican, the dormant prejudice against the Chinese made vocal now by the threat of action on the exclusion bills, anti-Semitism—all these things are different facets of the same thing, and they hang heavy on my mind and heart.[33]

The autumn 1943 issue contained the responses she received to similar pleas as well as unsolicited articles that also reverberated from the riots. Of the 20 articles in the Autumn 1943 issue, only five did not deal with racism, and 10 pieces—5 by blacks—concerned racial prejudice against African Americans. Langston Hughes, typically, saw a silver lining and shared it humorously with Arna Bontemps: "*Common Ground* is full of culled articles this issue!"[34]

The autumn 1943 number included a presentation contrasting African American press opinion on the riots with a sampling of racist comments in Congress, on the campaign stump, and in mainstream papers. The latter digest

Anderson titled incredulously, "Is This America Speaking?"   A second presentation juxtaposed two first-person accounts, one black and one white, of maturing in an America poisoned by racial prejudice.   Margaret Walker's "Growing Out of Shadow" told of the barriers, from the brutal to the banal, that she surmounted on her way to economic, political, social, and spiritual understanding as a young adult.   Lillian Smith's "Growing into Freedom" acknowledged the price of deep inner conflict she as a white paid to be human because she chose to reject the system of segregation that subtly misshaped her sensibilities in childhood.[35]

The issue's photo-essay, "The American Way," also dramatized the theme of race relations.   Facing the end of Smith's companion piece to Walker's, a pair of four-year-olds—one towheaded, the other nappy—sat solemnly but comfortably side by side on a sandbox at a New York City playground.   The striking vulnerability, yet dignity, of the photo demonstrated Smith's determination to bring about a healthy culture for whites as well as blacks.   This first photo in "The American Way" (where "color is only incidental in the deeper and rewarding business of human relationships") led to shots of Americans quietly enjoying interracial workplaces, schools, cafeterias, United Service Organization canteens, union meetings, and Brooklyn's integrated public housing.   The photo series demonstrated that in some places, the ideal was already a reality.[36]

The photographic essays in the middle of all but three of Common Ground's 37 issues are serious but upbeat, affirming the inclusive and positive vision of America-in-the-making.[37]   It is in this affirmative spirit that Langston Hughes proposed to do an essay on the absurdities of Jim Crow that Hughes had endured personally or heard in jokes then making the rounds.   Anderson welcomed Hughes's offer.   "White Folks Do the Funniest Things" (Winter 1944) includes a cartoon from a black New York newspaper to help illustrate the grim quality "Negro humor" had been led to:

This was the cartoon. Two little white boys are standing looking at one of the boys' father's collection of hunting trophies hanging on the wall in Papa's den—an elk head, a tiger head, a walrus. There among them, nicely mounted, is a human head—a Negro's. Proudly, the small son of the house explains, "Dad got *that* one in Detroit last week."[38]

Hughes noted that while blacks laughed, clipped the cartoon, and sent it to friends, none of the whites, out of a dozen or more to whom he showed it, even smiled.

The winter 1944 issue was barely published before letters began pouring in. Some praised Hughes's piece, as well as Anderson for printing it.   Lillian Smith recommended "White Folks Do the Funniest Things" to the readers of her monthly *South Today*, as a test of their mental health.   Publications as diverse as the *Canadian Magazine Digest*, the *Los Angeles Tribune*, and a church paper in St. Louis sought permission to reprint the piece. The *Negro Digest* announced its reprint on big placards all over Harlem.[39]

Offended readers objected. One found Hughes "a smart aleck," with no "constructive criticism." In one of several letters to Anderson, a reader from North Carolina labeled him "truculent," and she, in turn, wondered to Hughes, "If he finds you truculent and gets alienated, God knows what he'll consider me."[40] Nonetheless, Anderson was startled by the volume and vehemence of reader response to the quarterly's increased attention to people of color. The shift of emphasis in *Common Ground* had touched a nerve, and a good many readers were pained.

So many readers reacted, in fact, that Anderson decided that the spring 1944 issue would openly acknowledge the shift of emphasis. Her "Letter to the Reader" was without parallel: at no other time did an editor of *Common Ground* take to the magazine's pages to respond to readers. Although Hughes's "White Folks Do the Funniest Things" had stimulated the most comment of any piece printed in *Common Ground*, Anderson noted, letters with a "worried undercurrent" had been increasing, and many "who go the whole way with us on the foreign-language groups" begin to exhibit "very real emotional or intellectual withdrawal when we touch too frankly and too vigorously upon matters of color."[41]

Anderson defended attending to matters of color as merely responding to current events. The good effect of *Common Ground*'s focus and its advocacy of solutions at the national level, Anderson stressed, "lies ultimately in our own hearts, in our own creative imaginations, in reaching out across the barriers of color to what . . . are only other human beings like ourselves, now torn by fears and despair and bitterness and aspiration and yearning." Reaching out would involve realizing "we had nothing to do with being born white or colored" and "putting ourselves in the other fellow's place across the colorline and meditating how we would react were our situations reversed." Anderson offered to put readers in the same locality in touch with each other and asked to be kept posted on the groups' successes. *Common Ground* could then pass on the techniques for bettering communities that came out of the readers' groups.

The shift of emphasis and the attendant controversy did not go unnoticed by African Americans. Poet Melvin B. Tolson sent a sheaf of new work along with his words of encouragement: "Let nothing swerve *Common Ground* from its present course. It's the most vital thing of its kind anywhere. As long as a free-for-all goes on, okay! The crowd will investigate. And that's what you want."[42] By June 1944, Anderson found herself with enough excellent material by and about blacks that she could have done a wholly African-American issue. "The poor furrin-born," she confessed to Langston Hughes, "have got lost in the shuffle somehow."[43]

Despite the tensions surrounding *Common Ground*'s nonfiction, its fiction and visual images concentrated on an idealized life as it could be lived on common ground: the story of the coming and meeting of *all* the American peoples, even though the war had drawn increasing attention to the problems of Americans of color.   George and Helen Waite Papashvily, the magazine's second most frequent contributors after Langston Hughes, helped keep in perspective *Common Ground*'s attention to vulnerable minorities.   Eight of the Papashvilys' 15 *Common Ground* stories are autobiographical tales about George's acclimatization to America; the rest are drawn from Helen's family history—old-stock New Englanders on one side and more recent Irish Catholic and Scottish Presbyterian immigrants on the other.

Even though the emphasis in *Common Ground* had shifted from immigrants to Americans of color, by January 1945 the Papashvilys had become the quarterly's hottest contributors.   In nine months, *Anything Can Happen*, their best-seller about immigrant adjustment that had grown from their stories in *Common Ground*, sold 127,000 copies.   Harpers contracted for a second Papashvily book, a volume of Georgian folktales, and a movie producer was interested in the rights to their stories.   Orson Welles and other radio personalities negotiated for airtime with Helen and George.   During much of 1945 and 1946, the Papashvilys were regulars on the national lecture circuit.[44]

Another new but accomplished talent came to *Common Ground* in the spring of 1944.   A prize-winning artist from Riverside, California, with a master's degree from UCLA and two years of European travel, Miné Okubo had been interned with her Japanese-American family at the Topaz, Utah, concentration camp and was released in March 1944.   Shortly after the young artist arrived in New York, Anderson invited her to visit the *Common Ground* offices, where Okubo quickly became a fixture.[45]

Although 35 illustrators contributed to *Common Ground*, only 10 are in more than one issue, and just 5—Okubo, Bernadine Custer, David Fredenthal, Oliver Harrington, and Kurt Werth—account for 76 percent of the non-photographic visuals.   In these visuals, the illustrators emphasized primarily the texts' presentations of people who would be good to meet, who would be decent neighbors regardless of their background.   Although Miné Okubo followed the postwar resurgence of modernist abstraction and provided *Common Ground* with almost all of its few departures from a documentary aesthetic, she still delivered page after page of people good to know, most people of color such as Chinese-American Jon Wong, an unnamed Iroquois, African-American John Boscoe, and a young Los Angeles "pachuca."[46]

Miné Okubo depicted her Americans-worth-knowing for the most part positively; however, she occasionally conveyed the protest in the texts accompanying the illustrations.   Unlike Bernadine Custer's sanitized illustrations for Frank Yerby's "Homecoming," for example, Okubo's sketches for a similar story about a black veteran returned to the hostile South first show a sinister forest and then an alert African-American man on the run.   For Bradford Smith's "The Great American Swindle," which tells how Japanese-American evacuees had been cheated of personal and commercial property, Okubo drew two pictures: one showing a family's ordinary household belongings—suitcases, a rug, a lamp, a bedspring—all piled in a street, while in the other a mother turns away in embarrassed outrage as she sits on a duffel bag with her back against a crate, a furled umbrella in her hand, and a child at her knee.[47]

Despite occasional frankness in *Common Ground*, its visual images, like its fiction, projected an idealized view of reality. In nonfiction, however, differences of opinion on the appropriate means to achieve the ideal hardened and would contribute to the quarterly's demise.

Common Ground was always an open and busy forum for the "intercultural education" movement, which since the 1930s had advocated using both formal and informal education to foster mutual appreciation among American cultural groups.[48] From the very first issue through the issue of spring 1944, the "Schools and Teachers" column gathered news and practical suggestions. Between the autumn 1945 and the winter 1947 issues, Leo Shapiro's "Intergroup Education" columns differed only by being more compact and having a single author. "The Bookshelf" regularly included reviews of books on education and anthologies of classroom readings. Two other columns, "News Notes," between the issues of spring 1942 and winter 1943 (and then "Miscellany" for almost every issue thereafter), often included shorter announcements of new developments such as upcoming youth camps and workshops for teachers and group workers. Nine of the first 15 issues contained at least one article reporting on techniques used in schools and colleges.

Common Ground was clearly part of a burgeoning enterprise. The *Harvard Educational Review* for March 1945 reported that the publication of intercultural educational articles in education magazines for 1934–1944 increased steadily except during the initial mobilization for the war. In *Common Ground*'s autumn 1945 issue, Leo Shapiro pointed to the increasing number of workshops on intercultural techniques—fifteen across the country during the summer of 1945—as evidence of the expansion of intergroup education. So much attention was being paid, in fact, that he even lamented the proliferation of bibliographies and suggested that the Bureau for Intercultural Education publish a complete and annotated one. By the summer of 1947, with the number of short movie features growing steadily, the bureau could put out a bibliography as specialized as "Films in Intercultural Education."[49]

Margaret Anderson's strategy soon made *Common Ground* one of the central publications of the movement. The large intercultural education project of the American Council on Education in the mid-1940s sent 60 complete sets of *Common Ground* to teachers, librarians, and local coordinators in the project's cooperating school systems. Mordecai Grossman, a central figure among progressive educators, authored a lengthy 1946 article appraising the growing literature on intercultural education, and he listed *Common Ground* as the only magazine in the field. After 1945, general professional journals such as *Social Education* and *English Journal* regularly recommended *Common Ground* as a seminal resource for classroom teachers.[50]

V-E day in May and especially V-J day in August 1945 brought both the end of the war and recognition that much work remained. In private, Margaret Anderson confessed her inability to rejoice in the atom bomb's abrupt halt to hostilities: "What can a country like ours do constructively with such power when we have not ordinary decency toward each other so that we need things like the [Common] Council [for American Unity] and C[ommon] G[round], etc.?"[51] Langston Hughes sounded storm warnings from America's heartland:

The Middle West raw, cold, and prejudiced, trains crowded and smokey and travel the worst I've seen it so far, soldiers going home and mad, and an air like pre-cyclone weather in Kansas used to feel, with open and under-cover gusts of fascism blowing through forlorn streets in towns where desperate groups of interracial Negroes and whites are struggling to keep things half way decent.[52]

The end of one war brought merely a need for volunteers in another campaign.

Despite these misgivings, 1946 was *Common Ground*'s most robust year yet, with a paid circulation close to 9,000 (including 1,757 libraries and educational institutions) in some 1,745 communities in every state in the union. Of the 139 pieces that appeared outside the regular departments during 1945 and 1946, 64 (46 percent) were picked up as reprints by other publications. Given the size and concerns of *Common Ground*, a surprising number of publishers regularly scanned the quarterly for material that promised book-length work.[53]

Then, amid all the signs of vitality and appreciation, the Carnegie Corporation commissioned a comprehensive report on the Common Council for American Unity and *Common Ground*. Presented in late 1946, the report concluded that "the Council should explicitly exclude from its concerns any efforts whose primary function is to facilitate harmonious relationships between racial groups—the Jew and the Negro—and the old-stock Christian or 'general' American public."[54] That conclusion, of course, struck at the founding principle of *Common Ground*. What is more, it moved the fund to end its subsidy of the quarterly at the end of 1947. Three years after the Carnegie study, *Common Ground* folded, unable to get out the winter 1950 issue. Subscriptions had dropped from the all-time high of 8,747 in 1946 to 5,826 in 1949, the lowest level since 1942.[55]

The cutoff of funding from the Carnegie Corporation reflected the waning support for the national unity born of wartime fellow feeling. Within *Common Ground* this change was evident in the growing tension between the optimistic assumptions behind its commitment to intercultural education and the more confrontational approach to ethnic and racial inequity favored by activists like Carey McWilliams. His column, "Round-Up," which began in the winter 1947 issue, reviewed primarily pamphlets, government reports, and scholarly articles on race relations. The first "Round-Up" made a point of excluding intercultural education. McWilliams instead offered the publications of the Law and Social Action Commission of the American Jewish Congress as evidence of "a new realism, a toughness of attitude, a factual clarity, largely absent in the pre-war material which inclined toward the 'humanitarian' and the sentimental. The pleading, wistful note in race relations is being displaced by a militant forthrightness that avoids compromise and equivocation."[56] Praising briefs filed against journalistic race-baiting, restrictive covenants, and tax-exempt colleges practicing discrimination, McWilliams concluded, "I wouldn't trade one of these briefs for a truckload of materials on 'intercultural education.'"

Damaging blows to intercultural education in *Common Ground* came from other political activists besides McWilliams. Dan Dodson, the director of the New York City Mayor's Committee on Unity, for example, stopped just short of calling intercultural education the handmaiden of reaction. For Dodson, educational schemes often provided "an excuse to those who argue that education must precede action, by establishing self-serving agencies whose staffs' and major contributors' interests are not served by actual amelioration of intergroup relations, and by creating flashy, difficult to evaluate alternatives to direct social action."[57]

McWilliams called the effort among liberals impatient with education as a means to American unity "the civic unity council movement."[58] Rather than Adamic, whose attention had shifted to Yugoslavia, or Anderson, whose leadership never took hold under the pressures of the one-person editorship, McWilliams came to link *Common Ground* to this highly decentralized movement. McWilliams and others brought the civic unity council movement from approximately 200 national, state, and local bodies in 1945 to over 700 by August 1948. It was strongest in the cities and towns of the Midwest and Northeast, which together accounted for 60 percent of the local groups, and on the West Coast, which was home to an additional 20 percent of the locals. Hundreds of voluntary organizations drummed up community support, which seldom went beyond the municipal level. These local efforts stimulated scores of government agencies to promote harmony among racial, ethnic, and religious groups as well as to formulate public policy assuring equal opportunity and justice.[59]

Common Ground covered the movement regularly. "Miscellany" carried news and announcements aimed at "the interracial and unity committees organized in communities across the country"; "The Bookshelf" called attention to texts useful to discussion groups "stimulated by interracial committees across the land"; articles profiled locals from Seattle to Columbus, Ohio, to Boston; and McWilliams's "Round-Up" critiqued the locals' publications and activities.[60]

Political action—in fact, public action of any kind in support of interracialism—became more and more problematic for the civic unity councils after 1946. The Los Angeles Council for Civic Unity, a response to the 1943 riots, vanished not five years later, "unnoticed, unhonored, unsung," the decline hastened by the Council's decision in 1947 to exclude Communists and others on the political Left.[61] Returning to California from a national lecture tour in 1948, McWilliams sensed a full-blown witch-hunt against leftists.[62]

After 1947, Read Lewis could raise money for projects linked to the cold war, but he found little for *Common Ground*. Margaret Anderson attributed the lack of response to waning support for social reform. "Bookshelf" columnist Henry Tracy agreed, pointing to both pyramiding appeals from "Near East Relief, Displaced Persons, etc., etc., on top of the local Community Chest, and independent agencies" and disorienting postwar inflationary prosperity.[63] If folks with moderate means were unable to contribute, and some newly prosperous materialists were unwilling, sympathetic patrons with means were driven away by a postwar climate of opinion that made it risky to sponsor liberal causes.

The ground had shifted under the quarterly. To some it had become dispensable, to some it had become a disappointment, to some it was dangerous. All of this translated into declining numbers of subscriptions and no guardian angel to replace the Carnegie support. When Lewis and Anderson received word that their last-ditch appeals to the Independent Aid and the John Hay Whitney foundations would not be funded, Anderson set about closing up shop.[64]

The story of *Common Ground* qualifies some recent interpretations of the United States during the 1940s, and it confirms others. The existence of the quarterly challenges John Lowe's suggestion that ethnic writing went into eclipse in the Depression until the Black Power movement in the 1960s demonstrated the vitality of ethnicity. The quarterly also identifies some of the immigrants—and people sympathetic to their concerns—who opposed the cold war consensus developing in the late 1940s; the constituencies these immigrant Americans represent cannot be counted among those whom Richard Polenberg has seen affirming their patriotism at the expense of their interethnic and class interests.[65]

Above all, *Common Ground* reflects the persistence of a vision of the United States in the 1940s even as controversy intensified over how to realize that vision. The quarterly's authors, illustrators, and photographers envisioned an ideal America-in-the-making in which unity is possible amid diversity. They held to that ideal even as its nonfiction contributors increasingly differed over education or legislation as the surest bridge across the country's sociopolitical fissures in the 1940s—fissures that narrowed over class, nationality, and regional fault lines but yawned ever wider along color lines during the decade. World War II had given the magazine and its publisher, the Common Council for American Unity, the means to promote unity, but it also set in motion forces that intensified fragmentation and ultimately dispersed the magazine's support.

NOTES
The abbreviations of names recurring frequently in the notes are:

CMcW = Carey McWilliams
FSA = Frank Sebert Anderson
HWP = Helen Waite Papashvily
LA = Louis Adamic
LH = Langston Hughes
MMA = M. Margaret Anderson
RL = Read Lewis
WCB = William C. Beyer

1. [LA and MMA], "Editorial Aside," *Common Ground* 1 (Autumn 1940): 103. Anderson identified the editorial as a collaboration (MMA to WCB, August 2, 1977, M. Margaret Anderson Papers, Immigration History Research Center, University of Minnesota, St. Paul, MN (hereafter, Anderson Papers cited as "MMA Papers").

2. Morse L. Cartwright to Frederick P. Keppel, March 11, 1940, file folder: Common Council for American Unity—Support of *Common Ground* 1940-53, Carnegie Corporation of New York Papers, Carnegie Corporation of New York.

3. RL with Daniel Weinberg, November 19, 1971, and RL to LA, September 20 and 29, 1939, Shipment 6, Box 3, ff.: Adamic, Louis—Correspondence, Articles 1, American Council on Nationalities Services Papers, Immigration History Research Center, University of Minnesota, St. Paul, MN (hereafter American Council on Nationalities Services Papers cited as "ACNS Papers"; the numbers joined by a colon after "ACNS Papers" designate shipment and box; "ff.:" precedes the names of the file folder).

4. RL to LA, June 19 and September 14, 1939, 6:3, ff: Adamic, Louis—Correspondence, Articles 1, ACNS Papers; RL interview with WCB, June 22, 1977, and MMA interview with WCB, July 2, 1977, MMA Papers.

5. Marian Schibsby to LA, April 29, 1940, LA to Marian Schibsby, April 30, 1940, LA to RL, April 30, 1940, ff.: Adamic, Louis—Correspondence, Articles 1, ACNS Papers. See Richard Polenberg, *One Nation Divisible: Class, Race, and Ethnicity in the United States since 1938* (New York: Viking, 1980), 43-45; Geoffrey Perrett, *Days of Sadness, Years of Triumph: The American People 1939-1945* (New York: Coward, McCann, & Geoghegan, 1973), 87.

6. MMA to FSA, June 13, 1940, WCB's possession; LA to RL, May 23, 1940, 6:3, ff.: Adamic, Louis—Correspondence, Articles 1, ACNS Papers; MMA to LH, December 17, 1944, Langston Hughes Papers, James Weldon Johnson Memorial Collection, Yale University Library, New Haven, CT (Hughes Papers hereafter cited as "LH Papers"); LA to RL, August 10, 1940, 6:3, Adamic, Louis—Correspondence, Articles 1, ACNS Papers.

7. [LA and MMA], "Editorial Aside," 103. The articles by Van Wyck Brooks, Arthur M. Schlesinger, and George M. Stephenson were first published in 1921, 1922, and 1929, respectively. The articles in *Common Ground* 1 (Autumn 1940) mentioned in this paragraph of the text are: Van Wyck Brooks, "Taras Shevchenko," 15-17; Mary Ellen Chase, "Head and Hands Working Together," 3-6; Robert Maynard Hutchins, "On Democracy and Defense," 57-61; Arthur M. Schlesinger, "Immigrants in America," 19-28; LA, "This Crisis Is an Opportunity," 62-73; William Reilly, "Lost and Found," 7-

14; Lola Kinel, "On Becoming American," 44-48; Leon Surmelian, "I Ask You, Ladies and Gentlemen," 49-52; George S. Schuyler, "Who Is 'Negro'? Who Is 'White'?" 53-56; Marie Syrkin, "My Jewish Club Carries On," 86-89; Beatrice de Lima Meyers, "On Common Ground with Children's Books," 101-02; "Organizations and Their Work," 74-81; "Schools and Teachers," 86-92; "From the Immigrant Press," 93; "The Bookshelf," 94-102.

8. LA, "This Crisis Is an Opportunity," *Common Ground* 1 (Autumn 1940): 69; Jones, "American Literature and the Melting Pot," *Southwest Review* 26 (1941): 329-346; Alfred Kazin, *On Native Grounds* (New York: Reynal and Hitchcock, 1942), 518.

9. MMA to FSA, June 13, 1940, WCB's possession; RL to Frederick P. Keppel, February 28, 1941, 6:1. ff.: FLIS/CCAU Foundation Appeals—Carnegie Foundation, 1934-1949, ACNS Papers.

10. [LA and MMA], "Editorial Aside," 103.

11. MMA to FSA, February 25, 1941, WCB's possession (quotation from this letter); "The Classroom Reading Guide" (New York: Mayfair Agency, n.d.), 8:5, ff.: FL-FO-FR, ACNS Papers.

12. RL to Frederick P. Keppel, February 28, 1941, 6:1, ff.: FLIS/CCAU Foundation Appeals—Carnegie Foundation, 1934-1949, ACNS Papers; MMA, "Colleges and Courses," *Common Ground* 1 (Winter 1941): 81; [LA and MMA], "Editorial Aside," 103; MMA to FSA, February 25, 1941, WCB's possession.

13. [LA and MMA] to "American Writers and Literary Agents," [February 1941], ACNS Papers.

14. Ibid.

15. Cf. James D. Hart, *The Oxford Companion to American Literature*, 4th ed. (New York: Oxford University Press, 1965), pp. 4, 172; CMcW, *The Education of Carey McWilliams* (New York: Simon and Schuster, 1979), p. 179; Philip Gleason, "Minorities (Almost) All: The Minority Concept in American Social Thought," *American Quarterly* 43 (1991): 397.

16. LA, *Two-Way Passage* (New York: Harper, 1941), 184-185; LA to RL, June 13, 1941, Louis Adamic Papers, Princeton University Library, Princeton, NJ (hereafter Adamic Papers cited as "LA Papers"); LA to Freida S. Miller, June 11, 1941, 6:3, ff.: Adamic, Louis—Correspondence, Articles 3, ACNS Papers; LA, Untitled typescript, n.d. [Attached to LA to Alice Stetten, June 16, 1941], and LA to RL, June 17, 1941, LA Papers; Henry A. Christian, *Louis Adamic: A Checklist* (Kent, OH: Kent State University Press, 1971), xxxiii; RL to Stella Adamic, December 5, 1941, and Stella Adamic to RL, December 12, 1941, 6:3, ff.: Adamic, Louis—Correspondence, Articles 3, ACNS Papers.

17. MMA to George M. Stephenson, April 23, 1942, George Malcolm Stephenson Papers, University of Minnesota Archives, University of Minnesota, Minneapolis, MN; "The Work of the Common Council for American Unity in 1942," ff. CCAU Annual Report, 1942—"The Work of the C.C.A.U.," ACNS Papers; Blair Bolles to WCB, March 14,1986, WCB's possession; *Common Ground* 2 (Spring 1942): Eleanor Roosevelt, "The Democratic Effort," 9-10; Blair Bolles, "Disciples of Freedom," 3-8; Mike Masaoka, "The Japanese American Creed," 11; Mary Oyama, "After Pearl Harbor—Los Angeles," 12-13 (quotation from p. 13); Tooru Kanazawa, "After Pearl Harbor—New York City," 13-14; Satoko Murakami, "I Am Alive," 15-18; Roi Ottley, "A White Folks' War?" 28-31; Sigrid Undset, "Norway and Norwegian Americans," 73-76.

18. Woody Guthrie, "Ear Players," *Common Ground* 2 (Spring 1942): 32-43. Guthrie's other two contributions to *Common Ground* were "State Line to Skid Row," 3 (Autumn 1942): 35-44, and "Crossroads," 3 (Spring 1943): 50-56.

19. Perrett, *Days of Sadness*, 151, 153; Polenberg, *One Nation Divisible*, 73; CMcW, *Education*, 110.

20. "The Work of the Common Council for American Unity in 1942," 7, 5:4, ff.: CCAU Annual Report, 1942, ACNS Papers.

21. Martha Foley, ed., *The Best American Short Stories, 1943, and the Yearbook of the American Short Story* (Boston: Houghton Mifflin, 1943), x; Hershel Brickell, ed., *O. Henry Memorial Award Prize Stories of 1943* (Garden City, NY: Doubleday, Doran, 1943), xiv.

22. Alan Cranston, "The Registration of Aliens," *Common Ground* 1 (Autumn 1940), 82-85; Polenberg, *One Nation Divisible*, 59; John Higham, *Send These to Me: Jews and Other Immigrants in Urban America* (New York: Atheneum, 1975), 60-62; Perrett, *Days of Sadness*, 90.

23. Roger Daniels, *Concentration Camps: North American Japanese in the United States and Canada During World War II* (Malabar, FL: Krieger, 1981), 104; MMA to Eddie Shimano, May 26, 1942, 8:3, ff.: Shimano, Eddie, ACNS Papers (quotation from this letter).

24. Mary Oyama, "This Isn't Japan," *Common Ground* 3 (Autumn 1942): 34; Robert L. Brown, "Manzanar—Relocation Center," *Common Ground* 2 (Autumn 1942): 27; MMA to Eddie Shimano, November 9, 1942, 8:3, ff.: Shimano, Eddie, ACNS Papers; [MMA], "News Notes," *Common Ground* 3 (Winter 1943): 109.

25. Thomas R. Brooks, *Walls Come Tumbling Down: A History of the Civil Rights Movement, 1940-1970* (Englewood Cliffs, NJ: Prentice-Hall, 1974), 9-32; Richard M. Dalfiume, *Desegregation of the U.S. Armed Forces: Fighting on Two Fronts, 1939-1953* (Columbia: University of Missouri Press, 1969), 73.

26. LA to LH, May 23, 1940, LH Papers; MMA to WCB, June 1, 1976, MMA Papers; MMA to Margaret Walker, March 28, 1943, 8:4, ff.: wa-we-wh, ACNS Papers; MMA, "Langston Hughes Tours High Schools: A New Approach to Interracial Understanding" in California Elementary School Principals' Association, *Education for Cultural Unity*, 17th Yearbook (1945), 103-105; MMA to LH, December 28, 1942, LH Papers.

27. MMA to Larry Tajiri, March 22, 1943, and Larry Tajiri to MMA, March 31, 1943, 8:4, ff.: Tajiiri, L., ACNS Papers; MMA to FSA, February 27 1943, WCB's possession; MMA to Norman Thomas, March 23, 1943, 8:4, ff.: Thomas, Norman, ACNS Papers.

28. MMA, "Get the Evacuees Out!" *Common Ground* 3 (Summer 1943): 65.

29. Eddie Shimano, "Blueprint for a Slum," *Common Ground* 3 (Summer 1943): 78-85 (quotations from this paragraph are from pp. 84 and 85).

30. Yaroslav Chyz, "The War and the Foreign-Language Press," *Common Ground* 3 (Spring 1943): 3.

31. "'American Unity in the Present Crisis,'" *Common Ground* 1 (Spring 1941): 106; "'American Unity' Dinner," *Common Ground* 1 (Summer 1941): 111; Fadiman as quoted in Robert T. Howell, "The Writers' War Board: Writers and World War II" (Ph.D. diss., Louisiana State University, 1971), 379.

32. Mauricio Mazon, "Social Upheaval in World War II; 'Zoot-Suiters and Servicemen in Los Angeles, 1943" (Ph.D. diss., University of California, Los Angeles,

1976), 85; James S. Olson and Sharon Phair, "The Anatomy of a Race Riot: Beaumont, Texas, 1943," *Texana* 11:1 (1973): 64-66; Robert Shogan and Tom Craig, *The Detroit Race Riot: A Study in Violence* (New York: DeCapo Press, 1976), 89; Louis Martin, "Prelude to Disaster: Detroit," *Common Ground* 4 (Autumn 1943), 21.

33. MMA to Lin Yu Tang, June 29, 1943, 8:4, ff.: Y, ACNS Papers.

34. LH to Arna Bontemps, n.d. [October 1943], *Arna Bontemps-Langston Hughes Letters, 1925-1967*, ed. Charles H. Nichols (New York: Dodd, Mead, 1950), 146.

35. "The Negro Press on the Riots," 101-105; "Is This America Speaking?" 86-87; Walker, "Growing Out of Shadow," 42-46; Smith, "Growing into Freedom," 47-52.

36. "The American Way," 52-60 (the quotation is from the prefatory note, p. 52).

37. MMA with WCB, July 2, 1977, MMA Papers; John Szarkowski, "Introduction," *Walker Evans* (New York: Museum of Modern Art, 1971), 184-185; William Stott, *Documentary Expression and Thirties America* (New York: Oxford University Press, 1973), 53; Arthur Goldsmith, *The Encyclopedia of Photography*, vol. 15 (New York: Greystone Press, 1963-1974), 2785-2786; Beaumont Newhall, *The History of Photography: From 1834 to the Present Day*, rev. ed. (New York: Museum of Modern Art, 1964), 150.

38. LH to Arna Bontemps, September 23, 1943, *Letters, 1925-1967*, 143; MMA to LH, September 20, 1943, LH Papers; "White Folks," 46.

39. MMA to LH, February 8, 1944, LH Papers; MMA to Lillian Smith, January 23, 1944, and to Lillian Smith and Paula Snelling, February 1, 1944, 8:4, ff. Paula Snelling and Lillian Smith, ACNS Papers.

40. MMA to LH, February 8, 1944 and December 25, 1943, LH Papers.

41. MMA, "Letter to the Reader," *Common Ground* 4 (Spring 1944): 91, 92 (quotations in the next paragraph are from pp. 94 and 95).

42. Tolson to MMA, April 7, 1944, 8:4, ff.: Tolson, Melvin, ACNS Papers.

43. MMA to LH, June 1, 1944, LH Papers.

44. HWP to MMA, [September 1945], 8:3, ff.: George and Helen Papashvily, ACNS Papers; Arnold Rampersad, *The Life of Langston Hughes*, vol. 1 (New York: Oxford University Press, 1986), 383; HWP to MMA, [July 1945] and [April 1945], MMA to HWP, December 19, 1945, HWP to MMA, [June 1945], 8:3, ff.: George and Helen Papashvily, ACNS Papers.

45. Yvonne Grier Thiel, *Artists and People* (New York: Philosophical Library, 1959), pp. 260-267; Shirley Sun, "Commentary," in *Mine Okubo: An American Experience* (Oakland, CA: Oakland Museum, 1972), 11-51; MMA to WCB, June 1, 1976, MMA Papers; Mine Okubo to MMA, September 3, 1981, WCB's possession.

46. Mine Okubo, illustrations in *Common Ground* 6 (Autumn 1945): 41; 7 (Autumn 1946): 41; 7 (Spring 1947): 75; 8 (Winter 1948): 15.

47. Bernadine Custer, illustration in *Common Ground* 6 (Spring 1946): 41; Mine Okubo, illustrations in *Common Ground* 7 (Winter 1947): 35, 37, 79.

48. Nicholas V. Montalto, "The Forgotten Dream: A History of the Intercultural Education Movement, 1924-1941" (Ph.D. diss., 1978, University of Minnesota), 17-20, 50-56, 110-111, 132.

49. Abraham Citron, Collin Reynolds, and Sarah Tayler, "Ten Years of Intercultural Education in Educational Magazines," *Harvard Educational Review* 15 (March 1945): 130, 131; Leo Shapiro, "Intercultural Education," *Common Ground* 6 (Autumn 1945): 95, and 6 (Summer 1946): 105; [MMA], "Miscellany," *Common Ground* 7 (Summer 1947): 104.

50. Jeanne Schonberg to MMA, March 14 1946, 8:4, ff.: tab-taz, ACNS Papers; Mordecai Grossman, "The Schools Fight Prejudice," 36-37; "Report and Summary," *English Journal* 24 (December 1945): 569, and 38 (December 1949): 590; Ralph Adams Brown, "Pamphlets and Government Publications," *Social Education* 11 (May 1947): 225.

51. MMA to RL, August 10, 1945, 8:20, ff.: Anderson, Miss M. Margaret, ACNS Papers.

52. LH to Arna Bontemps, November 14, 1945, *Letters, 1925-1967*, 198.

53. [RL], "The Common Council at Work," *Common Ground* 6 (Autumn 1945): 100; "Reprints from *Common Ground*," 8:3, ff.: *Common Ground* Reprints, ACNS Papers; Henry C. Tracy to MMA, November, 30 1946, 8:4, ff.: Tracey, Henry, ACNS Papers; CMcW, "Once a Well-Kept Secret," *Pacific Historical Review* 42 (August 1973): 311; MMA to Sidney Wallach, June 14, 1943, 8:4, ff.: Wa-we-wh, ACNS Papers; MMA to Leon Z. Surmelian, January 28, 1944, 8:4, ff.: Surmelian, Leon, ACNS Papers; Frank Taylor to MMA, October 11, 1945, 8:4, ff.: tab-taz, ACNS Papers.

54. David Truman, "A Report on the Common Council for American Unity, August, 1946," 84, 7:2, ff.: Common Council for American Unity—A Report by David Truman, ACNS Papers.

55. Untitled sheet, 8:3, ff.: CG Stats, ACNS Papers; "Common Ground Circulation," 8:3, ff.: Common Ground—Miscellaneous, ACNS Papers.

56. CMcW, "Round-Up," *Common Ground* 7 (Winter 1947): 91. The other quotation in this paragraph of the text is from p. 92.

57. Dan W. Dodson, "Is Evaluation Much Ado about Nothing," *Journal of Educational Sociology* 21 (September 1947): 55-56. Cf. *Common Ground*: Rudolf M. Wittenberg, "Grass Roots and City Blocks," 7 (Summer 1947): 45; Carol Levene, "We Are Many People," 8 (Autumn 1947): 75-76.

58. I am following Carey McWilliams in referring to this diffuse effort as the "civic unity council movement" (cf. Roy Hoopes, *Americans Remember the Home Front: An Oral Narrative* [New York: Hawthorn Books, 1977], 192-93; CMcW, *Education*, 115). Others have called the local efforts identified with the movement "race relations committees," "interracial committees," and "commissions 'to promote better race relations'" (e.g., Larry Tajiri, "Farewell to Little Tokyo," *Common Ground* 4 [Winter 1944]: 92; Harvard Sitkoff, "Racial Militancy and Interracial Violence in the Second World War," *Journal of American History* 58 [December 1971]: 678).

59. Cf. *Directory of Agencies in Race Relations, National, State, and Local* (Chicago: Julius Rosenwald Fund, 1945); *Directory of Agencies in Intergroup Relations: National, Regional, State and Local, 1948-1949* (Chicago: American Council on Race Relations, c. 1949).

60. Cf. *Common Ground*: [MMA], "Miscellancy" 5 (Spring 1945): 99; Henry C. Tracy, "The Bookshelf," 6 (Spring 1946): 107; Robert W. O'Brien, "Seattle: Race Relations Frontier, 1949," 9 (Spring 1949): 18-23; Isabel Currier, "Monument of, for, and by the Living," 9 (Autumn 1948): 33-41; CMcW, "Round-Up" 9 (Summer 1949): 90, and 7 (Summer 1947): 95-96.

61. CMcW, "Los Angeles: An Emerging Pattern," *Common Ground* 9 (Spring 1949): 4.

62. MMA to Ruth Smith, February 14, 1947, 8:4, ff. Smith, Ruth, ACNS Papers; CMcW, *Education*, 129, 130.

63. Henry C. Tracy to MMA, January 1, 1950, 8:4, ff. Tracy, Henry C., ACNS Papers.

64. "Common Ground Report for Two Weeks Ending April 22, 1950," 5:7, ff.: CCAU Weekly Report of Activities, 1950.

65. "Theories of Ethnic Humor: How to Enter, Laughing," *American Quarterly* 38 (1986): 447; Polenberg, *One Nation Divisible*, p. 126.

5

"My Children Are My Jewels": Italian-American Generations during World War II

George E. Pozzetta

Although historians have long recognized war as an "engine of social change," remarkably little is known about the impact of war on ethnicity and ethnic group development. Anthony D. Smith of the London School of Economics noted this fact some years ago when he observed that a vast literature existed on both ethnic groups and warfare, but very scant analysis of the interrelationships existing between them had taken place.[1] With some notable exceptions, Smith's lament could still be taken as valid today.

Most studies of America during World War II either ignore white ethnic groups altogether or approach their inquiries from limited perspectives, usually emphasizing the foreign policy and political implications of ethnic loyalties.[2] Works that do engage ethnicity more broadly tend to take the view that World War II was "the fuel of the melting pot" for ethnic Americans.[3] This conception of the war's impact pictures white ethnics as succumbing to the inexorable pressures of the war crisis—which placed heavy demands on loyalty, conformity, and patriotism—by abandoning their ethnicity and embracing the dominant culture. Some authors have recognized that in pursuit of wartime unity, the nation did take steps toward "opening up American society to the ethnics in its midst" by supporting pluralism, but the standard narrative continues to depict social change and assimilation as being essentially unilinear in direction, with ethnics passively accepting directions from above while attempting to cope with the broader political, economic, and social changes wrought by the war.[4] Thus, few studies have looked within white ethnic groups to determine precisely how individuals responded to war conditions and, equally important, how they influenced the larger society by their actions.

This study explores the war's impact on one aspect of the Italian-American experience—the group's generational dynamics. It is part of a larger effort to understand how the Italian-American population confronted World War II and responded to its multifaceted demands. It adopts an internal view of the group and draws much of its evidence from Italian language sources such as newspapers, the records of ethnic institutions, and various local publications.[5]

On the eve of the war Italian Americans stood at a number of important crossroads. They constituted America's largest ethnic group stemming from the "new immigration," numbering perhaps 6 million residents in 1940. These individuals were still overwhelmingly urban in residence (88.1 percent, up from 87.9 percent in 1930) and working-class in occupation.[6] Living primarily in dozens of large "Little Italies," Italian Americans continued to support a dense network of Italian language institutions that underwrote their cultural values and their now distinctly Italian-American lifestyles. Italian- language newspapers, for example, totalled more than 150, with eight dailies and numerous weeklies and monthlies presenting an array of religious, ideological, and commercial points of view. Literally hundreds of mutual aid and fraternal organizations continued to exist, the greatest number of which were still the small regional clubs that perpetuated a sense of *campanilismo* (local identity) within the larger community. Joining these institutions were Italian- language parishes, theaters, recreational and athletic clubs; the newest mass medium, radio, had also become a integral part of the Italian-American world.

The group counted the greatest number of aliens—soon to become "alien enemies"—of any immigrant group in the United States (more than 600,000) and the largest total of foreign-born, of whom 65 percent, or slightly over 1 million, were illiterate.[7] Viewed through many native eyes, Italian Americans continued to be an embattled minority, beset by a lowly social status and notable for their alleged propensity for criminal activities, "hot-blooded, quick tempered" natures, and lower-class lifestyles. To some Americans, the notion that Italians were "not white" still held substantial currency.[8] Moreover, the group had achieved unwelcome notoriety for a cluster of generational problems, most prominent of which were high incidences of juvenile delinquency, violent youth gangs, and excessive school dropout rates.[9]

At the same time that Italian Americans were struggling with the unsettling processes of community and generational change, they were beset by an Italian fascist government that sponsored propaganda campaigns among Italians abroad, seeking to instill a political and ideological loyalty among immigrants. Benito Mussolini's claim that Italians remained subjects owing loyalty to the homeland "unto the seventh generation" was no idle boast; he buttressed it with a sophisticated propaganda machinery that honeycombed Italian settlements abroad with agents and programs. Thus, at a crucial phase of adjustment to their New World setting, Italian Americans were required to cope with vigorous outside intrusions designed to shape their identities, values, and ethnic institutions.[10]

Most Italian Americans, however, viewed fascism less as a political ideology and form of government than as a renewed Italianità—a vehicle for generating an ethnic respectability and acceptance that had much more to do with life in America than with events in Italy. But the outward forms of this Italianità in America were influenced by the fascist state. Fascism had managed to appropriate the symbols of Italian nationalism to itself—the flag, national heroes, traditional holidays, and patriotic legacies—and this co-optation was reflected in many Italian-American communities as residents came to equate the fascist regime with the Italian motherland. Since many people used Italian nationalist symbols to frame Italian-American ethnicity in the public sphere, the visible expressions of this ethnicity almost inevitably became connected in some fashion with fascist propaganda and glorification.[11]

None of these developments took place without challenge from within the group itself, and intense internal group contestation became a fact of daily life in the larger Little Italies. This was particularly true of the struggle against profascist elements in communities by the antifascists. Composed of an unlikely mix of groups and individuals, the antifascist opposition consisted mainly of labor activists (American Federation of Labor [AFL] and the Congress of Industrial Organizations [CIO]), leftist radicals (socialists, anarchists, Communists, syndicalists), liberal progressives, and Italian exiles. Despite having a common foe, these components were often deeply split among themselves. Moreover, those opposing the fascists always labored under the handicap of being viewed as antinationalist, unpatriotic, disloyal, and anti-Catholic by the mass of Italian Americans. Because of these problems, the committed antifascist cause was able to attract a only tiny following among Italian Americans.[12]

Although the fascist/antifascist split was easily the most visible fracture dividing Italian America, by 1941 other fault lines of regional background, ideology, class, and generation supplemented it. Given the size and diversity of the group, there were also meaningful distinctions across regions, cities, and neighborhoods within America. These internal variations, moreover, persisted throughout the war, even in the face of unprecedented intrusions from the larger society that aimed at creating a wartime unity. The outbreak of war struck at all these junctures, rearranging the makeup of Italian America and compelling Italian Americans to renegotiate their identities and positions within American society in special ways. Any generalizations made about the resulting accommodations, however, must be qualified by a consciousness of the differences existing within the group.

On war's eve the Italian-American population was at a generational transition point. In 1940, foreign-born residents from Italy (first generation) numbered 1,623,580, and native-born "foreign stock" Italian Americans (second generation) totaled over 2.9 million.[13] Added to these impressive figures were members of the third generation who escaped official attention in the census but surely numbered in the hundreds of thousands. Italian-American spokespeople consistently claimed for the group a total figure of 6 million, but this number cannot be verified in government records.[14]

Whatever the actual numbers of Italian Americans, the most critical generational dynamics taking place within the group occurred between the foreign-born immigrants and their children. The third generation was still quite youthful, and members of subsequent generations were too few in number to be important. By 1941, however, the first two generations were composed of adults who came into contact, and occasional conflict, in virtually every facet of life. The outcomes of these encounters were critical in determining the ways in which Italian America responded to the war.[15]

As the war drew off young men and women for service in the military and in war industries, members of the second generation often experienced a sense of liberation—an exhilarating release from the confining bonds of traditional families and isolated Little Italies. Stripped of their hyperbole, Mario Puzo's reminiscences surely spoke for many younger Italian-American males who went to war. He had spent his youth growing up in the constricted world of New York City's Hell's Kitchen, facing the prospect of a life with very limited horizons. When the war broke out, Puzo felt himself "delivered," describing the event as an "escape." He proclaimed, "I was delivered from my mother, my family, the girl I was loving passionately but did not love. And delivered WITHOUT GUILT. . . . The war made all my dreams come true."[16]

Numerous other Italian-American servicemen expressed similar sentiments. They were exposed to a greater cross section of the national population—to say nothing of new areas of the globe and the novel cultural experiences associated with them—than they had ever encountered before.[17] Testimony attesting to the expanding nature of these experiences is overwhelming. To pick from hundreds of such items: In 1941 Paul Garzone wrote from Fort McCellan, Alabama, mentioning that he "met up with fellows from all over the States here and believe me it is a wonderful experience." Michele Pepe of Providence, Rhode Island, sent a letter from his training camp in Texas City, Texas, and told of attending a square dance on the post. "I never in my life saw this dance done," he noted, "but after a little practice I finally mastered [it]." John Scungio of Rhode Island wrote from somewhere in the southwest Pacific in March 1944 and expressed his sense of what had happened to him—perhaps speaking for thousands of others in doing so. "In the last fifteen months," he noted, "I have learned more, seen more, and done more than I did in three or four years in the States. Yes, we are changing."[18]

Members of the older generation who remained home, however, generally took a less sanguine view of the war. For one thing, they were forced to cope with the government's decision at the beginning of the war to declare all unnaturalized Italians as "alien enemies." This designation mandated certain registration requirements and imposed limitations on travel and property ownership. The stigma struck hardest at the first generation, which supplied the greatest number of aliens.[19] The need for registering and surrendering banned possessions not only caused occasional physical hardship but also dramatically demonstrated the differences existing between aliens and their conationals who were citizens. Even if benignly administered, the rules governing alien enemies forced numerous humiliating accommodations that drove home the tenuous position in which aliens found themselves.[20] Although rare, there were instances in which regulations forced unnaturalized Italian residents to move out of family homes and evacuate restricted zones. [21]

Even older Italian Americans who had become citizens were not shielded from the transformations reshaping families and neighborhoods. Unlike Puzo, they often found wartime changes more troubling than liberating. As a result, they filled the pages of Italian-language papers and organizational records with concerns about the events that were intruding into their private domains and changing relationships with their children and grandchildren.

In exploring these materials, one is struck by the prominence given to issues centering on women. Italian-American culture had always manifested an intense concern over female behavior, and families typically were highly attentive to cultural mores that mandated chastity, close supervision, and proper domestic values. Moreover, since the older generation regarded women as the repositories of accepted Italian-American traditions, females came under particularly special scrutiny during periods of social change. [22]

Commentary on wartime marriage practices reflected these cultural values. During the conflict, marriage rates throughout the nation quickly increased, rapidly dwarfing the much slower pace characterizing the depression years, and Italian-American rates followed these trends. [23] Older Italian Americans were less concerned with marriage frequency, however, than with the character of the unions. Italian-language Catholic publications, for example, decried the incidence of women entering into "war marriages," frequently describing them as "hasty, [and] set up for divorces when the war is over." Commentators observed that the war crisis lessened time for proper courtship practices, while simultaneously giving young people more freedom to pursue their own wishes. [24]

Complaints against another wartime phenomenon, the "Dear John" letter, were also contexts for discussions of marital infidelity, lax moral standards, and improper female behavior. Pointedly, these commentaries almost never included specific disapprovals of male infidelity, especially with regard to military men serving overseas. [25] Other editorials condemned the increased rates of "birth control, divorce, and the masculinization of the fair sex," urging that the "old fashioned" attitudes of the parents be maintained in reference to these matters. [26]

So-called "mixed marriages" also generated substantial debate. [27] As young men and women left Little Italies, they encountered new pools of partners and increased the frequency of out-group marriages. To some extent, these new conditions only facilitated trends already in motion during previous years, but the war added fresh impetus. One spokesman in 1943 theorized that Italian young women knew only too well that their male counterparts were "still the embodiment of paternal attitudes," and carried with them "the dictatorial concepts of their fathers concerning women." Thus, with the new freedoms opened by the war, they were seeking "more liberal and intelligent group standards" and marrying outside. [28]

When it came to choosing new partners, the older generation foresaw problems for both men and women. Some commentators worried that too many

Italian-American women were not "equipped mentally to make sound judgments" with reference to such liaisons. In this view, the resulting unions were inherently unstable. A common complaint concerning Italian-American men held that they were making partner "selections from relatively low strata," a practice that led to the "weakening of the male species."[29]

Wartime conditions increased the more general concerns of the older generation over the growing impact of American notions of freedom and independence. With more younger women working out of the home and fewer men in residence to "enforce standards," complaints concerning violations of traditional practices jumped. As one disgruntled writer noted in 1944, "This unspanked generation of lip-stick, rouge, immodest dress and petting parties" was throwing away the "priceless ingredients of family harmony by not respecting the older people."[30]

Disrespect, of course, took many forms. The unwillingness of young women to turn over their paychecks to parents became more pronounced, as was the practice of married women with young children taking jobs in defense factories. The latter practice clearly grated on the nerves of members of the first generation. With working mothers absent from the home, fears of child neglect increased, and many analysts believed that ill health, loose morals, and increased crime were to be inevitable consequences. Such mothers were shirking "their principal patriotic duty to care for their children."[31]

The June 1943 program of the Italian Mothers' Club of Greenwich House in New York City captured the essence of these attitudes. Run by well-to-do women of the first generation, the club sought to maintain older family traditions. The theme of the June meeting was "My Children Are My Jewels" and the gathering climaxed with a dramatic reading of the following poem:

My mom goes out to work all day
to help to win the fight,
But who will look after us
Till she comes home at night.
Though your country needs you mom
Your children need you too
We're the future of the land
It's really up to you.[32]

Mary Concistre's 1942 study of 100 Italian-American families in East Harlem also documented a rise in internal familial tensions over changes in female roles. She found that "girls are breaking away from parental controls which have held full sway . . . until very recently." "The boys in the Italian immigrant areas," Concistre observed, "have presented problems ever since the turn of the century, but not the girls. Mothers are now meeting in groups to find answers."[33]

As Italian mothers met to discuss their daughters' behavior, they increasingly turned their attention to the problems of juvenile delinquency. During the first years of the war, anxiety over crime and juvenile delinquency increased nationally as Americans worried about "war-bred wildness," but Italian Americans approached the problem with special concerns.[34] Members of the older generation, of course, had long deplored the existence of youth gangs and crime within the group, believing that these troubling conditions adversely affected the status of Italian Americans.[35] Many now were convinced that the problems were worsening under wartime conditions since young people possessed increased affluence and freedom and were more disassociated from community mores.[36]

They were certain, moreover, that with the absence of so many men and women in the military and factories, parental supervision had dipped dangerously low. The publication of an Italian social agency in Brooklyn exemplified these concerns, indicating in May 1942 that "War or no War, juvenile delinquency marches on."[37] Another document written in the same year concluded: "Juvenile delinquency problems are at an all-time urgency. They must be dealt with!" With neighborhood attention directed fully to events overseas and with parents absent from the home, many Italian Americans believed youths were "running amuck and being led into lives of crime."[38]

Within this general flow of anxiety, there existed very clear subcurrents. The principal worry again centered on the actions of females, who now seemed to be competing with their male counterparts in pursuing lawbreaking ways. Put simply, older Italian Americans believed that delinquency among women was increasing rapidly, and the powerful voice of J. Edgar Hoover gave substance to their worries. In a series of press releases, the Federal Bureau of Investigation Director drew special attention to the "lack of interest in the fundamentals of matrimony, in the proper rearing of children" that he perceived as critical factors in producing "an ever increasing wave of lawlessness."[39]

Critics most often reproached the "Victory Girls" who loitered near camps, factories, and service clubs threatening community standards of morality and proper behavior.[40] Educator Angelo Patri offered advice to these young women, observing that they were "so inexperienced in the ways of a man with a maid, so ignorant of the ways of the world . . . as to be helpless in the face of a major mistake." "Watch yourself," was his admonition. "You and only you will have to suffer for any mistakes you make in association with a serviceman."[41] In searching for reasons to explain these troubling developments, writers invariably pointed the finger of blame at working mothers, who were not able to give their children proper supervision.[42]

Yet the evidence points two ways. Some individuals saw more positive relationships existing between the war and juvenile crime, at least as it referred to Italian-American males. As one analyst saw it: "At times when War and all of its horrors seem to tinge every perspective, one can see a faint spark of good. Those boys among us who terminated their educational courses early in life and those who were beginning to get out of hand, are now stymied. The discipline, socialization, education, and standardization of the armed forces, are causing an infiltration of other standards and glimpses of social life from everywhere." A second spokesman noted approvingly that "former candidates for reformatories are capable of acquiring a sense of army discipline and a willingness to risk their lives so that others may have a better and fuller life."[43] Indeed, many members of the older generation hoped fervently that the accomplishments of Italian Americans in the military would induce English-language newspapers to concentrate on these subjects and reduce coverage of criminality and delinquency, issues that previously had appeared with distressing frequency.[44]

As in all wars, military service struck members of the younger generation most directly, and the first thing recruits often noted was the degree of regimentation characterizing the armed forces. Military standardization, of course, affected all individuals who served, but it reshaped in particular ways ethnics who had spent their lives in isolated enclaves. One writer for an Italian-language newspaper described the process: "Our boys in the armed forces of our country all look alike, even though their names denote that they or their ancestors come from countries as far apart as the Antipodes." Italian Americans, he observed, "wear the same uniform, march under the same flag, obey the same orders, defend the same land, face a common enemy and fight for a common victory." He might have added that they ate the same diet, worshiped at the same standardized services, lived in the same barracks, and pursued the same forms of recreation as their fellow soldiers. These experiences tended to blunt feelings of distinctiveness commonly held by the second generation and worked to resolve the dilemmas of duality possessed by so many.[45]

To the extent that military service changed younger Italian Americans, it often added strains to their reinsertion into old neighborhoods and traditional families. Indeed, as individuals who were mustered out of the service during the war began to return, a new range of generational problems became evident. So obvious were they that some organizations began to plan for the much larger disruptions that would greet the mass return of veterans at war's end. Edith Terry Bremer of the American Federation of International Institutes, for example, prepared a detailed study for Boston in early 1945 that looked toward the imminent arrival of huge numbers of soldiers and sailors. She concluded: "War and the consequences thereof only sharpen the problems . . . of confusion, and unhappy adjustments by foreign born persons, and their children to America. . . . [they] precipitate new clashes." She was cognizant that many veterans had "experiences of travel, of mingling with men from many parts of the United States, and other experiences" that had widened their horizons. Much of this, she believed, was "beyond the experience and comprehension of the old-country parents."[46]

Bremer was not alone in comprehending that military service had implications for the entire group, not just those who were called to the colors. Italian

Americans used the experience of those who served in the military for a variety of ends. The younger generation, in particular, drew analogies between the unity and openness to advancement found in military units and the barriers and prejudice faced by many Italian Americans on the home front. As one individual phrased it, "When peace reigns once again, as our boys in uniform now look very much alike and are all called to make equal sacrifices, we hope that we may not forget the sacrifices of the minority groups to our common victory" and that we banish discrimination in public life.[47]

Italian Americans were not reluctant to make known the "sacrifices" of their group as a further reinforcement of their claims for greater inclusion in the dominant society.[48] The younger generation, in particular, pointed with great pride to the numbers of Italian Americans who entered the military, viewing their service as the ultimate test, not only of the loyalty of the group as a whole but also of the fact that they had definitively chosen America in the struggle over dual identities. Leonard Covello, who as a school administrator in New York City sat amid the greatest concentration of Italian Americans in the nation, wrote in 1943: "It has been rather amazing for me to observe with what zeal Italo-American young men enter the Service. Their apparent overanxiety to put on a uniform is undoubtedly a symptom of their eagerness to be identified with America, and to be given full recognition as Americans."[49]

In forum after forum, spokesmen claimed that Italian Americans served in the military in numbers far greater than their ratio of the total population. In early 1942, various estimates asserted that, on average, every American army division contained at least 500 men of Italian parentage, and by war's end, Italian publications routinely cited the fact that in excess of a million Italian Americans had served in the military.[50] A representative announcement proclaimed that "more than one million men of Italian blood are in the American army, navy, and air force, and hundreds have merited the highest honors for their bravery and the sacrifices of their life on the battlefields all over the world."[51] Notices of decorations bestowed on Italian Americans, promotions received, and other notable achievements in the military were front-page news in every Italian-language publication across the nation, further bolstering demands for greater inclusion.[52] That the point not be missed, one midwest journal noted, "These boys [Italian-American servicemen] give ample proof that heroism is not an exclusive characteristic of any particular group."[53]

There were sacrifices, however, that some Italian Americans believed should not be made in the war effort. Members of the older generation decried the spate of name changing that took place among Italian-American servicemen. Angelo Pace of Kansas City spoke for them when he pleaded, "We see no reason why anyone should wait for a war to change his name." He believed that such a practice had a devastating social impact on the group and urged that servicemen should "keep your name intact, at least for the duration."[54] Others failed to see cause for change at any time. P. A. Santosuosso, editor of the formerly profascist *Italian News* of Boston, branded the practice in 1943 as a "most shameful confession of inferiority," which he believed was increasing at an alarming rate. Although he was concerned about trends among servicemen, he was particularly critical of "young ladies who somehow think that the Americanization of their name will advance them socially."[55]   Another spokesman singled out soldiers, pointing out that "you need not be ashamed of your name, even if your superior officers have difficulty in pronouncing it; and if the tongue of the top sergeant goes into daily contortions when he calls the roll." "Just remember," this critic admonished, "that you are as much an American as those who claim that their ancestors came in the Mayflower."[56] Thus, claims for recognition and inclusion often contained two messages: accept us but let us retain our distinctiveness.

Perhaps no one in urban America had a more informed understanding of the conditions affecting younger-generation Italian Americans than Leonard Covello. A pioneer in secondary education among immigrant and racial groups, Covello had begun the "community-centered school" concept in New York during the 1930s. In his position as principal of Benjamin Franklin High School, located in East Harlem, he interacted on intimate terms with students and parents in this heavily Italian, black, and Puerto Rican district, gaining insights into community life from every possible perspective.

Convinced that the war was actually a "blessing" since it increased the interaction between Italian Americans and other Americans, Covello felt such contact would result in the removal of prejudices and the acquisition by youngsters of a "sense of social recognition and security," which they required for a balanced adjustment. The military services, he maintained, "are certainly splendid means for having young men see the country, meeting all kinds of Americans, establishing friendly relations with them." Such encounters, he maintained, would lead to mutual understanding and appreciation and ultimately accelerate the process of assimilation. Although in earlier years he had advised students to attend college or find work away from the neighborhood, he now urged "them to join the Armed Forces."[57]

He was always careful to point out, however, that the resulting interaction would *also* produce increased understanding by the larger society of Italian-American contributions to the war effort and the building of America. The process for him, therefore, involved a two-way exchange in which both the group and the dominant society underwent change.

Although Covello believed that servicemen would be most directly affected by the war, he observed important dynamics at work on the home front as well. Prior to the conflict, he noted that Italian Americans always placed "loyalty to one's family before everything else." In Covello's opinion, this exaggerated concern for family narrowed the social horizons of Italian Americans, restricting their contact with others and limiting their assimilation. The war, therefore, presented an opportunity to expand the contact points of Italian Americans by breaking the constricted focus on the family unit and extending the scope of care and concern outward.

Covello promoted these ends by establishing a neighborhood alliance of dozens of traditional small clubs, block societies, and family groupings existing in East Harlem, in order to publish a district newsletter, the *East Harlem News*. This publication supplied local news to servicemen from the area, wherever they might be stationed. Promoters sent it to all individuals from the community, not just the relatives and friends of those who worked on the project. He soon was able to enlist the participation of numerous student and parent volunteers, who collected soldiers' addresses, collated and stamped papers, and mailed out issues across the world. Covello believed that the project provided his students, in particular, with a new experience: "to do something for someone they do not know." In doing such work, he thought, the community discovered broader social vistas and began to think "not only in terms of their family or block, but in terms of national interest, for the Service men to whom they are writing are serving a great national cause."[58]

In many ways the hopes of Covello were realized in numerous Italian-American settlements throughout the nation. A study of Italian Americans in Carneta, Pennsylvania, concluded that "World War II gave the younger generation boys an experience that weakened the insularity of attitude fostered by the first generation." One veteran from this community observed: "The service gave me all I have, it gave me confidence. I found out the world outside Carneta wasn't hostile."[59] Elsewhere Italian Americans bought millions of dollars, worth of war bonds and stamps and participated actively in civilian defense programs, scrap drives, service flag raisings, and victory parades. Similarly, they observed rationing guidelines, planted victory gardens, and erected honor rolls in parish halls and community centers. Italian fraternal societies frequently established connections with service organizations and sponsored parties and dinners for soldiers, few of whom came from the local area. An investigator in New York, for example, found in 1943 "elderly Sicilian mothers—mostly non-citizens—feeding and caring for American soldiers at the USO." A single large mutual aid society in Brooklyn spent thousands of dollars equipping a special lounge and dancing center for servicemen.[60]

Expanded social horizons were not the only ways in which the war experience changed family and neighborhood life. Generational transformations also affected Italian-American community institutions. Even before the war there had been a power struggle taking place between the first and second generations for leadership within and among ethnic organizations. Part of the contest involved a competition for community authority between older institutions and newer organizations such as youth political associations, street-corner societies, and labor unions. On the eve of the conflict, the first generation still retained a hold on many of the largest and most influential traditional institutions within urban communities, particularly among the most active fraternal and mutual aid societies.

The outbreak of war intensified this contest for control. On the surface, members of the younger generation gained significant advantages from their greater degree of Americanization, their service in the military, and the increased suspicion under which the older generation came, particularly those who were aliens. But the struggle was not completely one-sided. Members of the older generation, even those who had strong profascist records in the prewar era, often managed to keep their grip on community power throughout the war.

Although many prewar *prominenti* retained their institutional control, the communities they resided in were too altered to permit a full continuation of old patterns. With the outbreak of hostilities, for example, numerous societies, clubs, and organizations in Italian-American settlements were transformed in ways designed to provide indications of war support. This was also true of the streets, monuments, buildings, and other emblems that marked the physical expressions of Italian-American ethnicity. In early January 1942, for example, Italian Americans in Providence changed the name of Mussolini Street to Russo Street in honor of Albert Russo, Rhode Island's first person of Italian extraction to give his life in the war. The Sons of Italy Lodge in Milford, Massachusetts, announced in the same month that hereafter the organization's meetings must be in English and that the Italian flag "must be put away" for all time. The same currents were evident in other large fraternal organizations, such as the Sons and Daughters of Italy. Shortly after Pearl Harbor, the men's lodge of this organization in Milford changed its name from the Vittorio Emmanuel Lodge to just simply the Milford Lodge, while the women's lodge adopted the same name, dropping the designation Salvezza d'Italia. The Society of Immaculate Conception in Bay St. Louis, Mississippi, burned the Italian flag—which had been the club's formal emblem—at ceremonies before the courthouse and substituted the American flag in its place. A reporter at the scene noted that "as the last bit of flame flickered out, heads were bared and the United States flag was raised." Examples such as these could be multiplied indefinitely.[61]

Other, smaller institutions simply closed their doors. The American Italian Community Center in Omaha, Nebraska, for example, found that its original members were "too sorrowed by the loss of some of their boys who are at War . . . and decided to discontinue operations until the war was over."[62] Most groups that made such decisions never became active again. Demographics played a role as well. La Societa Cittadina Calabro Americana, a New York City society that in 1934 "had to march four abreast in order to fit everyone in the parade," had "only a few old members" attending meetings in 1942. The president said that the members were dying off very fast, and the club was no longer able to hold balls or banquets to raise money. Earlier efforts to obtain younger members had failed since, "when the younger members had tried to introduce interesting activities for themselves, the older ones protested and they left the society."[63]

Despite the pressures of the war crisis, changes seldom occurred without substantial discussion, and generational splits often rested at the heart of these exchanges. Though few argued with the need to support actively the war effort, conflicts marred the meetings of many organizations over the precise means of accomplishing this goal. The issue of language use (Italian or English) was a common subtext to these tensions. A general pattern emerged that saw small, locally based groups invariably switching to English in their minutes and proceedings, while larger organizations at the state and national levels often retained Italian throughout the war.[64]

Yet, the overall trend was clear. English was winning out. Mary Concistre, for example, attended meetings of an Italian-American women's organization in East Harlem during the war and was "surprised to learn that everything is in English despite the fact that at least fifty percent of the members are older immigrants." She also found that "second generation Italian girls take the lead at the lodge meetings since business is in English and few of the older immigrants have mastered it."[65]

The dynamics that rearranged the relationships existing between the generations had important implications for the group as a whole. They highlighted the patterns of accommodation and resistance that characterized so much of the Italian-American experience during the war. As the generations struggled to cope with the rapid social change taking place at home and the unsettling impact of military service, they inevitably were forced to redefine their positions in American society and in the group itself. The dialogue taking place at these various levels, therefore, spoke to the larger issues of assimilation and ethnic group development.

On the surface, it is striking to observe how many Italian-American behaviors during the war mirrored those found in the general population. Like Americans everywhere, they supported the war effort enthusiastically, worried about the effects of wartime conditions on their families, children, neighborhoods, and institutions, and shared in concerns about crime and delinquency. In these respects, the record would seem to argue for the inexorable movement of Italian Americans into the melting pot. Yet these responses must be understood in light of the distinctive cultural, social, economic, and generational contexts that framed Italian-American life. The social forces unleashed by the war had different meanings for the various components of the national population even if the public behavior they elicited seemed similar.

In light of this fact, it would be a mistake to interpret what happened as simply another step in a straight-line movement of Italians along a continuum leading from "foreign" to "American." Although some of the changes that took place appeared to outside observers as clear evidence of inevitable assimilation and cultural decay, the reality was much more complicated. What was actually occurring was a complex, multipart process of negotiation within the group and between the group and the larger society. In the end, new sets of voices were heard from inside the group, with different perspectives and generational viewpoints, in the ongoing effort to frame an Italian-American ethnicity. A full comprehension of that identity and of the process by which Italian Americans were able to influence the dynamic changing of American nationality awaits the marriage of this analysis with additional evidence documenting the Italian-American experience during World War II.

NOTES

The author wishes to express his gratitude for assistance received in support of this research from the National Endowment for the Humanities, the American Philosophical Society, and the Division of Sponsored Research at the University of Florida.

1.   Anthony D. Smith, "War and Ethnicity: The Role of Warfare in the Formation, Self-Images and Cohesion of Ethnic Communities," *Ethnic and Racial Studies* 4 (October 1981): 375. Smith's work was concerned with structuring a general theory to account for these two factors in conflicts stretching from the time of the Egyptian kingdoms to the present.

2.   Studies that do deal with ethnic groups have tended to explore dramatic events such as the Japanese relocation and/or the aforementioned political and foreign policy implications of ethnic attachments.   See, for example, Roger Daniels, *Concentration Camps U.S.A.* (New York, 1971); James Miller, *The United States and Italy, 1940-1950: The Politics and Diplomacy of Stabilization* (Chapel Hill, NC, 1986); Maddalena Tirabassi, "La Mazzini Society (1940-1946): un associazione degli antifascisti italiani negli Stati Uniti," in Giorgio Spini, et al., eds., *Italia e America dalla grande guerra a oggi* (Venezia, 1976); Louis Gerson, *The Hyphenate in Recent American Politics and Diplomacy* (Lawrence, KS, 1964); John Jeffries, *Forging the Roosevelt Coalition* (Chapel Hill, NC, 1976); Winston Van Horne, ed., *Ethnicity and War* (Milwaukee, WI, 1984); and Antonio Varsori, *Gli alleati e l'emigrazione democratica antifascista, 1940-1943* (Firenze, 1982); Leo V. Kanawada, *Franklin Roosevelt's Diplomacy and American Catholics, Italians and Jews* (Ann Arbor, MI, 1982); Lorraine Lees, "National Security and Ethnicity: Contrasting Views During World War II," *Diplomatic History*, 11 (Winter 1987): 114-125.   The literature on Canada during World War II has been more attentive to the impact of war on European ethnic groups.   See Norman Hillmer et al., eds., *On Guard for Thee: War, Ethnicity, and the Canadian State, 1939-1945* (Ottawa, 1988); Luigi Bruti-Liberati, *Il Canada, l'Italia e il fascismo, 1919-1945* (Rome, 1984).

3.   John Diggins's excellent book, *Mussolini and Fascism: The View from America* (Princeton, 1972) is something of an exception, but, as he himself indicated, it rather narrowly concentrates on the nature of American public opinion toward fascism. See also Richard Polenberg, *One Nation Divisible: Class, Race, and Ethnicity in the United States Since 1938* (New York, 1980); LaVern J. Rippley, *The German Americans* (New York, 1984); Mike Davis, *Prisoners of the American Dream: Politics and Economy in the History of the U.S. Working Class* (London, 1986); John Blum, *V Was for Victory: Politics and American Culture* (New York, 1976); Howard F. Stein and Robert F. Hill, *The Ethnic Imperative* (University Park, PA, 1977), which sees the war as the "great crucible of amalgamation"; Allan M. Winkler, *Homefront U.S.A.: America during World War II* (Arlington Heights, IL, 1986); especially, Andrew Hacker, *The End of the American* Era (New York, 1970), which claims that "the war implanted in second and third generation immigrants an impatience to accelerate their assimilation into the mainstream of American life."

4.   See, in particular, Richard D. Alba, *Italian Americans: Into the Twilight of Ethnicity* (Englewood Cliffs, NJ, 1985).   Steven Fox's entertaining *The Unknown Internment: An Oral History of the Relocation of Italian Americans during World War II* (Boston, 1990) is largely silent on larger interpretations.   For more general treatments:

Allan Winkler, *Modern America: The United States from World War II to the Present* (New York, 1985); and Melvyn Dubofsky et al., *The United States in the Twentieth Century* (Englewood Cliffs, NJ, 1978), which claims the war worked to "diminish ethnicity among citizens of white immigrant origin." Philip Gleason's perceptive "Americans All: World War II and the Shaping of American Identity," *Review of Politics* 43 (October 1981): 511-15, offers the best explanation of dominant society change.

5. The broader study employs the concept of "the invention of ethnicity" to interpret the transformation of identities and institutions that took place during wartime conditions. Kathleen Conzen, et al., "The Invention of Ethnicity: A Perspective from the U.S.A.," *Altreitalie*, 3 (April 1990): 37-62; Werner Sollors, ed., *The Invention of Ethnicity* (New York, 1989).

6. U.S. Department of Commerce, Bureau of the Census, *Statistical Abstracts of the United States, 1946* (Washington, DC, 1946), Table 36, p. 36; Table 28, p. 33.

7. "Composition and Assimilation of Foreign Population of the United States," *Monthly Labor Review* 54 (January 1942): 73-75. This report indicated that the median age of the alien population was 48 years old, while that of the population as a whole was 28.

8. See Irving L. Child, *Italian or American: The Second Generation in Conflict* (New Haven, CT, 1943), 31-48, 81-83, for a psychological assessment of the culture and status of Italian America on the eve of the war.

9. Readers should be aware of the "We and Our Children" project carried out by the Foreign Language Information Service, which sought to discuss many of the problems arising between foreign-born parents and their children. Many of the resulting case files deal with Italians. See American Council for Nationality Services Records (ACNS), Immigration History Research Center (IHRC), University of Minnesota, St. Paul, MN.

10. See the insightful article by Bruno Ramirez, "Ethnicity on Trial: The Italians of Montreal and the Second World War," in Hillmer, *On Guard for Thee*, 77, for a discussion of these conditions in Montreal, Canada. In both the United States and Canada, support for fascism began to fall off after the Ethiopian War in 1936.

11. Gaetano Salvemini, *Italian Fascist Activities in the United States*, Philip Cannistraro, ed. (New York, 1977); Diggins, *Mussolini and Fascism*.

12. Salvemini, *Italian Fascist Activities*. Salvemini estimated that never more than 10percent of Italian Americans were openly antifascist.

13. *Statistical Abstracts of the United States 1946*, Table 36, p. 36. The Census Bureau also used the longer term "native white of foreign or mixed parentage" for individuals born in the United States to foreign-born parents.

14. For example, see *La Nuova Capitale*, February 6, 1942.

15. This analysis focuses on these two generations, while recognizing that, in doing so, the full complexity of the Italian-American reality is blunted. Diversity is narrowed in one other important respect. Members of all generations made different choices in their assimilation to American society, ranging from full acceptance to outright rejection. Irving Child's work on second-generation Italian males in New Haven, Connecticut, for example, noted three types of responses: "rebel," "in-group," and "apathetic." The arguments to follow will focus on the "rebel" position among younger elements and the "in-group" adaptation of older residents, while recognizing that there were adjustments that fit between these poles. See Child, *Italian or American*, 5, 60-81, 148-49, 151, 177.

16. Mario Puzo, *The Godfather Papers and Other Confessions* (Greenwich, CT, 1972), 25-26.

17. Neil Fligstein, "Who Served in the Military, 1940-1973," *Armed Forces and Society* 6 (Winter 1980): 297-312, reveals that a very broad cross-section of the population served during World War II.

18. All of these letters were reprinted in the Sunday Bulletin of St. Bartholomew's Parish, Providence, Rhode Island. The parish, called Silver Lake after the section of the city in which it was located, was an Italian-language parish run by the missionaries of St. Charles Borromeo (Scalabrinians), and by September 1943, it had already sent almost a thousand young men to the service. These records are contained at the Center for Migration Studies, Staten Island, NY, St. Bartholomew's Parish Records, Parish Bulletins, Box 3.

19. In part, the rates of naturalization among Italians during the war years give insight into the impact of the alien enemy status. During the period 1940-1945, some 281,354 Italian aliens became naturalized, by far the greatest total of any ethnic group. In 1944 alone, 106,626 became citizens, the largest single-year figure in American history.

20. Administrators found that the regulations opened up a bewildering array of situations in which very flexible interpretations were necessary. One such administrative ruling declared that in homes in which not all members are aliens, banned possessions such as shortwave radios, firearms, and explosives should be kept so as to be "out of reach of the alien members."

21. See Fox, *The Unknown Internment* 151-177. These instances occurred most frequently on the West Coast. The *Boston Post*, February 16, 1942, reports the case of Mrs. Rose C. Trovato, who lost a son at Pearl Harbor, who was forced to move from her home in a prohibited zone in Del Monte, California.

22. Many works on women in World War II have noted that concern over the changed roles of women was also prevalent in the larger society. What is striking is the fact that this literature has almost totally ignored any discussion of ethnicity in general and ethnic women in particular, as if all components of the American population shared the same attitudes toward women's roles. See Maureen Honey, *Creating Rosie the Riveter: Class, Gender and Propaganda during World War II* (Amherst, MA, 1984); Karen Anderson, *Wartime Women: Sex Roles, Family Relations and the Status of Women during World War II* (Westport, CT, 1981); Leila Rupp, *Mobilizing Women for War: German and American Propaganda, 1939-1945* (Princeton, NJ, 1978); Susan Hartmann, *The Home Front and Beyond: American Women in the 1940's* (Boston, 1982); D'Ann Campbell, *Women at War with America: Private Lives in a Patriotic Era* (Cambridge, MA, 1984); and Doris Weatherford, *American Women and World War II* (New York, 1990).

23. John Modell and Duane Steffey, "Waging War and Marriage: Military Service and Family Formation, 1940-950," *Journal of Family History* 13 (Spring 1988): 195-218.

24. *Il Crociato*, March 15, June 1, 1944.

25. See *Il Crociato* for the war years. Issues for July 25 and August 15, 1942, contain representative articles. Consult Anderson, *Wartime Women*, 80-84; Modell and Steffey, "Waging War," 211, for a discussion of national attitudes on these issues.

26. *The Italian News*, December 3, 1943; *Il Crociato*, July 25, 1942. For general attitudes on birth control see *The Italian News*, March 3, 1944, for a revealing incident involving the creation of a "Malthusian Bachelors Club" by a group of Italian-American

physicians in Boston. The group sought to keep the birthrate down among Italians. The Catholic Church and North End community leaders denounced the organization, labeling it "horrible," "insane," and "against religion and morality."

27. *The Italian News*, November 27, 1942. The St. Donatius Parish Book, IHRC and the Generations Project of Louis Adamic, ACNS, which contains numerous interviews with second-generation ethnics, are revealing of generational tensions over marriage patterns. See interview with Rose, Italian, 24 yrs. of age, as representative.

28. *Il Messaggiero*, September 1943. The bulk of comment on the question of out-group marriages identified the desire of the younger generation to "escape the moral and social standards of parents" as the primary reason for these weddings.

29. *Il Messaggiero*, February 1941; August 1943; *The Italian News*, March 10, June 30, 1944.

30. *The Italian News*, February 4, 1944; April 13, 1945; Child, *Italian or American*, 141. "Loyalty, respect, and honor" were the themes that appeared in commentary dealing with family values. Observers believed that the family was in the process of serious erosion. Representative editorials carried titles such as "Italian Home Life," "The Duty of Parents," "Italian Parents Failing," and "Respect Your Traditions!"

31. *Corriere d"America*, March 3, 1942; *Nazioni Unite*, October 22, 1942.

32. Program of Italian Mothers, Club, Greenwich House, New York City, June 8, 1943, Elba Farabegoli Gurzau Papers, Box 12, Balch Institute for Ethnic Studies, Philadelphia. Several more stanzas continue the themes outlined in the first two, which group members were instructed to "learn to the tune of 'Yankee Doodle'". The poem is believed to have been written by social worker Elba Farabegoli or by an anonymous member of the club. Reproduced by permission of the Balch Institute for Ethnic Studies.

33. Marie Concistre, "Adult Education in a Local Area: A Study of a Decade in the Life and Education of the Adult Italian Immigrant in East Harlem, New York City" (Ph.D. diss., New York University, 1943), 460. It should be noted that one area in which traditional mores seem to have held firm was in the realm of military service for women. So strong was Italian-American opposition to female service that the Office of War Information felt compelled to mount a publicity campaign in 1944 on behalf of the Women's Army Corps designed to overcome resistance. See Memorandum, Lew Frank, Jr., to Dave Frederick, April 14, 1944, Office of War Information Records, RG 208, Box 1118, Suitland Branch, National Archives, Washington, DC. This program reached out to other foreign groups, but it did focus on Italian sensibilities. It included a photo spread showing "special poses using foreign name WACs . . . to overcome resistance; foreign name WACs comfortably living in 'feminine barracks' and WACs with foreign names getting training in skills useful in peacetime occupations." The Office of War Information translated all program brochures into Italian, among other languages.

34. James Gilbert's excellent study, *Cycle of Outrage: America's Reaction to the Juvenile Delinquent in the 1950s* (New York, 1986), 24-37, believes that the war years were particularly important in defining delinquency. Interestingly, as delinquency became a significant public issue by 1943, national concerns increasingly centered on women. As with other works, however, Gilbert does not discern an ethnic dimension to this matter, assuming a homogeneity that did not exist. See also Eleanor T. Glueck, "Coping with Wartime Delinquency," *Journal of Educational Sociology* 16 (October 1942): 86-97.

35. Richard A. Cloward and Lloyd E. Ohlin, *Delinquency and Opportunity: A Theory of Delinquent Gangs* (New York, 1960), 100, cites children's court records from Cook County, Illinois, and New York City that reveal that Italian-American juveniles were

overrepresented among delinquents during the 1930s.

36. For general conditions see Elsa Castendyck, "Juvenile Delinquency in Wartime," *Federal Probation* 6 (July 1942): 45-48; C. L. Chute, "Is Juvenile Delinquency Increasing?" *Probation* 21 (December 1942): 59-60; M. S. Fischer, "Delinquent Behavior in Wartime," *Frontiers of Democracy* 9 (November 1942): 39-41; E. T. Glueck, "Wartime Delinquency," *Journal of Criminal Law and Criminology* 33 (July 1942): 119-35; Anderson, *Wartime Women*, 95-96; Gilbert, *Cycle of Outrage*, 25-41.

37. *The Guardian*, May 1942, contained in Leonard Covello Papers, Box 86, Balch Institute; John Slawson, "The Adolescent in a World at War," *Mental Hygiene*, 27 (October 1943): 532. But see Gary R. Mormino, *Immigrants on the Hill: Italian-Americans in St. Louis, 1882-1982* (Urbana, IL, 1986), 226, for an alternative view. Residents on the Hill did not complain of increased delinquency, and Mormino believed that the community's ethnic institutions were able to channel wartime behavior into acceptable forms.

38. *The Guardian*, November 1942; *The Italian News*, September 4, 1942; January 28, 1944; "Juvenile Delinquency in War Time," *State Government* 16 (November 1943): 230; Victor H. Evjen, "Delinquency and Crime in Wartime," *Journal of Criminal Law and Criminology* 33 (July 1942): 137. Along with various war-related activities, the Italian Board of Guardians launched a "1942 Membership and Fund Drive to Fight the War against Crime among American Youth of Italian Origin."

39. A. E. Fink, *Youth Problems in War Production and Camp Areas*, National Probation Association, Year Book, 1942, 60-74. For Hoover, see *New York Times*, November 28, 1941; July 7, 1946.

40. *The Italian News*, July 11, 1941; November 7, 1944. When a Boston municipal judge criticized servicemen who frequented "dives, dances, and the USO," he was in turn taken to task by an Italian-American editor who insisted that the problem also flowed from "teen age girls who chase the service men and the parents who are to blame for giving the kids so much liberty." *The Italian News*, August 21, 1942. For a different perspective, see Janann Sherman, "'The Vice Admiral': Margaret Chase Smith and the Investigation of Congested Areas in Wartime," in this volume.

41. Angelo Patri, *Your Children in Wartime* (Garden City, NY, 1943), 31.

42. *La Nuova Capitale*, March 20, 1940; January 31, 1941; *Il Messaggiero*, April, 1945; Gilbert, *Cycle of Outrage*, 32.

43. *Il Messaggiero*, January 1944; Leonard Covello, "Cultural Assimilation and the Church," *Religious Education* 39 (July-August 1944): 234.

44. Leonard Covello, "Cultural Minorities and the War Effort," typescript, speech delivered at American League for Tolerance Symposium, August 10, 1943, Covello Papers, Balch Institute.

45. Few scholars have studied these developments in any depth, but see Philip Gleason, "Americans All," 515; William McNeil, *American High: The Years of Confidence* (New York, 1986), 27. The first of these concluded that military service gave young men a pattern of "shared values and traditions" that helped to promote a "common sense of national belonging."

46. "Memorandum prepared for BOSTON SELF STUDY," May-June, 1945, Edith Terry Bremer, contained in ACNS, IHRC.

47. *Il Messaggiero*, March 1942; February 1943; *The Italian News*, May 30, 1941; November 5, 1943. On wider discrimination patterns, consult the two articles by Richard Steele, "The War on Intolerance: The Reformulation of American Nationalism,

1939-1941," *Journal of American Ethnic History* 9 (Fall 1989): 9-35; and "'No Racials': Discrimination against Ethnics in the American Defense Industry, 1940-1942," *Labor History* 32 (Winter 1991): 66-90.

48. From literally thousands of such items see "We Pledge Allegiance," *Il Crociato*, December 20, 1941.

49. Covello, "Cultural Minorities and the War Effort."

50. *Il Crociato*, October 24, 1942; *Il Progresso Italo-Americano*, October 13, 1942; *Gazzetta Italiana*, July 20, 1942; *L'Italia*, July 25, 1942; *New York Times*, October 18, 1942; *La Nuova Capitale*, February 6, 1942; *Il Messaggiero*, November 1943, February 1945. No records exist that break down those who served in the military by European ancestry, but these figures may have been correct. Because of the demographics and timing of Italian migration, Italian Americans were disproportionately of draftable age, and the tensions of their marginal status almost certainly induced members of the second generation to enlist at high rates.

51. *La Nuova Capitale*, August 24, 1945.

52. This conclusion is derived from reading scores of Italian-American newspapers for the war years. As one example, *Il Leone* of San Francisco regularly published a front-page section entitled "Il Nostro Album d'Onore" (Our Honor Roll), which contained pictures of local servicemen with notations of their service and honors. Although the motivation for such columns may seem obvious, the practice served other functions within the group. Joseph Tait's study of 743 Italians on the eve of the war, for example, found that 201 failed to name a single person of Italian origin who had become famous in the United States, and 411 failed to name any person who had become famous in Italy. This relative lack of role models and positive commentary was often decried by the older generation, and the war heroes may well have worked to fill these needs. See Joseph W. Tait, *Some Aspects of the Effect of the Dominant American Culture on Children of Italian-Born Parents* (New York, 1947), 46.

53. *Il Messaggiero*, November 1943.

54. *Il Messaggiero*, November 1942. See *The Italian News*, May 8, 1942 (Fiore to Flowers); July 11, 1941 (Cavagnaro to Cavanaugh); February 6, 1942 (Bevilacqua to Drinkwater). It is not possible to compare name-changing practices during the war with such practices in other periods or other groups, but what is clear is that Italian Americans believed the practice was increasing greatly.

55. *The Italian News*, April 2, 1943.

56. *Il Messaggiero*, January 1943; January 1945; *The Italian News*, July 4, 1942.

57. These sentiments appeared in numerous speeches delivered by Covello during the war, but see "Italo-American Youth in the War Crisis," March 23, 1943, as illustrative.

58. Covello, "Cultural Minorities and the War Effort." See Mormino, *Immigrants on the Hill*, 221-22, for a discussion of similar developments on the Hill. Residents began a wartime newsletter, the *Crusader Clarion*, to send news to servicemen. *La Nuova Capitale*, January 8, 1943, reports on the establishment of a Fulton Soldiers and Sailors Club in Newark, which provided cigarettes, news, and letters to men in the armed forces.

59. Clement L. Valleta, *A Study of Americanization in Carneta: Italian American Identity through Three Generations* (New York: Arno Press, 1975), 195. The author of this study also concluded that Italian-American servicemen came to accept their American nationality more firmly since they had to defend themselves in the service against the prejudice of non-Italians.

60. Paul Campisi, "The Adjustment of Italian Americans to the War Crisis" (M.A. Thesis, University of Chicago, 1942), 233.

61. From literally hundreds of such notices, see *La Nuova Capitale*, December 19, 1941; December 11, 1942; *The Italian Tribune*, September 11, 1942; *The Italian Citizen*, December 19, 1941; *The Italian News*, February 6, 1942; and clippings file, Box 8, Donnaruma Papers, IHRC. Occasionally, these sorts of decisions prompted bitter commentary from community members. See, for example, *The Italian News*, January 16, 23, 1942, which criticized the actions of the flag burners, deriding them as "morons" and insisting it was they who bore watching by the government.

62. Nebraska Grand Lodge Records, February 12, 1943, Order Sons of Italy in America (OSIA) Collection, Immigration History Research Center, University of Minnesota, St. Paul, MN.

63. Concistre, "Adult Education," 205.

64. Sons of Italy Venturia Lodge #1200, Massachusetts, minutes of April 12, 1945, OSIA Collection; Minutes of Meetings, Abraham Lincoln Mutual Aid Society of Peckville, PA, in the Balch Institute mark a switch to English; but see Maria Christina de Savoia Lodge, #1752; Christopher Columbus Lodge, West Virginia, and Roma Lodge, New York, OSIA Collection, for use of Italian.

65. Concistre, "Adult Education," 252-254.

6

Remembering Rosie: Advertising Images of Women in World War II

Maureen Honey

It is now 50 years since women were recruited to fill nontraditional occupations during World War II, and it is with mixed feelings that I reflect on that watershed event. Being the child of parents whose lives were shaped largely by the war, I feel an emotional connection to Americans who went through that conflict, suffered wartime separation, anxiety, and losses, and who believed in the validity of the struggle. It is, indeed, the one American war of the twentieth century for which I can fashion a moral perspective, given the terrifying nightmare of Nazism and genocide. On the other hand, I am a child of the 1960s as well, so I look back on the bombing of Hiroshima and Nagasaki, postwar McCarthyism, and the feminine mystique of the 1950s with deep misgivings about the outcome of the war and its legacy. The militarism that won the war was a double-edged sword that both defeated fascism and created new problems for America and the postwar world it dominated.

Here I will examine one facet of this complex knot of issues emerging from World War II: the changing roles of women. My work on wartime propaganda grew out of an initial interest in the contradiction between our image of Rosie the Riveter, a strong, capable woman in nontraditional work, and her ultimate replacement by Marilyn Monroe, Lucille Ball, and other stars of the 1950s, who embodied a childlike sexuality and comic naiveté that were far removed from the images of competence in wage work so recently highlighted by women's entry into war production.[1] How could we go from strength to weakness, worker to sexpot, muscles to mammary glands in such a short period of time? Did the public experience a mass amnesia that eliminated all memory of its reliance on women as home-front amazons? How were women themselves able to accept being stripped of so much power and authority? Finally, who or what was responsible for the change? Over the past 20 years, I have found partial answers to these questions, yet I must confess that World War II and its aftermath continue to pose unsettling feminist issues, with ongoing implications for today.

Let me begin with some important differences between then and now. We were at war in the 1940s, a long, global war that touched every part of the economy. We were at the tail end of an extended period of economic stagnation and massive union organization. We were a segregated society with legal separation of African Americans from white schools, businesses, restaurants, clubs, sections of town, and many other areas of life. The armed forces themselves were segregated. We were a society that condoned stripping Japanese Americans of their property and forcing them into desert encampments of great hardship and humiliation. I point out these conditions, not to pat ourselves on the back—because I believe racism, sexism, and militarism are still very much with us and in some ways on a more vicious level—but to provide a context for our understanding of media images then and now. Because we were at war, for instance, the media worked overtly, willingly, even eagerly with government policy-makers to fashion organized messages compatible with wartime plans. Certainly there is cooperation among media and government today, more than many of us like; certainly there is bias toward those in power, and there are messages many of us would consider propaganda, but the process during World War II was more visible, less self-conscious, and more focused than it is today.[2] I do not know that it is qualitatively different, but government-media cooperation during the war is easier to study, and therefore offers us a chance to demystify wartime images of women. Some of these images are still with us despite the vast amount of recent scholarship on who these women were and what happened to them. In addition, because antiracist and feminist movements have met with some success in recent years, we can look back at the war years with a sharper focus than was available to people 50 years ago and identify themes that ultimately destroyed the wartime potential for advancing gender equality beyond the war's end.[3]

Before describing the propaganda bureaucracy developed by the Roosevelt administration, I wish to emphasize the urgent nature of America's entry into the war. Telescoping the immense field of World War II military strategy into an outrageously small but nevertheless useful nutshell: the United States needed to supply its allies as well as itself, rebuild its navy, construct an air force, and mobilize all able-bodied men in as short a time as possible because in 1941-42 Germany and Japan were expanding their victories at an alarming rate. American planners felt that the war was to be won on the production front ultimately and that the U.S. was in a race to outproduce the Axis powers; indeed, with England huddled in bomb shelters, France already in defeat, and the Soviet Union under siege, the United States was the only country capable of mounting such a production drive.[4] The campaign for women workers, therefore, was framed by a larger effort to persuade the civilian population that what happened on the home front was crucial for victory overseas. Given the relative isolation of Americans from battle and the fact that this country had not been bombed or invaded, the government feared the connection would not be made without clear, persistent, emotional appeals by the media for collective action and personal sacrifice.[5]

There are two major reasons for the government's decision to engage in a massive propaganda effort after Pearl Harbor was bombed. The first of these is that the power of the government to influence or direct the economy was quite limited. Although the New Deal had initiated many reforms, for the most part the private sector still governed itself. The role of Washington was to coordinate corporate activities in such a way as to prevent or at least contain the damage done by catastrophes such as the Depression. In its role as overseer, the government could make suggestions to industry on how it should handle the labor shortage, but it had no way to enforce policies, a situation described by Eleanor Straub in her detailed account of labor policy during the war years. She relates, for example, the frustrations encountered by the War Manpower Commission (WMC) and the War Department when they urged defense industries to hire women and minorities. Employers resisted their instructions to hire such workers in aircraft, shipping, steel, and other essential industries strapped for labor power. As late as the end of 1942, she maintains, employers insisted that women were unsuitable for over half their labor needs. Despite continual pressure from the government, employers refused to remove prewar barriers against the employment of women until the last possible moment: "Prejudices against women, blacks, aliens, and Jews in the labor force were often not modified until in-migration had strained community facilities to the breaking point."[6] Straub concludes that in order to have administered an effective labor program, the government would have had to take unprecedented measures to control industry, measures that would have interfered with the prerogatives of business to hire whom it pleased. These steps, she asserts, the government was unwilling to take, and as a result, the program to get women into war production was not adequate to the task. Though the government could apply pressure on defense employers and the private sector as a whole through field offices and directives, it operated without powers to enforce WMC regulations. The best course open to it was publicity—contacting the public, enlisting its support in labor drives, and trying to change the attitudes that had interfered with hiring women. Such an approach enabled the WMC and the War Department to bypass the cumbersome and ineffectual procedures to bring employers into line.

The second reason for relying primarily on propaganda to meet labor requirements was that the government wanted to provide an ideological framework compatible with wartime conditions. Through emotional appeals, propaganda could perhaps accomplish what enrollment and registration drives were failing to do: impress upon the public the urgent need for production of war material. In addition, if production quotas were to be met, public resentment against dislocations dissipated, and the way paved for resumption of business as usual at the war's end, information to the media would have to be coordinated in such a way—so felt the government—that confusion would be kept to a minimum. It was thought that propaganda could help the government control public responses, not only to the labor shortage but to unsettling wartime phenomena as well—rationing, forced separations, housing shortages, strained community services, and overcrowded transportation facilities.

Despite the temptations to employ propaganda, however, Allan Winkler records there was initial government resistance to it.[7] One reason was that propaganda was equated with falsehood and illegitimate manipulation, in part because the Creel committee of World War I was perceived to have distorted the truth about that conflict and to have whipped up war hysteria.[8] Perhaps the most telling source of resistance came from New Dealers, who were reluctant to share their power with people they believed to be media hucksters. Washington's power elite was in no way opposed to private enterprise, but it was uncomfortable with certain aspects of it, such as high-pressure sales pitches.

Resistance to waging a propaganda campaign weakened under the pressure of advertisers, business leaders, and media representatives for direction. In addition, it became increasingly clear to the administration that fiscal, economic, and labor policy needed an ideological framework. Prior to Pearl Harbor, for instance, there had been significant isolationist sentiment on the part of the public. Although these feelings largely disappeared after the Japanese attack, there was still confusion over the purposes of the war, the reasons for rationing, and the seriousness of labor shortages in certain areas of the country. Communication between federal agencies and the media was unclear enough that some advertisers featured products whose sale would work against the production of war goods while others encouraged the public to hoard rationed materials.[9]

The pressure became overwhelming to bring the communication system into closer alignment with the country's needs and to mobilize the population. As a result, the Office of War Information (OWI) was established in the summer of 1942. Roosevelt attempted to sidestep the controversy over using the media for propaganda purposes by asserting that OWI would merely disseminate information about government programs in a neutral way. To underline his objectives, he appointed as head of the operation Elmer Davis, a respected news reporter who was opposed to government control of the press: "This is a people's war, and to win it the people should know as much about it as they can. This Office will do its best to tell the truth and nothing but the truth."[10] This elaborate bureaucracy coordinated government policy with information sent to the media until victory was finally declared in the fall of 1945. Several bureaus were set up that were responsible for dealing with various media industries. Bureau chiefs kept track of war agency requirements through regular contact with government information officers and through an interdepartmental liaison staff, which served as contact with war agencies for clarification of major policies. They sent detailed publications to, carried on extensive correspondence with, and visited representatives from, the radio, print, and film industries.[11]

Working closely with Roosevelt's wartime bureaucracy, major facets of the media—advertising, film, radio, magazines, even popular fiction writers —fashioned narratives and representations familiar to the public around the central message that civilians were as important to victory as were soldiers and that soldiers' lives depended on workers' meeting their production quotas. For many reasons, women become the chief iconographic deliverers of this exhortation, and the woman war worker, in particular, was the principal symbol of national unity and industrial mobilization. Part of this portrayal had some positive implications. Blue-collar work was elevated in stature throughout the media to convey the message that victory depended on production of war material. Muscles, hands, rolled-up shirtsleeves, functional clothing, sturdy shoes, sweat, and grime were prominent in portraits of home-front workers, female or male. People who worked with their hands and bodies, normally marginalized as colorful background to professional characters in popular culture, were center-staged and given heroic qualities in advertising, film, popular fiction, and other arenas. This was an especially big step for women because the work on display was traditionally defined as appropriate for men, requiring, as it did, physical strength, technological expertise, ease in handling tools, or male cooperation. Apart from the nearly total exclusion of non-white Americans, there is an egalitarian thrust to wartime images in terms of class and gender that attracts us today.

Illustrating this concept and the others I will discuss here are advertisements taken from the *Saturday Evening Post* from 1941 through 1945.[12] Since the *Post* had a subscriber circulation of over 3 million during the war years, we can see what image of war workers many Americans were given, and its handling of the recruitment campaign suggests the ways magazines of its kind were dealing with the subject. The beliefs and attitudes reflected in a magazine like the *Post* are especially important because they were part of the dominant middle-class American ethic. As such, they indicate what some of the prevailing myths have been in our culture during the war and how those myths related to conceptions of women.

The *Post* was connected to Washington via two facets of the Office of War Information: the War Advertising Council and the Magazine Bureau. Prior to the establishment of the OWI, leaders of the advertising industry approached government officials through a "defense committee" set up in the spring of 1940 concerning the use of advertising in support of the Allies. They met with little success and, in response to the lack of federal support, formed the War Advertising Council (WAC) in November 1941. Its purpose was to enlist advertisers, companies, and the government in a drive to get the issues of the war before the public. James Webb Young of one of the leading agencies, Young and Rubicam, proudly boasted at that founding meeting of the vast powers held by the advertising industry: "We have within our hands the greatest aggregate means of mass education and persuasion the world has ever seen."[13]

Advertising had everything to gain by making this move. The most pressing problem before advertisers was replacing accounts from consumer goods manufacturers who converted to war production. By June 1942, 29 percent of prewar production of consumer goods had been cut off due to conversion of manufacturing plants and to shortages of materials.[14] Without products to sell, advertisers were faced with a projected loss of 80 percent of their business over the course of the war. To survive, they undertook a sales campaign that featured advertising as an essential feature of successful prosecution of the war. If advertisers could convince the government that their services would boost public morale, they would have something to sell at a time when consumer sales were down.

The recruitment of women into war production was one of OWI's major projects, directed by the Bureau of Campaigns. When Gardner Cowles was made director of OWI's domestic branch, he appointed a former marketing head from NBC and advertising director of Colgate-Palmolive, Ken Dyke, as chief of the bureau, and Dyke became the WAC's principal contact with the government. Federal agencies funneled their publicity needs through his office to the Council, which made suggestions for a campaign guidebook and contacted an advertising agency for copy and layout. It also found a sponsor for the ad or campaign and an agency to place the ads in appropriate publications.[15]

The Council appointed a full-time consultant to the Bureau, sent representatives to its bimonthly meetings with Cowles, and maintained regular contact with the War Manpower Commission through Raymond Rubicam of Young and Rubicam, who assisted Paul McNutt, a member of the War Manpower Commission, with labor recruitment.[16] In addition to these direct links between the WAC and OWI, the Bureau of Campaigns attempted to coordinate government policy with magazine advertising through a monthly *War Guide for Advertisers* which identified campaign dates, objectives, and promotional methods while providing samples of ad layouts. It is clear from the influx of businessmen and media personnel into Washington and the extensive communication network set up between OWI and advertisers that cooperation among government agencies, propaganda organizations, and private industry was close. The ties extended to Treasury Department rulings that allowed war contractors to deduct publicity expenses from taxable income.[17] This key provision meant that businesses engaged in government contracts could run propaganda ads that were partially underwritten by the government.

The War Advertising Council created ads encouraging women to enter the labor force and the armed services throughout the war, but the most extensive cooperation between OWI and the Council concerning female labor recruitment occurred in early 1944, when the national "Women in the War" program was planned. This campaign, intended to last throughout the year, aimed to recruit women into civilian work and military service. The WAC asked advertisers to devote at least a portion of their ads to the theme of women war workers and advised them on appropriate appeals through booklets sent out in the winter of that year. In addition to these guidebooks with their thematic direction, the council provided the government with advertising agencies.[18]

This campaign is a good example of cooperation among the WAC, OWI, and government war agencies throughout the period. In November 1943, the Joint Army-Navy Personnel Board issued a directive requesting that the OWI use all its facilities to recruit women into the armed forces. It noted that women were reluctant to join the newly formed women's services and urged that the media be used to change public attitudes about female enlistment.[19] The Bureau of Campaigns responded by contacting the news, motion picture, graphics, magazine, and radio bureaus so that material could be adapted for different audiences. The News Bureau worked up special stories for the rural press, labor news, foreign-language and black newspapers, women's pages, and business house organs while distributing human interest pieces to press syndicates. Films from federal agencies were given to distributors for dispersal to churches, schools, war plants, and citizen groups. In addition, theaters agreed to show Hollywood films made in support of the campaign. The army produced recruitment posters, which were delivered twice a month to stores by the Boy Scout Dispatch Bearer Service and mailed to all post offices and cooperating businesses. Public transportation supported the campaign through displaying car cards in vehicles, which were paid for by the War Manpower

Commission, and the Outdoor Advertising Association provided posters to every community with a population of over 25,000. Under the National Spot and Regional Allocation Plan, radio stations agreed to transmit campaign messages on 75 programs a week for two months, and each station agreed to carry three announcements a day.[20] The WAC made a major effort to support this campaign, preparing ad guides for the Women's Army Corps, the Navy, and the War Manpower Commission. Some of the ads to which I refer are a product of this campaign, and they reflect prominent themes in the recruitment drive as a whole.

The propaganda strategies of the advertising industry were more blatant than those of the magazine industry, although the participation of writers, publishers, and editors in OWI campaigns was just as complete. As with advertisers, publishers and editors pressured government officials to organize the media after Pearl Harbor and requested that Washington give them accurate information about the war front while telling them what needed to be done at home. In the spring of 1942, a representative was sent to New York from the Office of Facts and Figures, predecessor to the Office of War Information, in order to get some idea of how magazine editors felt about the proposed establishment of a magazine division. She found that they all favored the plan and believed it "long overdue." Because most could not afford to send correspondents to Washington, they suggested that someone frequently meet with them in New York and that they be sent "a regular memo as to themes the government wants stressed."[21]

As a result of the spring meetings with editors, the Magazine Bureau was established with the reorganization of government information offices in June 1942. Bureau officials quickly grasped the utility of creating efficient lines of communication with the magazine industry, pressing for greater funds and authority to disseminate information for the purposes of influencing the public. The chief of the Magazine Bureau was Dorothy Ducas, a journalist and personal friend of Eleanor Roosevelt. She had discovered in her visits to editors that stories concerning war news were frequently delayed by lack of government information, while inadequate and sometimes conflicting directives from Washington interfered with the Magazine Bureau's aid to government programs. Concerned that they would give up trying to cooperate altogether, she asked Gardner Cowles to give her more power throughout the summer of 1942 and insisted that magazines were well suited for influencing large numbers of people.[22]

Ducas and her staff carried on a voluminous correspondence with government officials while answering an average of 600 letters a month from editors and writers requesting background material for stories. They took an active role in ascertaining the publicity of war agencies, information about which was then sent out as suggestions for specific stories to individual writers. To illustrate campaign goals and strategies, they sent photographs, pamphlets, posters, and guidebooks to editors. Ducas tried to further minimize public misunderstanding of government programs by arranging meetings between editors and heads of agencies. So that she could get accurate information out to writers, Ducas attended all such meetings and met regularly with the War Department, the Navy Department, and the War Manpower Commission.

Because so few publications had stationed correspondents in Washington, Ducas made frequent visits to their New York offices both to ensure that stories were not working against policy goals and to suggest taking up subjects that were useful to the government. A typical visit occurred in March 1943, when she contacted editors of Fawcett Publications, This Week Home Institute, the Russian War Relief Committee, *McCall's*, *Click*, Dell Publishers, and *Ladies' Home Journal*. She arranged a meeting between a writer for the *Journal* and a member of the Russian War Relief Committee, smoothed the feathers of a pulp editor who was denied clearance for a story he saw in another magazine, obtained information for the WMC on a story it considered damaging to labor recruitment, met with a writer concerning an article on "combatting race hatred" while suggesting to *Click* that it publish the story, and encouraged the planned publication of an article on teenage war workers.[23] Later, these contacts were systematized by assigning staff members to specific magazine groups so that the special needs of each market could be incorporated into propaganda appeals.

The major activity of the Bureau was publication of the bimonthly *Magazine War Guide*, which was the main avenue of communication between OWI and the magazine industry. It began publication in July 1942 and ran until April 1945. Published and circulated three months in advance of the desired publication date of stories, the *Guide* gave editors time to contact writers who would put together an appropriate piece. This wartime agenda was widely circulated, reaching 400 to 600 magazines with a combined readership of over 140 million people. By the end of 1943, the *Guide* was being sent to more than 900 people on magazine staffs and 400 government information officers. One thousand copies were distributed to freelance writers.[24]

According to OWI files, magazines were major supporters of the "womanpower" campaign, perhaps because their audience was primarily female. Their extensive involvement was early indicated in the summer of 1942, when editors asked Dorothy Ducas for information about the employment of women; she, in turn, urged Elmer Davis to develop a coordinated policy on the subject—how many women were needed for what kinds of jobs and where they could go for training. She also mentioned that magazines were taking the lead in mobilizing women through anticipating the need for day-care centers: "Magazine editors have been convinced that nurseries are necessary before the full womanpower of the country can be tapped." They had complained that there was no central source to consult for a list of centers and for procedures to get them established in war production areas.[25]

The Magazine Bureau reacted quickly to these requests, taking credit for a number of stories on womanpower and labor needs that appeared in national magazines in the fall of 1942. In addition to providing information through pamphlets on how to get women into the workforce, many of Ducas's activities in New York concerned this subject. She encouraged several magazines to print stories on nursing, for example, because the Bureau made nurse recruitment one of its major efforts. She provided *Harper's Bazaar* and all the Sunday supplements with a picture spread and suggested stories to *Cosmopolitan* and

Life. Similarly, to recruit clerical workers, Ducas agreed to help *Woman's Day* with a story on housing for government workers, congratulated *Redbook* for serializing a novel in support of the campaign, and provided a suggestion to Fawcett Publications that a story be written about a worker who "sacrificed for her country and was rewarded." She also discussed pieces with *Mademoiselle* that glorified working in Washington and finally succeeded in placing material on the subject in several magazines.[26]

These reports indicate that the recruitment campaign was of prime concern to the Bureau and to magazines; they worked closely together in developing stories that would encourage placement of women in jobs where they were needed. Ducas took an active role in making suggestions to magazines with certain audiences for stories suited to those markets, in answering requests from editors and writers for background information, and in seeing that magazines were moving in the right direction. A New York liaison office, set up in August 1943, provided editors with freer access to government information, although the visits from Bureau officials to writers and magazine editors continued until it folded in August 1945.

The image of women in magazine stories and advertising from the *Saturday Evening Post* resulted from a number of factors: imagined needs and attitudes of the audience, experiences and values of the artists, marketing decisions by editors, business interests of companies, and propaganda requests from the government. It is difficult, if not impossible, to sort these out and state which factor produced which part of the picture. We do know, however, that *Post* editors and writers participated extensively in the recruitment campaign. For instance, the editors met regularly with government officials concerning home-front campaigns, and the *Post* was a member of the Magazine Advisory Committee to the Magazine Bureau. It also carried advertisements from major companies that bear the stamp of the War Advertising Council. In addition, it had long employed writers who became members of the Writers' War Board (WWB), a private group that included Rex Stout, whose popular Nero Wolfe mysteries had appeared in the *Post* for many years.[27] The magazine also participated in the two major drives conducted by the OWI. To support the "Women in Necessary Services" campaign in the fall of 1943, it asked its foremost illustrator, Norman Rockwell, to create an appropriate Labor Day cover. His illustration was featured on the September 4 issue, which showed a woman dressed in red, white, and blue coveralls, rolling up her sleeve and striding purposefully toward a distant goal while loaded down with the bric-a-brac of defense work—air raid warning equipment, a wrench, and a service hat. Rockwell's figure reflects the campaign's emphasis on service jobs with her milk bottles, railroad lantern, farming tools, conductor's change carrier, oilcan, and mop. Six stories (out of eight) that month concerned women in defense work, and five lead stories on the subject appeared from September through December 1943. Similarly, in apparent response to the "Women in the War" campaign of 1944, the *Post* ran 10 lead stories concerning women in war work; 6 of them appeared in the spring when the campaign was officially launched. An additional 10 pieces during this period focused on women in military service, a significant increase over 1943, when only 2 concerned the services, thus reflecting the campaign's emphasis on the armed forces.

Between 1943 and 1945, the *Post* ran many advertisements that made no product pitch and devoted the entire copy to recruitment messages. Advertisements that were designed specifically to attract women to war work constituted 16 percent of the total number appearing during this three-year period. The impact of the campaign is understated by this figure, however, because such ads received prime space in the magazine as full- or half-page copy, a position occupied by a minority of the advertisements. The proportion of recruitment ads in this category was 55 percent.[28]

Companies that devoted 75 to 100 percent of their advertising space at various times during the war to the campaign were generally those that no longer produced consumer goods—especially household appliances—or that were directed to a female clientele. Eureka vacuum cleaners, for example, ran a series celebrating all aspects of women's war work. Crosley and Servel refrigerators and Easy washers featured war workers manufacturing or using their products. Wayne gas and Kelly tires devoted much space to women performing male jobs in service and trade. Food product ads, such as those for Maxwell House coffee, Canada Dry ginger ale, and 7-Up, also glorified women in war work, while the paper shortage freed Kleenex to play a major part in the "Women at War" campaign.[29]

Companies that most needed female workers (with the exception of the national railroads) generally stayed out of the recruitment campaign, preferring instead to celebrate the weapons of war they were manufacturing and postwar products. Advertisements for De Soto, Pontiac, and Nash-Kelvinator, for example, featured battle scenes rather than pleas for women workers. Likewise, the aircraft companies were more likely to feature strides made in aviation than to feature female riveters. These companies had a traditionally male clientele and their images are in line with appeals to masculinity. On the other hand, companies with a female market carried the bulk of recruitment copy, perhaps because their advertisers were more familiar with female images and because their audience was the group that needed to be reached.

The images of war workers in advertising during the recruitment campaign served the purpose of attracting women into fields drained by the enlistment of men and encouraging public acceptance of women in new roles. This was accomplished by demonstrating that women were capable of nondomestic work and, in fact, had been engaged in arduous labor outside the home throughout American history. The prevailing image of women as reliable, tough, efficient guardians of the home front, seeing to it that society functioned smoothly in the absence of men, was in part due to the War Advertising Council's strategy for enlisting civilian support of government programs. It suggested to the OWI that civilians who planted victory gardens, salvaged tin, paper, and fat, stayed within rationed allocations of scarce resources, and took war jobs should be highlighted in order to encourage compliance with economic and social goals: "[OWI must encourage] the development of a militant spirit—a desire to excel on the Home Front. We want more than just favorable compliance. We want zeal, enthusiasm, and individual initiative that will raise the standard of the whole effort. We Need Home Front Heroes."[30]

Presumably because the role of women was so vital, they became the symbol of this militant spirit and the model for proper civilian attitudes. An advertisement by Kraft Food Company is representative of the way women were featured. It shows a mother pitching hay while her daughter drives a tractor, with the caption: "Heroines . . . U.S.A." The text reads: "Always on our dairy farms, women and girls have had plenty of chores to do. . . . But what they are doing now would amaze you."[31] This ad was designed to attract women into farm work, one of OWI's major campaigns in the summers of 1943 and 1944, but at the same time it glorifies women's work as heroic service to the nation. Other tributes to women praised them for their efficiency, intelligence, and uncomplaining performance of their job. Bell Telephone, for instance, labeled its operators "Soldiers of Service"; Crosley refrigerators applauded the "resourcefulness and ingenuity of American women;" and Eureka proclaimed, "You're a Good Soldier, Mrs. America."[32] Bibb Manufacturing pictured women and men marching with determination toward victory, Arvin Manufacturing declared that "Women are doing their part to help win the war . . . working shoulder to shoulder with men," and an optical company praised women who "fight beside their men."[33]

Many ads placed war workers in a long tradition of heroines who helped their men in wartime. The Pennsylvania Railroad, for instance, informed readers that women were filling jobs that required strength and coolness and had "proved they can fill these roles most capably" while, at the same time, it linked them to patriotic heroines of the past by referring to a larger-than-life railroad worker as "Molly Pitcher, 1944."[34] An Armco ad referred to a female truck driver as "a 'covered wagon' girl: 'I got a job driving a truck when Paul went across. I'm hauling the stuff they fight with.' . . . Hers is the spirit of the women who reloaded the long rifles as their men fought off the Indians . . . the courage that helped build the kind of America we have today."[35] Through these associations of women with past struggles, the woman in a nontraditional job was portrayed as valiantly leading the nation to victory. Advertisers attempted in this way to provide women with positive role models for entering male occupations and to give the public a standard-bearer of home-front solidarity and protection.

Other ads promoted confidence in women's ability to do a "man-size" job by emphasizing that femininity was not incompatible with arduous high-pressure work, a theme that simultaneously assured the public that inhabiting masculine roles did not destroy female sexuality or "womanliness." A utility ad, for instance, pictures a diminutive female worker operating a huge machine and describes her as follows: "Five feet one from her 4A slippers to her spun-gold hair. She loves flower-hats, veils, smooth orchestras—and being kissed by a boy who's now in North Africa. . . . How can 110 pounds of beauty boss 147,000 pounds of steel? . . . . through the modern magic of electric power. The magic that makes it possible for a girl's slim fingers to lift mountains of metal."[36]

Although the intent of such messages was to associate women with durable goods production and heavy labor, they reinforced the traditional notion that women were essentially delicate and sexually alluring. This was a theme prominently stressed in military recruitment ads, which usually pictured servicewomen in the company of attractive men in uniform and emphasized the beauty of the women themselves. Camel cigarettes ran a series on women in the armed forces that showed women in fatigues in one part of the ad and off duty in evening gowns with officers in another part. Canada Dry made a similar attempt to maintain feminine identities of servicewomen; the company participated extensively in military recruitment and frequently ran advertisements saluting women in uniform. One of its 1944 ads illustrates the way feminine desirability was paired with military roles. It shows soldiers raising a toast to photos of women in various branches of the armed services with the caption "To the Ladies."[37] A Whitman's chocolate ad uses a similar technique by showing a beautiful WAC receiving the traditional gift a suitor brings to his sweetheart—a box of chocolates.[38] Though the economy required that women assume male roles, don functional clothing, and engage in physically demanding work, the emphasis on female sexuality gave the message that these new roles did not signify fundamental changes in the sexual orientation of women themselves or in their customary image as sexual objects. The feminization of women in the military reflects, as well, opposition in the armed forces toward lesbianism in the military, an institution that segregated large numbers of women into domestic quarters and provided opportunities for female camaraderie and affectional ties. In fact, a campaign on the part of the military to discourage lesbian and gay relationships during the war was subtly reflected in such advertisements.[39]

Heterosexual imagery was also prominent in advertising that depicted women in overalls on the production line, with the subliminal message that the war worker's real life had merely been suspended or postponed and lay waiting to be reanimated by the return of its missing fiance, husband, or yet-to-be-encountered sweetheart. Indeed, overt romantic connections were made between the woman riveter or welder at home and the soldier for whom she was working and waiting, so that the home front and battlefield were conceptualized in terms of heterosexual bonding, female and male fighting to reunite their severed halves. For instance, a riveter in a Texaco ad completes her task with determination and mentally signs the plane she is working on "From Alice to Eddie to Adolf."[40] Another ad shows an electrical worker in aircraft extending her hand aloft to a vision of a combat plane as the text characterizes the diamonds she is holding as follows: "Small things perhaps, these jewels a woman gives a man—but in war, as in love, there are no little things."[41] In a Eureka vacuum cleaner layout, a drill press operator gazes wistfully into the future as she contemplates her sweetheart's return: "She's not so very tall . . . just as high as a man's heart. But there's nothing helpless about her hands on a press. You should see her assembling parts for the starter motor that whirls the props of the plane Jimmy flies. . . . she works to the rhythm of a little tuneless song. . . . she hears it in the great war plant's thud and hum. . . . This is bringing Jimmy back . . . bringing Jimmy back."[42]

On a deeper level, the female warrior in her blue-collar uniform, inspired by her love of a man, blurred into traditional images of women as nurturers, not only of men but of the nation's morality and its spiritual well-being. Harking back to Victorian conceptions of women as spiritually pure domestic guardians, wartime propaganda connected skilled technological and physically demanding labor with cooking nutritious meals for the family, writing letters to men overseas, saving money for the postwar home occupied by a full-time homemaker, and other feminized occupations in which women devoted themselves to caring for others. Welding a ship hull was no different than sewing a patch on a little boy's torn pant leg. Karen Anderson describes a strategy developed by the WAC for encouraging housewives to enter war production factories that reinforced the image of war workers as dutiful wives performing the same function in the factory that they had at home.[43] Two examples illustrate this approach quite well. A Wayne gasoline ad features a woman gas station attendant with the caption, "The Missus Takes Over"; she is described as follows: "Giving your car the same care she used in keeping house and not a bit afraid of soiling her pretty hands."[44] In another ad encouraging both the womanpower and the victory mail campaigns run by Mazda electric, a factory worker on her break writes a letter to her husband overseas and compares the plant to her kitchen: "Here's a picture of me in my uniform. Remember how you used to wipe the flour smudges off my nose? Well, you ought to see me now—I'm a regular grease monkey. . . . The plant's as bright and cheery as my own kitchen."[45]

Assuming that housewives would not enter the labor force for economic reasons or be prepared to perform anything but simple household chores reflects ignorance of the working histories most women shared.[46] Employment outside the home was a normal, if irregular, feature of many women's lives, and many families required two incomes to achieve a middle-class standard of living. By casting nontraditional work into domestic images, propaganda implied that war workers had experience with nothing except homemaking and subtly undermined the idea that women and men could do the same work. As Karen Anderson perceptively observed when discussing this aspect of the recruitment campaign: "The demonstration by women that they could perform jobs hitherto assigned primarily or solely to men caused a reassessment not of the nature of women, but rather of the nature of the jobs they were doing so that they more nearly conformed to traditional preconceptions regarding women."[47]

Reinforcing associations of women with domestic roles were ads that portrayed women as responsible for housework even if they were in a plant. A Westinghouse ad, for example, congratulated a married aircraft worker for both building planes and running a home.[48] A Eureka advertisement described a soldier's mother making gas masks as "a two-job woman, running a house for Dad O'Rourke of a morning, and making gas masks on Eureka's 4-12 shift."[49] War workers were often shown in housewife/mother roles—working with, or taking care of, children or doing housework in factory coveralls. Children pictured in these scenes cheerfully helped their mothers with household tasks, especially young daughters, who were frequently dressed in coveralls and kerchiefs themselves.

Not only did such advertisements try to encourage women to stick by their posts even though the demands of a two-job lifestyle were considerable, but they implied that children and husbands would be well cared for. Maxwell House coffee recruitment ads portrayed war workers in warm domestic scenes to attract middle-class women into the labor force, yet the subliminal message was that pulling women out of the home would not damage family life. A representative ad from this series appeared in March 1944. A war worker in her 20s or early 30s is resting after a hard day's work at the factory, still wearing her coveralls and identification badge; her lunch bucket is prominently displayed on the dining room table. She is flanked by her parents and a little girl, her daughter perhaps, who hugs her closely while she sips the coffee that her mother has just poured. All three are eagerly listening to her working-day tales and are clearly full of respect for what she is doing.[50] In much the same vein, a Greyhound advertisement shows a young—evidently single—woman, lunch box in hand, dressed for work. She stands for those who have left home to find employment in war industries and is surrounded by photos intended for her family that portray her in various aspects of war work, all with captions that point to how proud such women are of the work they are doing: "I helped build this ship! . . . I'm helping pour hot steel. . . . You should see me handle this tractor."[51] While publicizing work in labor-short fields, the ad delivers the message that war workers come from respectable families and that their wartime duties will not interfere with close family ties. Similarly, a Kellogg advertisement shows a WAVE serving breakfast to her parents, while the manufacturers of Pontiac feature a fresh-faced WAC described as "your daughter, sister, sweetheart, or wife."[52] These ads reflect advertisers' attempts to enlist women without economic need into the struggle, to pair positive family images with nontraditional work, and to counter long-standing beliefs that proper, stable homes required a full-time homemaker. Wartime advertising temporarily adjusted woman's home role to the demands of outside employment but made it clear that the role would not be abandoned.

Reinforcing the traditional underpinnings of war workers as guardians of the republic was the highlighting of the white, middle-class, heterosexual nuclear family in propaganda in order to give the war a metaphorical focus. The family at home, with its noticeably absent breadwinner, was the spiritual center of the mobilization campaign and the image most clearly associated with victory and peace. The protection of the family came to be the soldier's job as he formed the first line of defense to keep the enemy from reaching his manless, unprotected, vulnerable family. Masculine strength preserving feminine purity and softness, then, was the flip side of Rosie with her riveting gun. Rosie could replace a man on the production line, but her ultimate well-being depended not on herself but on a stronger male savior to whom she subordinated whatever autonomous drives she may have had before the emergency.

The creation of expanded roles for women, in other words, took place within a context that neglected to connect new work opportunities with women's rights or even individual rights. Because the work was conceptualized ideologically as sacrifice for a national cause, and women were used as representations of sacrifice, the implicit message that women could do all kinds of work was muted and eventually silenced altogether. The need for feminine sacrifice, in fact, was developed into a postwar theme to hammer home the plight of the returning veteran, jobless, traumatized by battle, sometimes badly wounded. He who had risked his life to protect the American family and save the civilized world from a barbaric enemy deserved first place in a woman's heart and first priority in whatever plans she had made during his absence.[53] Accordingly, by the second half of 1944, advertisers began to reverse the direction of the social change they had tried to effect in the recruitment campaign. One issue the OWI was careful to emphasize was the return of the battle-scarred veterans, who would need care and understanding in their readjustment to civilian life. Concerned especially about job placement, it asked that publicity be given to the Selective Service requirement specifying that servicemen be guaranteed their former jobs.[54] Ads reflected this orientation by assuring soldiers that their rightful place was reserved and that employers eagerly awaited their return. Mobil Oil, for instance, trumpeted this message: "Yes—your job is waiting for you, Soldier!" while an advertisement for Greyhound pictured a soldier writing home about the good news he had just received: "My old dispatcher at Greyhound writes me that they're planning the finest passenger buses the U.S.A. has ever seen—and he says they'll want me back there to pilot one of 'em."[55]

Conversely, believing that wartime employment patterns for women were merely a stopgap measure, necessary only while the men were gone, advertisers assumed female war workers would either go home or seek jobs in pink-collar areas. Taking advantage of this presumably automatic shift and eager to facilitate the changeover to peacetime production, typewriter companies encouraged working women to enter clerical work, one of the areas, along with teaching and nursing, that OWI had indicated would need large numbers of women in the postwar period.[56] A Smith-Corona ad, for instance, pictures a metal assembly worker contemplating her factory badge and asks: "When it becomes a souvenir, what then? . . . Like our fighting men, you've earned the right to choose the work you enjoy."[57] The message supports the notion that one may work where one pleases, but it also advises women to learn to type and suggests that women naturally prefer office to factory work. Another Smith-Corona ad shows several hands and asks the reader the question, "Are yours ready for that post-war job?" while urging her "to learn to type today and get ahead tomorrow."[58] Others made it clear that the future for women workers lay in clerical fields by focusing on little girls. An ad for Underwood typewriters, for instance, featured a child who was designated "Young Lady with a Future" because "she loves to type" while entitling her "Future Secretary of America."[59] Another Underwood ad relays to the reader how lucky a girl will be to grow up in the new world: "Whether she becomes secretary to the President of the United States or to the president of some one-man business, her mind and her hands will help speed and influence whatever projects cross her desk."[60]

By 1945, advertisers had completely dropped recruitment themes of the previous two years, and women in ads were all—with the exception of servicewomen—in traditional fields or had no occupational role. Most ads implied that currently employed women would have no outside job in the postwar world but would instead take up full-time homemaking at the first opportunity. Two themes used throughout the recruitment campaign facilitated this portrayal.   One was the praise of war workers for their remarkable achievements as double-duty workers—taking a war job and maintaining the home.   Though the initial effect of this message was to foster positive attitudes toward employed wives and mothers and to reassure women that they could handle home responsibilities even if they entered the labor force, its implication was that the exhausting load could not be borne indefinitely.   This idea was later brought out in ads that showed war workers eager to rest at home after victory and to use their high wages for purchasing a domestic paradise wherein work was kept to a minimum.   A Briggs home appliance ad, for example, featured a woman in factory coveralls motivating herself to go to work every day by looking at a picture of the modern kitchen she would some day have, while a Monsanto ad proclaimed: "There'll come a day . . . when a lot of the good new things of peacetime will become important to Rosie the Housewife."[61] Similarly, Thermos bottle advertised its product by showing a war worker pouring coffee for herself at the factory in one picture and serving coffee to her husband and friends as a housewife in another as she says: "This is what I'm working for—the carefree home parties we used to have."[62]   Leaving her war job in favor of the home was shown as the woman worker's reward for a job well done.

There was an element of truth in what advertisers were saying about wartime work.   It frequently was exhausting, and there is evidence that many women could not cope well with the demands of families and enormous workloads at the factory.   Reports of the Women's Bureau showed that one-half of married workers bore full responsibility for housework and were in desperate need of increased community services.   To support its request for more government funding of such services in 1943, it cited cases like the following:

A 45 year old woman, living on a farm fifteen miles from the plants, gets up at four, packs lunches for herself and two sons in high school, gets the family breakfast, and leaves home at six o'clock. For her ride home she has to wait for men who work longer hours, so regardless of the hours worked it is after six when she reaches home. Then she has dinner to get, dishes to wash, and the whole round of household work to do. . . . It is eleven p.m. when she retires, allowing only five hours for rest.[63]

Drained by factory workweeks averaging 44 to 48 hours, pressured by husbands—if they were married—to continue their roles as homemakers, hampered by inadequate transportation, and forced to shop in crowded stores, women workers were often faced with intolerable workloads, a situation that the Bureau noted led to high absenteeism and dropout rates. Undoubtedly, many women gladly left war work for a less rigorous work schedule.   Most, however, needed an income either for survival or to improve their family's living standard—50 percent of the women in war production areas who described themselves as former homemakers voiced a desire to keep their jobs, and 80 percent of all women workers in war jobs indicated in government surveys that they would remain in the labor force after the war.[64]   More important, the media's proposed solution to this problem changed from recommending ways during the recruiting effort that women workers could cut down on housework to implying wage work was so distasteful that they would drop out when things were back to normal.

A related thematic change was the shift from the wartime idea that working mothers could raise happy children to that suggested by tragic portraits of families breaking under the strain of mother's being away. By the spring of 1944, ads began dramatizing the unhappiness of children with war-working mothers. An Armco ad, for instance, featured a little boy in tears being comforted by his mother as she leaves for the factory: "Chin up soldier . . . just like Daddy said."[65] Another company that manufactured war material, Adel Co., used the same idea when it showed a mother in coveralls and factory badge stopping on her way to work to answer her daughter's plaintive question: "Mother, when will you stay home again?" The text provides an answer for her: "Some jubilant day mother will stay home again, doing the job she likes best—making a home for you and daddy, when he gets back." The ad goes on to discuss the company's plan to convert to peacetime production in a way that illustrates advertisers' postwar focus on women as consumers rather than producers: "She's learning the vital importance of precision equipment made by Adel. In her post-war home she'll want appliances with the same high degree of precision and she will get them when Adel converts its famous Design Simplicity to products of equal dependability for home and industry."[66] As manufacturers began to convert to production of consumer goods, advertisers intensified the attack on working mothers. A factory worker has to plead before a judge for her teenage son, who is labeled a "Victory Vandal" by Yale and Towne locks, and in a State Farm insurance ad a hysterical girl is carted away to a foster home because her mother has to work.[67] These traumatic scenes contrasted dramatically with ads showing mothers at home with their children playing happily nearby.

The full-time homemaker was an integral part of the ideal American family, which meant that two conflicting images of women existed during the war: the strong, dependable patriot who could run a machine, and the innocent, vulnerable mother outside the realm of technology who was depending on soldiers to protect her way of life. Reinforcing the traditional image was the way advertisers made homemakers into the living embodiment of every value America safeguarded; they thus became symbolic of the besieged nation. A good example of this representation is an Adel Manufacturing ad that shows a young mother and a little girl gently playing with kittens in a field of flowers. The pastoral scene conveys the beauty, peace, and innocence that war has temporarily obliterated, and the ad makes clear that this is the way of life America is trying to preserve: "It's to keep that world and to bring back the birthright of millions of children elsewhere that American men and machines are fighting on every battle front."[68] This ad reflects the vulnerable image of women that resulted from focusing on the family as the key element of endangered American beliefs, as does the following American Radiator advertisement, appearing early in the war, which pictures a young mother and baby surrounded by the violence of warfare: "Now, as in the past—the home is the bulwark of the nation."[69] This simultaneous glorification of women as

symbols of the nation under attack and of soldiers as their champions strength-
ened traditional gender roles wherein men protected women from a harsh and
brutal world.

An important related function served by images of women during the war
was their role as guardians of a way of life temporarily disrupted by uncertainty,
violence, and prolonged separation from loved ones. The desire for something
stable to hold onto is evident in wartime popular culture. A 1943
Nash-Kelvinator ad, for instance, features a soldier in a combat zone wistfully
daydreaming about the peaceful world he has left behind and yearning for the
familiarity of home: "I want my girl back, just as she is, and that bungalow on
Maple Avenue."[70] A Eureka ad captures this aspect of women's symbolic
function quite well. A mother is holding her baby, and both are looking into the
distance, metaphorically seeking the young father overseas while bravely facing
up to the possibility that he may be dead. Though she looks vulnerable, the text
praises her for carrying on without her husband and bravely keeping her home
secure even as the fabric of her life has been torn asunder: "Face to face with
you, my little son . . . I know there will be bright tomorrows. . . . [Your
father] may never see you now . . . but we must live in hope, always. That
makes you and me very special kind of partners. Building together the kind of
life he would want for both of us."[71] The ad illustrates the double function
women served as faithful comrades trusting their men to safeguard them from
harm while courageously keeping their home intact though it was without a
leader and provider and facing an uncertain future.

An image that combined the contradictory concepts of women as home-front
fighters and women as gentle caretakers of the family was that of the pioneer
woman. This was a common figure in ads of the war years and one with which
the public was familiar from iconography of the New Deal.[72] Frontier wives
were lauded as appropriate role models for contemporary women trying to
manage without men. The National Life Insurance Company, for instance, ran
a series entitled "Protecting the American Home," which stressed the bravery
and strength of women of the Old West. Pillsbury also ran a series of pioneer
ads emphasizing women's ability to withstand deprivation and to care for their
families in the midst of danger, while Eureka featured a welder who urged
readers to "Keep the home fires blazing."[73] Using the image of the pioneer
woman was one way to increase the acceptability of women in important,
demanding roles since it established the idea of female strength and toughness
as a vital part of American history. At the same time, the pioneer represented
a capable, supportive, and stoic partner who could keep the home going
single-handedly until things returned to normal.

Just as the servicewoman represented civilian patriotism, so did the
housewife, both historical and contemporary, stand for what made America
strong: the family. Viewing history as a linear progression, propagandists
during the war located the family in a specific historical context that encom-
passed both the essentialist belief in woman's biological destiny to be
wife/mother and the portrait of America as advancing force of civilization. To
fashion an inspirational image that would frame America's role in the war, they
drew on mythology of the western frontier and pioneer settlement with man the

explorer/defender and woman the faithful follower. Beginning with the Revolutionary War and ending with the fight to tame a western wilderness, propaganda depicted women as loyal partners in men's struggle to defeat both foreign and indigenous enemies standing in the way of progress and freedom. Betsy Ross, Molly Pitcher, and pioneer homesteaders were associated with, and embodied in, war workers, modern-day guardians of a civilization formed by women on the cutting edge of those early battles to establish families in the new land. The actual, historical opposition during these periods—England, Native Americans, Mexico—were obviously not the point, particularly with England as an ally, but the mythology of America as advancing civilization and women its hearth builder very much was. The essentialism that lay at the core of wartime propaganda, despite its overt efforts to recruit women into male-defined jobs, consigned to women the role of family guardian and peacetime consumer of prosperity's bounty, which ultimately rendered the androgynous image of woman as Jill-of-all-trades both irrelevant and dangerous. The war was fought and won, according to propaganda, to advance the human race, which meant restoring to men their rightful place as innovators, breadwinners, protectors of the innocent and vulnerable. Women's superior nurturing ability, so the message went, was needed to heal the wounds of war and humanize the warrior hero necessarily calloused by his bruising battle with tyranny.

The antifeminist backlash of the 1950s, popularly known as the feminine mystique, did not need a conscious policy to push Rosie out of the factory into the home, although one existed, according to Eleanor Straub.[74] The more compelling force, I believe, was a cultural mythology first developed in the nineteenth century to rationalize male control of the marketplace and industrial expansion in a Victorian context. While seriously challenged by feminists, socialists, and progressive movements, an ideology that equated civilized advancement with a separate, domestic sphere remained available to media experts of the 1940s searching for ways to dramatize the war for a population insulated from its direct impact. The role of women, in particular, was a necessary subject for propaganda designed to mobilize this population, and therefore it was at the forefront of media portrayals that attempted to mythologize the war's aims. Wartime images of women grasping the tools of modern civilization and handling them with grace and competence suggest a potential in American culture for seeing gender as one component of strength, not its inevitable determinant, but a closer examination of those images reveals an equally strong tendency to masculinize the human quality of assertiveness and, more alarmingly, to pair virility with progress. In addition, the absence of black women in advertising propaganda, despite the fact that they made up approximately 10 percent of women workers in war production areas, starkly illustrates the exclusionary nature of women's images in World War II.[75] Heroism and concepts of womanliness could be associated with white women in nontraditional roles, but racism proved to be an impenetrable barrier in creating expanded images of women.

The militaristic context of wartime propaganda inevitably distorts its relevance to us 50 years later, we who are not embroiled in a world war, not mobilized for production of war material. At the same time, idealization of the bourgeois family with its bipolar model of gendered capabilities has been a prominent feature of American life since at least the nineteenth century, and I think it is important to recognize the deep cultural assumptions upon which it rests. World War II provides us with an example of the connection between essentialist notions of women as selfless nurturers and a kind of chauvinist patriotism that conceives of America as the vanguard of civilization and evolutionary progress. Both ideas have been seriously challenged in the last 20 years, but we need to examine the full legacy of World War II, its aftermath as well as its striking innovations, lest we forget the power of these images to destroy the potential for egalitarian work roles in American life.

NOTES

1. Maureen Honey, *Creating Rosie the Riveter: Class, Gender, and Propaganda during World War II* (Amherst: University of Massachusetts Press, 1984). Other analyses of women's role in the war include Karen Anderson, *Wartime Women: Sex Roles, Family Relations and the Status of Women during World War II* (Westport, CT: Greenwood Press, 1981); William Chafe, *The American Woman: Her Changing Social, Economic and Political Roles 1920–1970* (New York: Oxford University Press, 1972); Sherna Gluck, *Rosie the Riveter Revisited: Women, the War, and Social Change* (Boston: Twayne, 1987); Susan Hartmann, *The Home Front and Beyond: American Women in the 1940s* (Boston: Twayne, 1982); Leila Rupp, *Mobilizing Women for War: German and American Propaganda 1939-1945* (Princeton: Princeton University Press, 1978).

2. Critiques of the bias in contemporary popular culture include Todd Gittin, *Inside Prime Time* (New York: Pantheon Books, 1983); Chandra Mukerji and Michael Schudson, eds., *Rethinking Popular Culture: Contemporary Perspectives in Cultural Studies* (Berkeley: University of California Press, 1991).

3. By the 1940s, the feminist movement had fizzled as an effective political force and would not be revived until the 1960s. For a discussion of how it lapsed, see William O'Neill, *Everyone Was Brave: A History of Feminism in America* (New York: Quadrangle Books, 1968).

4. Studies that stress the importance of American production capacity in winning the war are *Industrial Mobilization for War: History of the War Production Board and Predecessor Agencies 1940–1945*, vol. 1 (Washington, DC: Government Printing Office, 1947); Eliot Janeway, *The Struggle for Survival: A Chronicle of Economic Mobilization in World War II* (New Haven, CT: Yale University Press, 1951); Sumner Slichter, *Economic Factors Affecting Industrial Relations Policy in National Defense, Industrial Relations Monography*, no. 6 (New York: Industrial Relations, 1941).

5. There is evidence of this concern in government documents from the period directed at magazine editors. See "War Production Drive," "Toughening Up for War," *Magazine War Guide* (December/January 1943) entry 345, box 1700; "Discomfort," *Magazine War Guide* (March/April 1943), entry 345, box 1700. All government documents cited in this chapter are from Records of the Office of War Information, Record Group 208, National Records Center, Suitland, MD.

6. Eleanor Straub, "U.S. Government Policy toward Civilian Women during World War II" (Ph.D. diss., Emory University, 1973), 170, 33.

7. Allan Winkler, "Politics and Propaganda: The Office of War Information, 1942–1945" (Ph.D. diss., Yale University, 1974), 1–46. This study was published by Yale University Press in 1978 under the title *The Politics of Propaganda: The Office of War Information 1942–1945.*

8. A brief account of this organization is given in George Creel, *How We Advertised America* (1920; rpt. New York: Arno Press, 1972). See also James Mock and Cedric Larson, eds., *Words That Won the War: The Story of the Committee on Public Information 1917–1919* (Princeton: Princeton University Press, 1939).

9. Frank Fox, *Madison Avenue Goes to War: The Strange Military Career of American Advertising 1941–1945*, Charles E. Merrill Monograph Series (Provo, UT: Brigham Young University Press 1975), 68.

10. Winkler, "Politics and Propaganda," 47.

11. The best sources of information on OWI are Winkler's study and David Jones, "The U.S. Office of War Information and American Public Opinion during World War II, 1939–1945" (Ph.D. diss., State University of New York—Binghamton, 1976).

12. The conclusions in this study are based on all the advertisements carried in the lead issue for every month of the *Saturday Evening Post* from January 1941 through March 1946.

13. Fox, *Madison Avenue*, 22.

14. Richard Polenberg, *War and Society: The U.S. 1941–1945* (Philadelphia: J. B. Lippincott, 1972), 11.

15. Fox, *Madison Avenue*, 50.

16. These extensive links are described in records of the Office of War Information. See Manpower Campaigns file, "Report from the War Advertising Council," September 1942, entry 90, box 588.

17. Fox, *Madison Avenue*, 41.

18. J. Walter Thompson was the advertising agency for the War Manpower Commission; "Words That Work for Victory," March 1, 1944–March 1, 1945, "Report of the War Advertising Council," entry 90, box 588.

19. Women in the War Campaign file, entry 90, box 591.

20. Ibid. This is just a small sample of the amount of recruitment propaganda created and disseminated by the media under OWI direction. In 1944 alone, 50 radio programs on the "womanpower" campaign were broadcast each week for 26 weeks.

21. Memo, Dorothy Ducas to Ulric Bell, May 11, 1942, Magazine Bureau Organization file, entry 339, box 1695.

22. Memo, Ducas to Cowles, August 4, 1942, Magazine Bureau Organization file, entry 339, box 1695.

23. Report, Ducas to Harold Guinzburg, March 25, 1943, Magazine Bureau Organization file, entry 339, box 1695.

24. Memos, Ducas to F. Girardot, September 17, and December 11, 1943, Magazine Bureau Organization file, entry 339, box 1695.

25. Memo, Ducas to Elmer Davis, September 23, 1943, Magazine Bureau Organization file, entry 339, box 1695.

26. Report, Ducas, December 16, 1942; memos, Ducas to Bell, May 19, 1942, June 30, 1942, May 11, 1942, December 21, 1942, Magazine Bureau Organization file, entry 339, box 1695.

27. Regular contributors of fiction to the *Post* who were executive members of the Writers' War Board include Rita Halle Kleeman, J. P. Marquand, Stephen Vincent Benet, Walter D. Edmonds, Mary Roberts Rinehart, Kenneth Roberts, Sophie Kerr, Robert Pinkerton, and Paul Gallico. Although the authors of other stories with clear propaganda purposes were not members of the board's advisory committee, it is likely that they were asked by fellow writers to write stories for OWI campaigns. Though these writers do not appear on the rosters of board committees, the nature and quality of the stories they wrote suggest contact with board members. Robert Carson, for example, wrote stories that glorified heroines in war work, yet he does not appear on WWB lists. Similarly, Margaret Craven and Phyllis Duganne contributed fiction with strong recruitment themes but were not official members.

28. Information coded included the occupation, activity, and dress of all women in any advertisement in which they appeared. If a woman's clothing or activity did not reflect her employment as either wage worker or housewife, she was placed in the category "no occupation." The occupational status was coded as follows: traditional pink-collar roles (including housewife) or nontraditional jobs (including male occupations and the armed services); and war work (including volunteer activities) or employment unrelated to the war effort (housework was placed in this category). Products being advertised and company names were noted for all advertisements picturing women. If children appeared in the ad or if reference was made to a woman's family, she was considered a mother. In addition, I noted the attitude expressed toward the woman's role in the illustration, text, and caption, that is, how her activity was presented to the reader, how her contribution to the war effort was interpreted, and what motivation she was pictured as having for playing the role in which she was cast.

29. Advertisements containing women were categorized into two major groupings: those that concerned war workers and those that did not. An ad was judged to be in the former category if it featured at least one woman in clothing appropriate for factory work, ship construction, the armed forces, male service and transportation jobs, farm labor, and volunteer services or if the work she did was clearly identified as paid employment that was related to the war effort (such as clerical worker, nurse, child care supervisor, telephone operator, draftsperson, or service and trade worker). Advertisements that featured women but did not describe them as having paid employment (in home roles, planting victory gardens, buying goods, or serving as decorative figures) were not considered to be about war work. Finally, the size of the advertisement was noted, and whether it was a full, half, or quarter page was also noted. Full-page ads were given more weight in the analysis than the others, which were judged to have less of an impact on the reader.

30. La Roche to Cowles, January 3, 1943, Young and Rubicam file, entry 20, box 15.

31. July 1, 1944, 87.

32. February 12, 1944, 75; January 9, 1943, 50.

33. March 27, 1943, 95; June 5, 1943, 93; May 27, 1944, 1.

34. May 13, 1944, 64; October 21, 1944, 90.

35. April 15, 1944, 103. The strategy to develop a militant spirit in civilians also explains the observation made by Leila Rupp that "magazine illustrations and advertisements pictured women in uniform in an extent out of all proportion to their actual numbers." Rupp, *Mobilizing Women*, 150.   Rupp concludes that the overpresentation of servicewomen resulted from public fascination with them as an exotic wartime phenomenon. However, the emphasis on women in uniform grew largely out of the War Advertising Council's plan to equate civilian support of home-front campaigns with the brave and loyal actions of soldiers in the thick of battle. Since women were the major representatives of home-front militancy, it makes sense that female military imagery abounded during the war.

36. June 12, 1943, 55.

37. November 11, 1944, 76.

38. January 9, 1943, 8.

39. Allan Berube, "Coming Out under Fire," Mother Jones (February–March 1983): 23–29.

40. March 20, 1943, 36.

41. February 26, 1944, 33.

42. October 30, 1943, 67.

43. Anderson, *Wartime Women*, 82.

44. April 29, 1944, 70.

45. January 30, 1943, 7.

46. Leila Rupp makes this point in *Mobilizing Women*, 152.

47. Anderson, *Wartime Women*, 61.

48. January 16, 1943, 41.

49. November 29, 1943, 94.

50. March 25, 1944, 51.

51. June 24, 1944, 65.

52. November 20, 1943, 60; September 30, 1944, 33.

53. A full discussion of this theme is provided in Susan Hartmann, "Prescriptions for Penelope: Literature on Women's Obligations to Returning World War II Veterans," *Women's Studies* 5:3 (1978): 223–39.

54. *Magazine War Guide*, September/October 1943, entry 345, box 1700.

55. September 23, 1944, 41; August 12, 1944, 78.

56. "Women in the Post-War Jobs," *Magazine War Guide*, January 1945, entry 345, box 1700.

57. November 4, 1944, 92.

58. September 16, 1944, 108.

59. September 9, 1944, 74.

60. May 27, 1944, 84.

61. May 6, 1944, 94; November 27, 1943, 113.

62. July 8, 1944, 88.

63. U.S. Department of Labor, Women's Bureau, Women's *Wartime Hours of Work: The Effect on Their Factory Performance and Home Life*, bulletin 208 (Washington, DC: Government Printing Office, 1947). See also Janann Sherman, "'The Vice Admiral':

Margaret Chase Smith and the Investigation of Congested Areas in Wartime," in this volume.

64. U.S. Women's Bureau, *Women Workers in Ten War Production Areas and Their Postwar Employment Plans*, bulletin 209 (Washington, DC: Government Printing Office, 1946).

65. March 4, 1944, 103.

66. May 6, 1944, 99.

67. June 17, 1944, 91; March 17, 1945, 93.

68. June 10, 1944, 101.

69. January 3, 1942, 1.

70. February 27, 1943, 7.

71. January 29, 1944, 56.

72. The pioneer family was a prominent image in public art during the depression of the 1930s, symbolizing cooperation, self-sufficiency, and American initiative. Barbara Melash, *Engendering Culture: Manhood and Womanhood in New Deal Public Art and Theater* (Washington, DC: Smithsonian Institution Press, 1991), 33–82.

73. June 26, 1943, 77.

74. Straub, "U.S. Government Policy," 10.

75. Hartmann, *The Home Front*, 216. See also Karen Anderson, "Last Hired, First Fired: The Black Women Workers during World War II," *Journal of American History* 69 (June 1982): 82–97.

7

Women Defense Workers in World War II: Views on Gender Equality in Indiana

Nancy Felice Gabin

The significance of World War II for American women remains a central question in analyses of the female experience in this century. Scholars have evaluated the short- and long-term impact of the war, debating the extent of change and continuity in social, political, and economic terms. There is much grist for the mill.. Nearly half of the 11 million women employed in the United States in 1940 worked in low-paid, low-status clerical, sales, and service jobs. The 20 percent who worked in manufacturing were concentrated in a few low-paid industries such as textiles and garments. World War II substantially improved the economic prospects of women as the demand for labor to meet the nation's wartime needs exceeded the available supply of male labor and opened occupations formerly closed to them. Of the 18 million women employed in 1944, 36 percent held clerical, sales, and service jobs, while the proportion employed in manufacturing had increased in relative terms to 34 percent. The entrance of over 3 million women into manufacturing represented a striking 140 percent increase over the figure for 1940, but the 460 percent increase in the number of women employed in male-dominated basic industries that converted to war production was even more dramatic. The war also offered many women upward occupational mobility. Although 49 percent of the women employed in defense industries in March 1944 had not worked before the war, 27 percent of those so employed, attracted by higher wages, better working conditions, and the opportunity to learn new skills, had shifted from other occupations.[1]

Many of the changes associated with World War II were only temporary, but their impact on the attitudes and behavior of women and men, unionists and employers, and policymakers and politicians has been hotly contested. The extent to which women for the first time took male-defined jobs in basic industries and challenged assumptions about the "naturalness" of the gender division of labor has been a principal concern in the debate over the impact of the war. The scholarship on this issue generally divides between those who view the influx of women into the nation's factories as a historical "watershed" because it validated their labor force participation—especially that of married, middle-class women—and those who regard the circumstances of the war as reinforcing, rather than subverting, occupational segregation by sex. This chapter assesses that debate by examining ideas about gender equality in Indiana workplaces during the war. Emphasizing the importance of change as well as continuity, it contends that the greater visibility of women factory workers during World War II prompted popular consideration of gender equality, compelled unionists and employers to confront their commitments to gender hierarchy, and offered at least some working women the novel experience of equality. Focusing on working-class, rather than middle-class, women and men in factories, the chapter highlights the extent to which the war years were more volatile on the question of gender equality than scholars generally have acknowledged. [2]

Indiana offers a rich field for an analysis of ideas about gender equality in the 1940s. The state received a much larger than average share of war contracts, ranking eighth in the nation, and its manufacturing industry grew more rapidly than that of most states. In 1944, payrolls of war industries accounted for nearly one-third of all Indiana income payments, ranking the state fourth nationally behind only Michigan, Connecticut, and Ohio in this regard. Women made up a significant proportion of those payrolls. In 1940, women represented 18 percent of those employed in manufacturing in the state. By the end of 1943, more than one-third of all factory workers in Indiana were women. The greatest increase in female employment in the state occurred in the defense industries, not only in machinery plants (mostly converted auto and electrical goods plants), where women on average made up one-third of the labor force, but also in iron and steel mills, where the number of women employed increased 260 percent by 1944. In some factories, such as a tank armor plant in Gary, an RCA factory in Bloomington, and most of the ordnance plants, women constituted the majority of workers. [3]

The influx of women demolished some of the barriers to their greater integration into industry. The trend was evident in the employment of women in industries and plants that before the war had employed men almost exclusively. Women employed in steel mills before World War II tended to work only on sorting and inspecting tinplate. The demand for labor expanded women's opportunities in the mills; women could be found in almost every department, working at the ore docks, in the storage yards handling raw materials, on the coal and ore trestles, in the coke plants, in the blast furnaces, in the steel furnaces, in the rolling mills, and in the finishing mills. Women held untraditional jobs ranging from bricklayer to furnace door operator to truck driver to crane operator. At the peak of wartime employment, women's share of the steel labor force averaged 20 percent, varying from a low of 6 percent to a high of 55 percent in the different divisions of the industry. Although the new presence of women in enormous plants such as U. S. Steel in Gary and Alcoa in Lafayette raised eyebrows, the labor forces of smaller factories throughout the state were similarly transformed. To cite just one example, the Brown Rubber Company in Lafayette employed approximately 500 people before World War II, 75 percent of whom were male, in the production of rubber auto parts. Having secured defense contracts for the manufacture of self-sealing gasoline tanks for bombers and rubber fittings for army air corps vehicles, the factory in 1944 employed 400 people, 85 percent of whom now were female. [4]

The employment of women in defense industries new to Indiana highlighted the changes wrought by the war. At the inland shipyards at Evansville and Jeffersonville, for example, women proved adept at burning, chipping, and welding. Nearly 3,000 women, constituting one-sixth of the workforce, were employed in production jobs at the peak of wartime employment at the Evansville shipyard alone. Like the shipyards that had no prewar history in Indiana, newly constructed ordnance factories transformed small rural villages into teeming cities almost overnight. The most notable examples were a powder plant at Charlestown, the Kingsbury Ordnance Works in La Porte County, and the Wabash River Ordnance Works in Vigo County, which together employed thousands of women. Although the work itself—dangerous and unusual— attracted attention and made ordnance plants and their employees novelties, the sudden appearance of the huge installations employing great numbers of women also made women workers visible in new ways and to an unprecedented extent. This phenomenon reinforced the popular perception that women were inhabiting new and previously male public space. [5]

Even factory work that was regarded as traditionally women's was accorded greater respect and higher value during World War II, as Indiana cannery operatives discovered. In the 1930s, Indiana ranked second in the United States in terms of the number of wage earners in canneries and had the fourth largest number of canning factories of any state in the nation. Because of the location of the canning plants near the fields and the relatively brief but highly labor-intensive packing season, most Indiana canners relied on local women from the towns and surrounding farms. The annual stint in the canneries was a mainstay of the rural family economy in Indiana. Yet, women cannery workers were largely invisible, regarded as members rather than heads of households, as insulated by their rural isolation from a restive urban working class, and as too dependent on the canneries for cash income to protest their exploitation. During World War II, if only for a brief moment, women cannery workers became highly and newly visible. Opportunities for higher-paid and less seasonal jobs in defense plants attracted Indiana women and diminished the available supply of labor for the vegetable-packing season. "Older men, boys, and girls if properly trained can help in harvesting," advised an Indiana trade journal in March 1943. "Housewives and others not regularly employed may if enrolled and given some pre-season training," it lamely suggested to canners who had long depended on, and exploited, just such people as a source of labor, "provide enough labor in the canneries to get us through 1943." Growers and packers cooperated with the state office of the War Manpower Commission and the Indiana Employment Security Division to recruit still-unemployed women. When demand continued to exceed supply, they turned to German prisoners of war, a practice that attracted a great deal of public attention and highlighted the importance of women as workers. Another indication of the new respect paid women's role in the industry was the introduction at the annual state tomato festival in 1944 of a tomato-peeling contest. Noting the event's "enthusiastic" crowd of 3,500, industry coverage made clear that the champion tomato peelers—all women—were canning factory employees. These and other efforts publicly to esteem work that before the war was trivialized or invisible indicate the higher profile of women factory workers in Indiana during World War II.[6]

World War II, however, did not so much erase the boundaries separating women's and men's work as much as redraw them. Job segregation by sex persisted, women still making up the principal labor force in female-dominated industries or being unevenly distributed through the occupational structure of particular plants. For example, although not considered a war industry, the garment industry—whose Indiana labor force was predominantly female before and during the war—acquired defense contracts for such items as uniforms, military bedding, and parachutes. Although women did hold untraditional jobs in war plants, many worked on operations that were the same as or similar to those performed by women in peacetime. Automotive parts and equipment factories and electrical goods plants had always hired women in production jobs. Their conversion to defense production usually entailed few changes in the work process and required simply the hiring of more women for jobs already labeled as "female." Where women did take men's jobs, the job often had been altered in ways that justified and rationalized the hiring of women and maintained the notion that gender distinctions were essential and fundamental. The use of hoists and conveyors or the modification of a press to accommodate the smaller stature of women was regarded as having transformed a male-defined job into a female-defined one. The preservation of the gender division of labor seemed to validate the continued use of separate and unequal wage rates and job classifications based on sex.

The technological changes and sometimes dramatic shift in the composition of the labor force that attended the conversion process in industry, however, at least made the once-rigid boundaries separating women's and men's work ambiguous. As employers remapped the occupational structure, employees challenged decisions about wage rates and job classifications. At issue were wage standards as well as jobs. Simply put, male workers did not want defense jobs labeled as female because it would justify lower wages and jeopardize employment for men. The response of female workers was more complex but, at least during the period of conversion to defense production, was not as influential as that of men. Close examination of wage and job classification disputes at several Indiana automotive parts and equipment plants between 1941 and 1943 illuminates the dynamics of wartime conflicts over gender equality in the workplace.[7]

The first response of male workers in plants in which they were dominant generally was to prevent the employment of women on defense production. Before the United States actually entered the war, conflict developed, for example, between the Bendix Corporation in South Bend, Indiana, and the union representing workers in the plant, United Auto Workers (UAW) Local 9, over defense employment. The company always had employed women, but only in certain female-labeled jobs. On September 4, 1941, the local took a strike vote to protest the placement of women in aircraft parts inspection, a new defense operation similar, it claimed, to work long performed by higher-paid male auto parts inspectors in the plant. The union later concluded an agreement with

Bendix that endorsed the customary practice of segregating women in particular departments, classifying jobs according to the sex of the operator, and paying women an hourly rate 25¢ less than that paid men in the same or similar jobs. The contract, however, also contained a new feature that limited the future employment of women except in already demarcated "female" departments. Union leaders pressed for this provision because management refused to equalize the wages of women and men in defense jobs. Seeking to protect men's jobs and wage standards, Local 9 conceded women's lower rates but compelled management to obtain the local's permission before hiring more women.[8]

As the attempt to exclude women from defense jobs became an untenable strategy for maintaining wage standards, workers generally pressed vigorously for application of the principle of equal pay for equal work. There was, however, uncertainty in many minds about the correct application of the principle. The classification of newly created defense jobs that closely resembled prewar operations to which both sexes had been assigned but for which sex-differentiated wage scales had been established particularly confounded interpreters of the equal-pay principle. Workers tended to argue that if a man had ever performed a job, it was, *ipso facto,* a "male" job, and women now employed in it should receive the higher "male" rate negotiated before conversion. But employers feminized disputed operations and accorded them the lower "female" rate, claiming that the process of conversion had simplified the tasks once assigned to men, making them more like those done by women before the war. Both sides were somewhat disingenuous since neither would admit the flimsy and esoteric basis for many prewar differentials. It became, however, increasingly difficult to distinguish between operations performed by men and women. Even management was uncertain. Operating a honing machine at the General Motors Delco Remy plant in Anderson, Indiana, one woman, for example, found it easy and convenient to do her own setup, the task that differentiated the work of women and men on the machine and justified a lower wage rate for women. When it was brought to his attention, the foreman was surprised that she could do the setup, but rather than grant her the higher rate of pay and thereby acknowledge the arbitrary character of the sexual division of labor, he simply took her off the job. Another baffled foreman at the same plant referred an equal-pay grievance on an aircraft part assembly job to higher management because both sexes had performed and were performing the operations associated with the job. "I am unable to determine which is to be done by men and which to be done by women," he confessed. In this confused and confusing environment, disputes over job classification and wage determination proliferated.[9]

The endorsement by the National War Labor Board (NWLB) of the equal-pay-for-equal-work principle in the fall of 1942 promised to resolve the conflict between labor and industry over wartime wage policies. The decision of the NWLB in the landmark case brought by the UAW and the United Electrical Workers (UE) against General Motors (GM) also disallowed slight disparities in job content as justification for wage differentials. Directing the company and the unions to include in their contracts a clause stating that "wage rates for women shall be the same as for men where they do work of comparable quantity and quality in comparable operations," the NWLB rejected GM's claim that the necessity of employing male helpers to assist women on certain operations warranted its paying women less than men and asserted that "wage-setting on such a basis is not compatible with the principle of equal pay for equal work." By ordering GM to establish wage rates for women and men on the basis of comparable quality and quantity of output rather than differences in the physical characteristics of the operations, the NWLB not only removed the opprobrium from the term "job dilution" but also called into question the legitimacy of sex-based job classifications and the pervasive devaluing of women's work.[10]

The NWLB intended its equal-pay policy to fulfill its mandate to settle labor disputes, but the ambiguous boundaries between women's and men's prewar and wartime work continued to make the determination of job classifications and wage rates difficult, and conflict persisted, as a NWLB case involving Bendix and UAW Local 9 demonstrates. As war production intensified in 1942, Bendix sought to revise the agreement that restricted both the hiring and placement of women at its South Bend plant. The company now wanted the freedom to hire more women without the consent of the local, to place them in departments of the plant designated for men only, and to pay them the lower rate accorded women in the same jobs in so-named "female departments." Fearing a wholesale reduction in wage rates, the local demanded that women placed in male departments in jobs also performed by men receive the higher male rate before it would agree to eliminate the contract clause restricting the employment of women. Bendix refused to equalize wages, maintaining that implicit in the prewar agreement to classify the work of women and men separately was the assumption that the two sexes performed different and unequal work. Now to pay some women higher wages simply because they would be performing jobs elsewhere in the plant, the company asserted, would violate not only the contract but long-standing principles of wage determination.[11]

Local 9 then placed itself in the unusual position of discrediting the sexual division of labor in the plant. Arguing that there were no "female classifications" *per se*, the local insisted that wage rates should be determined on the basis of the content of the job, not the sex, of the operator, and that even women employed in "female jobs" in "female departments" should receive the same pay as men and women similarly employed elsewhere in the plant. Bendix rejected this demand, claiming that to raise so many women's wage rates would place the company at a competitive disadvantage in the industry. Management did call the union's bluff and proposed an independent, plant-wide, evaluation of the disputed jobs to eliminate sex labels and differentials. Confronted with the prospect of wage increases for some women but wage reductions for many men, Local 9 balked, withdrew its demand for wage equalization and called instead for a 10¢ differential between men and women in the same jobs. Bendix countered with an offer to increase the hourly rates of women in those jobs by 8¢.[12]

Unable to compromise, both sides invited NWLB arbitration of the dispute. In his decision, Harry Shulman, the board-appointed arbitrator, declared that "the differential between male and female rates was in origin and in its continuance based on nothing else but sex." Shulman agreed in principle with the company proposal for systematic job evaluation but rejected it as both impractical in wartime and offensive to the union. Stating that "were this differential not agreed upon and were it not of long standing there would be little doubt that it should be completely eliminated," Shulman reduced it but did not erase it. He granted the union's offer and pegged the hourly rate for women in the disputed classifications 10¢ below that already negotiated for men. Shulman also removed the restriction on the company's freedom to employ women.[13]

The Bendix decision reflected the NWLB's retreat from the broadly defined position on equal pay that it had adopted in the fall of 1942. In May 1943, William Davis, chair of the NWLB, criticized unions' use of the equal-pay-for-equal-work policy to increase wages in job classifications to which only women had been assigned in the past. In a decision on another case, Wayne Morse further ruled that the equal-pay doctrine "is not to be invoked to abolish wage differences between jobs which have historically been performed by women almost entirely and jobs which have been recognized in the industry as jobs limited for the most part to men." In July 1943, the NWLB settled an ongoing dispute between GM and the UAW by eliminating sex labels on jobs but substituting the terms "light" and "heavy" for the controversial "female" and "male" and establishing a 10¢ wage differential to reflect alleged job disparities. "Rates of each classification," Edwin Witte of the Regional War Labor Board later explained, "imply whether the employees are men or women." The board was not unmindful of the extent to which wages in women's jobs were artificially low. The slippery and inconsistent character of the gender division of labor also undermined NWLB attempts to render clear and unambiguous decisions. The board, however, like other federal agencies during World War II, chose not to lead a revolt against long-standing and deeply rooted ideas about women's place and gender hierarchy in American industry.[14]

But together with the process of conversion and the increased employment of women, NWLB rulings—despite their limitations—disturbed workers' equanimity with respect to the gender division of labor. In combination, they compelled unions to make the case for higher wages for the growing share of their membership that was female by acknowledging the extent to which distinctions between women's and men's work had been, and still were, arbitrary and irrelevant. The UAW, for example, was placed in the novel position of proving that women's jobs were the same as men's jobs despite the prewar practice, in which the UAW had concurred, of distinguishing among jobs on the basis of sex. In its exception to the NWLB's 1943 decision in the GM case, the UAW insisted that no discrimination should be made between "light" and "heavy" operations, disagreeing that the work performed by women and men in same-titled jobs was dissimilar enough to warrant wage differentials and noting that within any job or rate classification there were tasks that ranged in difficulty. This was a considerable advance over the UAW's position before and during the period of conversion, when it had sought to preserve wage standards by restricting women to a small number of jobs and excluding them from the larger number of male jobs. The new perspective suggested a revision of the union's rather limited notion of equal pay for equal work to include the idea of equal pay for comparable work or work of comparable value, a concept better able to address the problem of occupational segregation by sex in industry.[15]

The UAW did not wholly endorse gender neutrality in this period. In other instances, the union continued to think in customary ways and to describe the wage and occupational structure in the auto industry in gender-specific terms, even though doing so played into the hands of employers who also asserted the importance of difference in establishing lower rates for women regardless of occupation. Industry members of the Regional War Labor Board, for example, objected to the 1943 decision because it used a standard of comparability in narrowing the differential between women and men in same-titled jobs. "There is different work being done by women than that being done by men," they insisted. By talking in terms of men's jobs that women could do and women's jobs that men did not do, the UAW confirmed, rather than challenged, management's position. The equivocal position held by the UAW would bedevil its efforts late in the war and afterwards to challenge occupational segregation by sex and eliminate sexual discrimination.[16]

But the significance of the reconceptualization of gender and the work process in industry during World War II ought not be underestimated. The UAW at least began to rethink its approach to wage determination. The UE, which represented thousands of electrical goods workers throughout Indiana in the 1940s, went even further, guarding against wage cutting by challenging the very basis for wage discrimination by sex. In another landmark NWLB case, the UE charged General Electric and Westinghouse with systematically undervaluing the work performed by women. Endorsed by the NWLB in a 1945 decision, the UE's position essentially advanced the same argument as our contemporary concept of equal pay for work of comparable worth. The union and the board assailed the practice of both firms of systematically and neutrally evaluating all jobs in their plants but arbitrarily reducing wage rates by as much as one-third if women performed them. On the basis of documented evidence as well as the personal observations of jobs made by NWLB members, the board concluded that Westinghouse and General Electric had deliberately paid women less than men for jobs involving equal or greater skill, effort, and responsibility. The board thus found, at least in the case of the two largest electrical goods manufacturers, that sex alone explained the low wages paid to women and that the companies had discriminated in setting lower rates for women. The board went out of existence before it could design and implement a remedy, and the UE's campaign failed in the short run. Like the NWLB and the UAW, the UE's own position on gender equality in industry was limited in certain respects; the union, for example, did not then advocate sex-blind job assignments. But even if World War II was not the time for permanent change in the status of women in the labor market and for gender equality in the workplace, it was important in establishing precedent for reconsideration of wage disparities specifically and occupational segregation by sex generally.[17]

The response of women to the issues raised by the war emergency was varied and not easy or simple to interpret. There is abundant evidence that women in Indiana defense factories recognized the prospect for, and actually fought hard to obtain, equal opportunity and equal treatment in the workplace. The myriad complaints of employers about the difficulty of recruiting and retaining women for still low-paid jobs in female-dominated occupations attest to the intent of women to take advantage of the demand for their labor and the higher wages in basic industry. It is also apparent that women not only agreed that women who replaced men during the war should receive the same rate previously paid male employees but also were keen on capitalizing on the opportunity to challenge the separate and unequal status of women in industry. Some volunteered for transfer to male-defined jobs to file equal-pay grievances. Other women charged that men did not press for equal pay because they wanted to preserve their gender's dominant position in the labor force and sought NWLB arbitration on their own. A U.S. Women's Bureau investigator reported that even in plants where women were a small minority, they pressed for equity, if necessary to the point of threatening to strike.[18]

Women, however, did not speak in one voice or act as a unified group. Some women blamed the limited extent of change on other women who were new to basic industry and saw no reason to complain about unequal pay because their wages already were significantly higher than those they were accustomed to receiving in conventional women's jobs like waitressing, sales and clerical work, and garment manufacturing. Recounting how her local ratified Delco-Remy's offer to increase all women's hourly rates by 10¢ rather than grant equal pay to women in those jobs also performed by men, one woman told a U.S. Women's Bureau investigator that "many were young girls, others did not expect to work after the war. All they could see," she complained bitterly, "was the ten cents right then." When a majority of the women employed at the Chevrolet Commercial Body plant in Indianapolis similarly acceded to management's offer to raise their hourly rate of 82¢ to 96¢ rather than demand the $1.09 rate paid to men in the same jobs, women who had worked in the plant before the war claimed that they were "out of heart." Distressed by the disinterest among younger women in the issue of equal pay for equal work, they were reluctant to continue pressing for equal pay.[19]

It is undeniable that many women, like men, continued to think in terms of gender hierarchy when they contemplated the structure and organization of work. But to be fair, there also is evidence that even women who recognized the larger, long-term implications of equal-pay disputes simply found the burden of protest too onerous. Women employed at a company producing aircraft bearings in South Bend "fuss and fume among themselves [about unequal pay]," a female union officer complained, "but will not go to a meeting and do something." The women, however, countered that they were willing to tolerate inequality in wages in return for postwar job security; the plant in which they were employed did not expand as much as others in the city, such as Bendix and Studebaker, and so they felt more confident about their prospects for retaining their jobs when the war was over. Seeking support or action from men who viewed them as temporary coworkers or, worse, as interlopers, and who dismissed them as "hotheads" or troublemakers as well, was a challenge many women chose not to meet. Other women felt it simply was not worth the effort only to be cheated in pay. For instance, after the War Labor Board promoted light-heavy distinctions and sanctioned essentially sex-based wage differentials, women who may have wished to defy expectations and seek a man's job, particularly one that required some additional skill or training, saw no practical reason for doing so. "Women have not bid for men's jobs as they would just have to do harder work for less money than the men get and for the same as they get on the women's jobs," explained one woman. As another put it, "Women feel proud of being able to do men's work, [but] after working awhile, they don't like it because of the unequal pay." In other words, the absence of protest ought not be interpreted necessarily as either agreement or even acquiescence on the part of women in their own subordination.[20]

The attitudes of working women in this period and the impact of World War II on them defy simple explanation. It is still a task of research to define the views on gender equality held by working-class women—those women who would have worked even had there been no war or who, because of the conditions of working-class life, were accustomed to a lifetime of employment. The extent of the evidence of women's acceptance of, and commitment to, wage work and their recognition, even if unspoken, of the problems of gender inequality and hierarchy in the workplace indicate that the middle third of this century was a critical period in the history of women and work. Marked by change as well as continuity, the decades were more volatile on the question of gender equality in the labor market and the workplace than we once thought.[21] By examining the history of working-class women, we alter our understanding of the years between the achievement of women's suffrage and the birth of the National Organization for Women, the period often referred to as "the doldrums" or "the nadir" for American women. Despite the large body of scholarship on women's experience during World War II, there still are important things to be said about women and work on the home front.

NOTES

1. Mary Elizabeth Pidgeon, *Changes in Women's Employment During the War*, Special Bulletin No. 20, Women's Bureau (Washington, DC: Government Printing Office, 1944), 9, 12, 15.

2. The secondary literature on women and World War II is vast. For assessments of the impact of the war on women in the labor market and the workplace see William Chafe, *The American Woman: Her Changing Social, Economic, and Political Roles, 1920-1970* (London: Oxford University Press, 1972), 135-95; William Chafe, *The Paradox of Change: American Women in the 20th Century* (New York: Oxford University Press, 1991), 121-72; Ruth Milkman, *Gender at Work: The Dynamics of Job Segregation by Sex during World War II* (Urbana: University of Illinois Press, 1987); Sherna Gluck, ed., *Rosie the Riveter Revisited: Women, the War, and Social Change* (Boston: Twayne Publishers, 1987); Susan Hartmann, *The Home Front and Beyond: American Women in the 1940's* (Boston: Twayne, 1982), 53-99; Karen Anderson, *Wartime Women: Sex Roles, Family Relations and the Status of Women during World War II* (Westport, CT: Greenwood Press, 1981); Leila Rupp, *Mobilizing Women for War: German and American Propaganda, 1939-1945* (Princeton: Princeton University Press,

1978), 167-81; Amy Kesselman, *Fleeting Opportunities: Women Shipyard Workers in Portland and Vancouver during World War II and Reconversion* (Albany: State University of New York Press, 1990); and D'Ann Campbell, *Women at War with America: Private Lives in a Patriotic Era* (Cambridge: Harvard University Press, 1984), 101-61.

3. Indiana Economic Council, *Hoosiers at Work* (Indianapolis: Indiana Economic Council, 1944) 8, 22; *USES Labor Market Letter* 1 (November 1945); Hugh M. Ayer, "Hoosier Labor in the Second World War," *Indiana Magazine of History* 59 (June 1963): 97. At the Vigo County ordnance plant, 85 percent of the 5,000 employees were women; the labor force of the Chrysler ordnance plant in Evansville was 60 percent female. More than 50 percent of the workers at the Gary tank armor plate mill were women. Hugh M. Ayer, "Hoosier Labor in the Second World War" (Ph.D. diss., Indiana University, 1957), 362.

4. Ethel Erickson, *Women's Employment in the Making of Steel, 1943*, Women's Bureau Bulletin No. 192-5 (Washington, DC: Government Printing Office, 1944), 1-20; John K. Jennings, *The War Manpower Commission in Indiana, 1943-1945* (Indianapolis: War Manpower Commission, 1946), 89-90; Donna Penning, "Iron Yard," *Steel Shavings* 7 (1981): 24; Joan Souther, "Dozen Different Jobs," *Steel Shavings* 7 (1981): 32-33; Brown Rubber report, Indiana War History Commission Collection, Box 4, Folder L, Indiana Division, Indiana State Library, Indianapolis, Indiana.

5. Evansville Report, Indiana War History Commission Collection, Box 3, Folder E; Ayer, "Hoosier Labor in the Second World War II," 117-19; Max Cavnes, *The Hoosier Community at War* (Bloomington: Indiana University Press, 1961), 15-54, 79-107.

6. Lotys Benning, *The Vegetable Canning Industry* (Indianapolis: National Youth Administration of Indiana, 1938); Nancy Gabin, "Labor and Gender Relations in the Indiana Food Processing Industry: Women in Tomato Canning Factories, 1920-1950," paper presented at the North American Labor History Conference, Wayne State University, Detroit, Michigan, October 17, 1992; *The Canners' Wail* 10 (1943); 11 (1944).

7. The following discussion of wage and job-classification disputes at Indiana auto plants settled by the National War Labor Board is drawn in part from my book, *Feminism in the Labor Movement: Women and the United Auto Workers, 1935-1975* (Ithaca: Cornell University Press, 1990).

8. *United Auto Worker* (September 15, 1941); Decision of the National Board in case of Bendix Aviation and UAW Local 9, July 26, 1943, *War Labor Reports* 10 (1944): 45-46.

9. "Engineers of Womanpower," *Automotive War Production* 2 (October 1943): 4-5; "Women Work for Victory," *Automotive War Production* 1 (November 1942): 4; minutes of Management-Local 662 meeting, November 11, 1942, Neal Edwards Collection, Box 3, September-November Meetings Minutes Folder, Walter P. Reuther Library, Archives of Labor and Urban Affairs, Wayne State University, Detroit, Michigan (hereafter cited as ALUA).

10. Opinion of the Board in the GM case, *War Labor Reports* 3 (1943): 355-56.

11. Decision of the National Board in the Bendix case, September 20, 1943, *War Labor Reports* 11 (1944): 669-77.

12. Ibid.

13. Ibid.

14. National War Labor Board, *The Termination Report of the National War Labor Board*, Vol. 1 (Washington, DC: Government Printing Office, 1947), 293-96; decision of the National Board in Rotary Cut Box case, *War Labor Reports* 12 (1944): 605-9; arbitrator's decision on women's rates in the GM case, July 31, 1943, Walter P. Reuther Collection, Box 28, Folder 5, ALUA; decision of Regional Board XI, October 9, 1943, *War Labor Reports* 11 (1944): 745; Eleanor Straub, "U. S. Government Policy toward Civilian Women During World War II," *Prologue* 5 (1973): 240-54.

15. UAW exception to arbitrator's decision in GM case, August 18, 1943, Walter P. Reuther Collection, Box 28, Folder 4. The process whereby the union came to acknowledge the arbitrary character of the sexual division of labor is illustrated in minutes of meetings between Local 599 and the Buick Motor Division in Flint, Michigan, during May 1943 as both sides debated application of the NWLB's equal-pay order. UAW Local 599 Collection (unprocessed), Box 3, Women's Rates Folder, ALUA. For the UAW's prewar record on gender issues, see Gabin, *Feminism in the Labor Movement*, 8-46.

16. UAW exception, August 18, 1943, Walter P. Reuther Collection, Box 28, Folder 4; decision of Regional Board, October 9, 1943, *War Labor Reports* 11 (1946), 746.

17. Milkman, *Gender at Work*, 80-83, 147-49; Winn Newman and Jeanne M. Vonhof, "'Separate But Equal'—Job Segregation and Pay Equity in the Wake of *Gunther*," *University of Illinois Law Review* (1981): 269-331; Nancy Gabin, "The Issue of the Eighties: Comparable Worth and the Labor Movement," *Indiana Academy of the Social Sciences Proceedings, 1988* 23 (February 1989): 51-58.

18. See, for example, UAW Local 97 report, U. S. Women's Bureau Records (RG 86), Box 1703, Union Schedules Folder, National Archives and Records Administration, Washington, DC.

19. Ibid., UAW Local 662 Schedule, May 1944; Ibid., May Bagwell to Mary Anderson, March 18, 1944.

20. Ibid., UAW Local 590 Schedule; UAW Local 662 Schedule, May 1944.

21. Important recent scholarship that is reshaping our thinking about women, work, and equality in the twentieth century includes Elizabeth Faue, *Community of Suffering and Struggle: Women, Men, and the Labor Movement in Minneapolis, 1915-1945* (Chapel Hill: University of North Carolina Press, 1991); Eileen Boris, "Regulating Industrial Homework: The Triumph of 'Sacred Motherhood,'" *Journal of American History* 71 (March 1985): 745-63; Dorothy Sue Cobble, *Dishing It Out: Waitresses and Their Unions in the Twentieth Century* (Urbana: University of Illinois Press, 1991); Alice Kessler-Harris, *A Woman's Wage: Historical Meanings and Social Consequences* (Lexington: University Press of Kentucky, 1990).

8

"The Vice Admiral": Margaret Chase Smith and the Investigation of Congested Areas in Wartime

Janann Sherman

The total mobilization of Americans for World War II blurred the boundaries between home front and battle front and, at least temporarily, blurred the lines between genders. The ensuing public discourse about proper activities for women underscored the competing visions of women's place in American society and the remarkable tenacity of traditional roles.

The president's wife and eight congresswomen were among the very few females in positions of public power in American government. Most took it upon themselves to speak for women, often working across partisan lines for the advancement of their sex. One of them, Congresswoman Margaret Chase Smith of Maine, was just beginning her tenure on her first major committee, and one of the most powerful committees in wartime, the House Committee for Naval Affairs.[1] Smith worked on a wide variety of military and home-front issues on this committee. But her role as spokesperson and advocate for women was foremost in those war years. Distinguished by her gender, Smith used her unique access to the public eye, in both the media and congressional hearings, to lobby for the amelioration of the particular problems of working women. From her strategic position on the Naval Affairs Committee, she wrote and forcefully pursued a series of measures to expand women's roles in military service. Smith's efforts on behalf of military women have been detailed elsewhere.[2] What follows is an analysis of Smith's work on the Naval Affairs Subcommittee for Congested Areas and its implications for the role of women in the public sphere.

It was "vice"—a euphemism for prostitution—and a rising venereal disease rate that prompted a congressional response to congested conditions in communities expanded by military activities and war industry and pulled Smith into the center of discussions about women in wartime. Her subcommittee toured military installations, schools, neighborhoods, war industries, hospitals, and jails. They heard from 421 witnesses during 33 days of hearings in 13 cities on both coasts and Hawaii. The hearings generated more than 2,400 pages of testimony and reports from city and state officials, industry management, federal agency representatives, military leaders, and interested citizens.[3] These hearings provided a window on the wartime home front in its most extreme conditions. Did it matter that there was a woman at the window?

As the war effort escalated, the resulting social transformation provoked an alarming sense of dislocation and disorder. People were literally on the move. In addition to those men and women who left home to join the military, over 15 million Americans relocated during the war years, most of them responding to the lure of jobs in defense industries. Over 1.5 million blacks and large numbers of poor white "hillbillies" left the South for industrial urban areas; millions of women moved into jobs previously held by men. People seemed to be abandoning their "place" in society, disrupting long-standing communal arrangements.[4]

Widespread concern about women moving into public spaces, free of controlling males and cut off from familial and community restraints, played itself out in efforts to control women's sexuality. Assumptions of promiscuity followed women in any but the traditional role of homemaker, since all other functions were inherently "unnatural." Women in war industry, particularly single women, were presumed to be subject to extraordinary sexual temptations. Responses from industry and government included the imposition of restrictive dress codes—forbidding makeup and mandating coveralls in the place of tight sweaters, for example—and curfews for unescorted females. Rumors of salacious activities in the workplace served to discredit women as serious workers.[5]

Similarly, a vicious smear campaign against women in the military began in 1943, as it became clear that they were in for the duration. Rumors and gossip portrayed women as either prostitutes intended to "service the troops" or lesbians intent upon staging orgies in the barracks.[6] Both First Lady Eleanor Roosevelt and Congresswoman Edith Rogers, author of WAAC legislation, denounced reports of immorality as "Nazi inspired" attempts to "get all women back into the home and out of the war effort."[7] The rumors were, in fact, spread by American G.I.s, hoping the slander would get women out of the military.[8] The smear campaign drastically affected recruitment, in addition to humiliating and demoralizing women already in the service of their country.[9]

"Victory girls," who supposedly pursued sexual relations with soldiers out of misplaced patriotism, were frequently arrested and subjected to venereal disease examinations on the pretext of protecting soldiers' health. Federal Bureau of Investigation statistics reveal a 95 percent increase in the number of American women officially charged with morals violations between 1940 and 1944, but only 17.3 percent of them were found to be infected. The harassment of "promiscuous" women continued throughout the war. There was, of course, no similar epithet applied to sexually active men.[10]

Early in 1941, with the draft bringing thousands—soon to be millions—of young men into camps and ports, the problem of "vice" took on new urgency. Smith, along with other congresspeople and public officials, fielded a flurry of concerned letters urging government action against the twin evils of liquor and vice. A Joint Army-Navy Committee held a conference of morals officers in late February to draft a unified policy for suppressing organized vice around military establishments and to press for legislation giving them the power to force compliance from local communities.[11] The result was the May Act, making vice activities near military installations a federal offense.[12]

Once armed with the power to police areas designated hazardous to the troops, however, the military was extremely reluctant to use it. Ambivalent about the benefits of closing down organized prostitution, many military officials believed that the sex urge was uncontrollable and that men required sex to be good soldiers.[13] Without access to professionals, young men might seek other more dangerous outlets—causing increasing hazards for innocent women—or even turn to homosexuality: "a blight which had been known to ravage European armies. . . ."[14] Hence, military responses to vice problems featured a complex mix of urging local communities to control them, providing education on potential hazards to their men, and supplying both mechanical and chemical prophylactics when warnings failed.

Local authorities, too, were less than wholeheartedly committed to eradicating vice. Political machines had an important source of revenue at stake in vice operations. Further, some local health officials sincerely believed that designated areas were the most effective way to control prostitution. Perhaps not least, there was widespread ideological resistance to eliminating a policy that seemed to protect virtuous females in the community by minimizing incidents of rape and molestation.[15] Meanwhile the problem escalated. According to the sensationalist press, vice and venereal disease were reaching epidemic proportions.[16] Prostitutes were allegedly very busy spreading the contagion. With the number of sexual contacts per prostitute said to be averaging 50–75 per evening, "a diseased prostitute can do far more damage than a 500-pound bomb dropped squarely in the middle of an Army Camp."[17] Readers were reminded that in the last war, despite heroic efforts to make the U.S. Army the cleanest in the world, 338,746 men were treated for venereal disease, the equivalent of 23 divisions.[18]

Under increasing public pressure, Surgeon General Thomas Parren published a stinging attack on the military's anti-VD policy, which, he said, was no policy at all. Calling venereal disease the "No. 1 Saboteur of Our Defense," Parren's book contained lurid descriptions of "our country's newly organized panzer prostitutes." The press gleefully reprinted portions of the Parren polemic, and public opinion forced an angry Franklin Roosevelt to demand a full report from the Army and Navy.[19]

On February 23, 1943, Secretary of the Navy Frank Knox met in closed session with the House Committee for Naval Affairs. He brought two documents: an article from the current issue of the popular *American Mercury* magazine entitled "Norfolk—Our Worst War Town," detailing appalling living conditions and the ease with which one could obtain illicit liquor and sex, and a secret report from Robert Moses concerning vice conditions in five congested areas.[20] Secretary Knox requested a thorough congressional investigation of vice around naval bases on the East and West Coasts. At the same time, Knox submitted a plan to the White House calling for executive action to alleviate these conditions.[21] After the meeting with Knox, Naval Affairs Committee

Chairman Carl Vinson immediately dispatched a seven-"man" subcommittee, headed by Ed Izac (D-CA) and including Congresswoman Smith, to Virginia.[22]

Vice was at the heart of the investigations as hearings opened in Norfolk. The Navy's principal East Coast port had become a symbol in the popular press for a national scandal.[23] Intent on disclaiming press reports, military and local health officials peppered their testimony with venereal disease rates, assumed to be an "objective" measure of the scope of the problem. The figures varied widely, depending on the "population" base used, but were invariably lower than average and steadily dropping. Virginia officials reported that "despite stories of drunken sailors and vice," their rate had fallen from a high of 92 per 1,000 in 1940 to below the shore-station average of 40 per 1,000. Some areas reported rates as low as 2 per 1,000.[24] Unfortunately, the figures were not very reliable and could be expected to increase in proportion to the amount of interest in finding them. One police chief admitted, "The harder one tries to find cases, the more one finds."[25]

Officials credited their improving statistics to the closing of red-light districts, although the net effect, they were forced to admit, was not the elimination of prostitution but its dispersal. No longer under the control and scrutiny of police and doctors, prostitution had moved out of their reach into the jurisdiction of the county sheriff and a few scattered deputies. Taxi drivers acted as procurers, ferrying soldiers and sailors to the "hot spots" that had sprung up just outside the city limits.[26]

Disturbing testimony made it plain that the prostitute's place as a major source of contagion was rapidly being taken by transient young girls. Variously called "patriotic amateurs," "Khaki-wackies," "cuddle bunnies," and "good-time Charlottes," these girls, sometimes only 12 to 14 years old, were assumed to be unable to resist a uniform, considering it their patriotic duty to comfort the serviceman.[27] A third group of women straddled the line between professional and amateur. These semiprofessionals were chiefly waitresses in restaurants and beer parlors supplementing their meager wages.[28]

The rationale for the attack on prostitution was the connection between health and military efficiency. The problem was consistently defined as a medical, not a moral, issue. However it was defined, it was a problem as old as armies, and attempts to control it had changed little over time. The response has always been to control the consequences of male sexuality by controlling the women.[29]

The underlying assumption was that all women were potentially contagious. Because the police were seeking control over a broad spectrum of the female population, legal definitions were intentionally vague to allow them to assume extensive discretionary authority. Local ordinances providing for curfews and the arrest of women with "no visible means of support" were applied to those whom the arresting officer judged to be "promiscuous."[30] Despite critical shortages of police, spokesmen assured the subcommittee of their commitment to rounding up "potentially infected" women, even "stretching the law just a little" in the interest of vigorous enforcement. Virginia officials decided that since testing for venereal disease was 65 to 75 percent inaccurate anyway, "any girl that is promiscuous should be sent to an institution where she can be treated."[31] In short, all women without a male escort were subject to arrest, and those arrested were assumed to be infected or "potentially infected" and compelled to undergo medical examination for venereal disease requiring a minimum of 72 hours. All investigated areas mandated these degrading examinations and the forcible detainment of those infected, often for as long as six months. No legal procedures were begun until health authorities cleared the women as disease-free; even then, they might be detained if they were believed to remain promiscuous.[32]

City authorities pleaded for funds for new and more secure detention facilities, not so much to keep the women in as to keep the sailors out. "You know how naval personnel is [sic]," said the Norfolk Police Chief. "Men are more or less indiscriminate at certain times and we have found that a herd of women in a particular area would create a dangerous situation." His men were under intense pressure "to see that no undue advances were made or a riot would result."[33]

Sitting at the end of the long hearing table, surrounded by a roomful of men, Margaret Chase Smith was distinctly uncomfortable with the topic of discussion and fainthearted about participating. Yet, as the only woman on the subcommittee, she felt compelled to respond to what seemed to her to be the unrelenting denigration of women. Most of all, she wanted to see the conditions for herself. Enlisting the aid of the subcommittee's counsel to help her gain access to forbidden places, Smith donned a disguise and attempted to slip out one evening to visit a "hot spot." But the male subcommittee members got wind of her plan and insisted upon joining her, turning it into an official visit, not at all what she had in mind. She was disappointed, in any event, to find out it was "only a bar."[34]

Similarly, Smith later missed out on a night tour of the fleshpots of Tijuana while hearings were held in San Diego. Half the subcommittee ducked out to see the border town "in the raw" one evening. The other members, including Smith, made an official visit the next day. When the congresswoman complained that she might have learned something useful on the nocturnal excursion, she was told that her male colleagues had merely shielded her from unpleasantness. What they saw "were not the kind of things generally observed by feminine members of Congress."[35]

In Virginia, Smith was dismayed at reports of hundreds of women being rounded up and thrown into overcrowded jails. She did manage to escape alone, between sessions, to visit the Norfolk jail and attracted considerable attention from the press, who dubbed her the "Vice Admiral." After her visit, she made use of the public forum to expose the plight of these women.[36]

Smith told the press she had found 91 women and girls at the Norfolk jail detained in space for 25. Scattered mattresses lay about the floor, topped with filthy blankets. There was one lavatory and one table. Forced to wait weeks, even months, before being sentenced or diverted to their home authorities, the women, Smith reported, "had absolutely nothing to do, not even a place to sit down."[37]

Most of the younger girls had been arrested for being alone on the street, trying to find a brother or a boyfriend in the hustle-bustle of boomtown.

Married women told Smith of finding themselves stranded when their soldier-husbands moved to another area, of being bored and lonely. They went out unescorted and were promptly arrested.[38] The towns were teeming with large numbers of men in uniform. Liberty parties averaged 70,000–80,000 men in Norfolk, nearly 150,000 on an average weekend in Los Angeles.[39]

Vice raids fell most heavily upon lower- and working-class women. Many of the detainees Smith observed were girls and women of few means. She pointed out during hearings that a girl in Norfolk did not have a chance to survive by waiting on tables or working in beer parlors at starvation wages of only $10–12 a week.[40] Waitresses were specifically exempted from minimum wage laws. They and other young women without skills often found prostitution an economic necessity. Most of the young women Smith talked to, she said, seemed to be farm girls from poor homes and every one of them certainly deserved a better chance.[41]

In addressing the press and the subcommittee, Smith vigorously protested the unsanitary and neglected condition of the female inmates, the wrongful detention of innocent girls, and the absence of programs for training and rehabilitation. "I can't think of anything less effective," Smith told authorities, "than sending them home at random."[42] Nonetheless, military and civilian officials were concerned about these women only to the extent of their effect on the war effort. While many expressed concern for the increasing delinquency of younger girls, authorities believed repression and detention had proven to be "a practical and thoroughly effective police procedure for the control of venereal disease."[43]

Although vice and its impact on the progress of the war had been the primary reason for the subcommittee's investigation, conditions in Norfolk prompted it to widen its focus to include the entire range of problems associated with the expansion of naval base facilities and increased war industry production. The subcommittee found massive increases in population, coupled with limited community resources, threatening both war production and social stability. Seriously overcrowded industrial port areas were plagued with substandard housing, food shortages, war profiteering, and rampant crime.

Cities and towns had been transformed from largely residential communities into booming industrial centers almost overnight. Few knew how to determine precisely how many people had flooded into their towns. Municipalities tried to arrive at accurate estimates using ration book distribution data, unemployment figures, housing applications, and military personnel counts. But nearly all of them testified to increases of at least 100 percent since the war began. Several had exploded into five and six times their normal size within two years. For example, Newport, Rhode Island, grew from about 30,000 to 77,000; in Maine, Portland's payrolls increased from an annual rate of $6 million in 1940 to $73 million at the beginning of 1943. West Coast cities grew the most and, at the time of the hearings, were expected to increase significantly as the war heated up in the Pacific. Vallejo, California, changed from a small agricultural center of 20,000 to a boomtown of over 100,000, and her sister-city Richmond swelled from a 1940 census of 23,642 to an estimated August 1943 population of over 145,000.[44]

These cities experienced almost unimaginable scarcity of all essential goods and services. Food shortages of monumental proportions resulted from rationing allocations based upon prewar population figures. Grocery shelves cleared within an hour of opening in Virginia. Bremerton, Washington, which had grown from 15,134 to over 65,000 in two years, saw 51 of its 108 grocery stores closed there in the same period. Two hundred restaurants in San Francisco closed in 1943 when their food allowances were cut in half.[45]

Manpower shortages left municipalities without adequate fire and police protection, transportation services, or garbage collection. Raw sewage flowed directly into beach areas, foreclosing recreation and polluting seafood sources. Communities threatened with epidemics of typhus, bubonic plague, and malaria reported critical shortages of doctors and hospital beds.[46]

Witnesses came before the subcommittee to complain, to explain, to justify, and to plead for help, greeting yet another federal presence with a mixture of hope and skepticism. For while the federal government was unquestionably responsible for the relief of problems caused by war-related activities, local officials found federal agencies—especially the Office of Price Administration and the War Production Board—more often than not the chief obstructionists to solutions.[47] Discussion of their arbitrary decisions and dilatory methods made for some of the more impassioned testimony at the hearings. Local officials told of countless instances of their pleas for assistance falling on deaf ears in Washington. Applications disappeared into the black hole of the federal bureaucracy, whose procedures sometimes required them to pass 30 desks before approval, the final decision resting with officials far removed from local situations.[48] The subcommittee repeatedly criticized Washington's "expediters of delay." Congresswoman Smith sharply reproached federal agencies which, she said, had "interpreted the word 'execute' to mean 'kill' rather than 'carry out.'"[49]

This constellation of problems was manifested in individual lives. A man recruited to work in war industry would arrive to find no housing. He lived out of his car or shared a "hot bed"—rotating an eight-hour sleep shift—in a stifling dormitory. The subcommittee found as many as 18 men sharing hot beds in a single room.[50] Since a man's 10-hour war job often took two to three hours to reach, he left too early to get breakfast at one of the very few restaurants that had enough food to open. Come lunchtime, he could hope for a meager meal at work—the cafeteria at the Bethlehem Shipyards, for example, was issued exactly 1/10th of an ounce of meat per meal per person.[51] It was nearly impossible to get food after work because restaurants were constantly running out, and most food stores closed before workers could reach them.[52] The war worker was tired and he was hungry.

Women war workers had the same problems as the men, plus another full set. Their new jobs in industry did not significantly alter the sexual division of labor in either the factory or the home. Women suffered a good deal of petty harassment in the workplace as well as significantly lower wage rates.[53] The subcommittee found women working 13 days on, 1 day off, then 6 days the following week. Moreover, a Woman's Bureau survey found two-thirds of all working women and three-fourths of all working mothers carried the additional load of housework.[54] Working wives and mothers in wartime were further burdened by stores that closed early, meal preparation complicated by rationing and shortages, inadequate child care arrangements, insufficient medical services for themselves and their children, long lines, and shoddy merchandise. Women accomplished their two jobs at the expense of their sleep and their health. The result was increasing absenteeism—often nearly 20 percent of the workforce—and labor turnover rates approaching nearly 100 percent in most West Coast ports. Chronic absenteeism in war industry was seriously hampering the war effort, and the initial congressional response had been to treat it as sabotage.[55]

In their search for solutions, the Civilian Personnel Subcommittee of the Naval Affairs Committee, chaired by Congressman Lyndon B. Johnson, had earlier debated a bill requiring war plants to keep records of absentees and report their names to the Selective Service.[56] The guiding assumption was that absentees were slackers, sneaking days off to spend their newly inflated wages. Subcommittee member Smith and Labor Secretary Frances Perkins, who testified before the subcommittee, objected to using the draft as punishment for chronic absenteeism, urging a more compassionate assessment of the problems that workers faced.

When one committee member suggested that high wages were leading to more drinking and to "Monday pneumonia," Perkins countered with a chronicle of poor safety practices, substandard housing, and overtaxed transportation systems. For women war workers, Perkins suggested "Monday pneumonia" was most likely caused by exhaustion from trying to do all the housework and laundry on Sunday. Secretary of War Robert Patterson thought women's higher rates of absenteeism were due to their lack of work experience and their strong inclination to go shopping. Smith retorted, "Perhaps the real reason is that most women . . . are trying to do two jobs at once, taking care of the home and working in industry."[57] Congresswoman Smith urged her colleagues to "stop smearing . . . workers who work long hours under difficult conditions." She was the only member of the subcommittee, and one of seven on the full Naval Affairs Committee, to reject the absentee-registration measure, which she said would only add to government red tape and do nothing to address the underlying problems. The full committee reported the bill favorably, 19–7, but no further action was taken.[58]

Uncovering the reasons for women's significantly higher absenteeism became a mission for Smith throughout the Congested Areas Hearings. A steady stream of war industry representatives complained to the subcommittee that women were unreliable, often took a day off without warning, and frequently and capriciously quit their jobs.[59]

Despite an early reluctance to hire women, the need for their labor had become so great that both government and industry launched massive recruiting campaigns.[60] Framed in patriotic slogans, programs stressed self-sacrifice and a glamorization of war work. Ignoring women who had to work from economic necessity, wartime propaganda focused on the middle-class housewife and created a surface image without challenging basic assumptions about women. The government attested, and personal reports confirmed, that there was no job a woman could not do. Mobilization information emphasized the similarities between industrial work and housework—if a woman could operate an electric mixer, she could run a drill press—reinforcing the idea that female talents lay primarily in housekeeping. Another major theme, the promotion of female self-subordination to the collective effort, discouraged expressions of women's rights as selfish and divisive. The message was unmistakable: women could, and should, retain their femininity while making the sacrifice to do "men's" work for the duration to help end the war and bring their men home.[61]

Society's attachment to traditional ideas about women was most apparent in the resistance to creating child care centers and other support services for working mothers. Early mobilization efforts specifically exempted mothers from their appeals for employees in war industries. Mothers were charged with perpetuating the American ideals of home and family, the very reasons for which the men were fighting the war. Wartime mobilization depended heavily on the behavior of housewives, who had to deal with rationing, shortages, price controls, scarcity and extra work involved in shopping, gardening, and canning, in addition to the control of the children in the absence of their father. The assumption that juvenile delinquency was the fault of mothers who worked was abundantly evident. An alarming increase in truancy and petty crime, as well as juvenile prostitution, was believed caused by the changing nature of the family: the high percentage of homes where the father was absent and the increase in the number of working mothers. The family was regarded as a key link in the nation's defense. Women, in their customary roles, were essential to the family's stability and survival.[62]

As a consequence of these attitudes, industry and government did not formulate any special policies for women in the workplace, assuming that their needs were identical to those of male employees, except, of course, in the design of rest rooms. These same attitudes ensured women's absence from war manpower councils. Despite the considerable activities of women's organizations and women in high office, they had little opportunity to direct policy. Women's Bureau chief Mary Anderson complained that her agency was never consulted about women's employment policies, and while the War Manpower Commission finally created a Woman's Advisory Board, members were not allowed to formulate policy.[63]

In Great Britain, where the greater emergency increased the need to recruit mothers, there was a significantly greater effort to provide services. Though Britain had a third of the population of the United States, English child care centers cared for three times as many children. Priority certificates permitted housewives to order food in the morning and pick it up on their way home to ease the burden of grocery shopping. The British Food Ministry set up over 2,000 central kitchens, which prepared 3 million hot meals a week for women to carry home at cost. Some war industry plants and some communities in the United States set up programs of this type, but they were spotty and inefficient.[64]

World War II provided the stage for the first serious assault on the sex-segregated labor force, and many feared the radical implications of freeing women from family responsibilities. Once begun, services to smooth women's employment opportunities would be extremely difficult to discontinue, encouraging still more women to take permanent jobs extending beyond "the duration." "Our entire concept of what constitutes 'a good home' will be changed by this war," said Suzan Laughlin, a woman's counsel for Vega Aircraft. "There is great danger that many of our married women now working in factories, having once tasted economic freedom, will have a difficult time going back into the 'rut' of housekeeping."[65] Nonetheless, as the draft drained off most of the young and able-bodied men, industry leaders found themselves desperate for female labor at a time when women had ceased responding to their fervent appeals. Some discussion of the needs of working mothers began to enter the public debate.[66]

Numerous exit interviews and surveys compiled for employers and submitted to the Congested Areas Subcommittee indicated that many mothers would work if safe, convenient, affordable child care was provided. For example, a San Diego survey indicated that 20 percent of local women would take jobs if child care was available; exit interviews at one Detroit plant revealed that 15 percent of women quit because of inadequate child care; one-third of New England mothers not working indicated they would take war jobs if they had someone to care for their children; and lack of child care facilities was determined to be a major factor in termination of employment in Hawaii.[67] In addition, government-sponsored studies found the turnover rate for women was higher than that of men only where there were no adequate services to help women carry the double burden of home and job.[68] Yet, despite a rising and insistent demand for child service centers to care for children whose mothers were employed in work essential to the war effort, industries as well as federal and state authorities proved remarkably reluctant to provide them.

During the hearings, Smith repeatedly pointed to studies demonstrating that women who did have access to child care were dependable workers. To industries failing to provide services, Smith asked what was being done to help women handle their dual responsibilities of home and work. Was part-time work available, and what about programs for child care? Part-time work was simply too complicated to offer, replied the employment manager from Consolidated Vultee Aircraft Corporation, in a typical response. As for child care, he said, "We have felt that should be handled outside the company," and he referred obliquely to "undue obligations to employees." Another manager declared that child care was not his concern: "If she has children, she has to farm them out or get someone to look after them."[69]

The hearings were filled with employers arguing that state, local, or federal agencies should provide childcare facilities. Local agencies found it easy to demonstrate that they were shorthanded or that they had applied for funding that had not been forthcoming. Federal agencies refused applications for funds or simply lost them in the bureaucratic morass.[70] The ideological underpinnings of this buck-passing were often revealed by the manner in which child care was discussed. Some, like a man named Beal of South Portland, were bluntly opposed to assisting a potentially hazardous social transformation. "School officials would not advocate a nursery school. It constitutes juvenile delinquency," Beal said. Smith suggested that surely there were some women who had to work. What happened to their children? "In most cases a grandmother or some other person is in the home. . . . I still maintain the home should be kept up."[71]

The manifold problems with child care centers—slow and insufficient funding, problems with staffing, scattered and inconvenient locations, hours too short and fees too high—were a function of conventional ideology, which women as well as men supported. Mothers, too, were uncomfortable with leaving their children with strangers. Most mothers saw child rearing as their responsibility and primary to their self-identity.[72] Another factor was the stigma attached to institutionalized child care, a legacy of Works Progress Administration programs that featured prying social workers.[73] While the subcommittee found that some child care centers were being underutilized because they were inconvenient or expensive, they also learned that many women preferred to leave their children with a relative or close friend.[74]

Clearly, the problem of warworker absenteeism, particularly among women, was much more complicated than either subcommittee members or witnesses initially believed. After seven months of hearings, Smith was beginning to lose patience with unresponsive officials. Women's absenteeism was not intentional, Smith insisted; the women were just too tired. It was not fair, she said, to say that "the employment of women is pulling down the production rate . . . when, as a matter of fact, it is due to reasons beyond their control. . . . Shouldn't we be doing something to take care of that?"[75]

Official recommendations of the Congested Areas Subcommittee reflected the concerns Smith raised throughout the hearings, although they fell far short of what she might have wished. While not challenging the need or the effectiveness of rounding up scores of suspected prostitutes, the subcommittee, in the initial report authored by Smith, asked that federal funds "be allocated to provide for the detention, treatment, and rehabilitation of venereally infected women."[76] But it was apparent from concluding reports that the subcommittee as a whole was primarily concerned with improving confinement conditions and medical treatment. Shortages of personnel and funding, plus an absence of any real commitment, effectively halted the possibility of significant efforts for reeducation or rehabilitation. Detention for the duration solved the immediate problem.

To aid working mothers, the subcommittee stressed the immediate need for child care and the responsibility of the federal government to provide it. Their sole purpose, stated explicitly in their report, was *not* to foster "social reform", but to expedite the war effort by reducing juvenile delinquency and increasing the population of available war workers.[77] The subcommittee also concluded that a major cause of absenteeism, particularly among women, was the need to take time from work to obtain groceries and other provisions. They recommended later hours of operation for food stores and banks, checks against depletion of supplies by earlier shoppers, and the establishment of shopping centers in closer proximity to war plants.[78]

Complaints aside, a congressional subcommittee has little power to force action from either industry or executive departments. Smith's subcommittee was an exception. Shortly after their hearings began, spurred by an incendiary press, an outraged Congress, and pressure from the Secretary of the Navy, the White House created an Executive Committee for Congested Production Areas with the authority to prescribe binding policies.[79] As the Naval Affairs Congested Area Subcommittee completed its investigations, its reports were increasingly addressed to this committee. The resulting division of labor brought significant action.[80] The subcommittee's final reports listed a success rate of nearly 90 percent, that is, only 24 of 283 recommendations failed to be accomplished. These varied widely, from urging the rapid completion of public housing, hospitals, and sewage projects, to Chairman Edouard Izac's personal favorite: raising the ice cream quota so that "a young man can come to town and get ice cream instead of hard liquor."[81]

Congresswoman Smith had raised issues that would not otherwise have been addressed by the congressional subcommittee or their witnesses. Very few women testified at the Congested Areas Hearings (only 13 of 421 witnesses), most of them as representatives of federal, state, or local authorities. No one spoke for working-class women, whether prostitute or aircraft welder; no one spoke for women and children, except for Smith. Her suggestions for child care, for housing planned for families with two working parents, for flexible hours, for equal pay, and for a recognition that working women worked at least two jobs reflected a sensitivity to women's situations not available to the men on or before the subcommittee. She seemed, too, to raise the consciousness of her colleagues. After a few hearings, Chairman Izac and Congressman Fogarty started sounding like her, seizing the opportunity to point out to industry representatives that women war workers needed assistance, not blame.[82]

Margaret Chase Smith's "gender consciousness," her awareness of her position on the committee as "the woman," and her sense of fairness combined to bring about an alternative perspective on women's problems in the congested areas and elsewhere. Because of her concern and her power Smith managed to change the shape of the war's impact on women. Her successes and failures illuminate the complex intersections of gender and power, and demonstrate the limits and possibilities of one woman's leadership in the midst of World War II.

NOTES

1. Elected in 1940, a congressional widow stepping into her husband's empty shoes, Smith went on to serve just over four two-year terms in the U.S. House of Representatives (1940 to 1948) and four six-year terms in the U.S. Senate (1949 to 1973). The bulk of the primary source material for this chapter was provided by the Margaret Chase Smith Library Center, Skowhegan, Maine; hereinafter referred to as the MCSLC.

2. See Janann Sherman, "'They Either Need These Women or They Do Not': Margaret Chase Smith and the Fight for Regular Status for Women in the Military," *Journal of Military History* 54 (January 1990): 47–78.

3. Hearings were held in Virginia, California, Rhode Island, and Maine. They were published: U.S. House of Representatives, 78th Congress, 1st Session, *Investigation of Congested Areas*, by a Subcommittee of the Committee on Naval Affairs, Hearings pursuant to H. Res. 30, parts 1–8, respectively (hereafter, *I.C.A. Hearings*). In March

1945, the subcommittee held hearings in the Pearl Harbor-Honolulu area, pursuant to H. Res. 154, 79th Congress, 1st Session, Part 1. *I.C.A.* Reports were also published: No. 66, Hampton Roads, March 30, 1943; No. 91, San Diego, May 3, 1943; No. 96, San Francisco, May 17, 1943; No. 113, Newport, May 24, 1943; No. 118, Portland, June 7, 1943; Summary Report No. 144, October 1943; No. 164, Puget Sound, January 5, 1944; No. 172, Columbia River, January 25, 1944; No. 162, Los Angeles-Long Beach, December 21, 1943; Summary Report No. 272, November 1944; No. 39, Pearl Harbor-Honolulu, April 8, 1945. Statistics from *I.C.A.* Summary Reports, No. 144, October 1943, 1083, No. 272, November 1944, 2493, and *I.C.A.* Report No. 39, Pearl Harbor-Honolulu, 500.

4. In 1944, 16 percent of all working women held jobs in war industry. Between 1940 and 1944, the number of women employed increased from 12 million to 18.2 million. In the heavy industries of steel, machinery, shipbuilding, and aircraft and auto factories, the number of women workers increased from 230,000 in 1939 to 1.7 million in 1944. Data from Susan M. Hartmann, *The Home Front and Beyond: American Women in the 1940's* (Boston: Twayne, 1982), 6; Sherna Gluck, *Rosie the Riveter Revisited: Women, the War, and Social Change* (Boston: Twayne, 1987), 10; D'Ann Campbell, *Women at War with America: Private Lives in a Patriotic Era* (Cambridge: Harvard University Press, 1984), 67.

5. John Costello, *Virtue under Fire: How World War II Changed Our Social and Sexual Attitudes* (Boston: Little, Brown, 1985), 183–90.

6. Author's notes from a roundtable discussion of former military women, "In the Service of Their Country: Women during the Eisenhower Era," a conference held at the Dwight D. Eisenhower Presidential Library, Abilene, Kansas, October 21, 1988.

7. Eleanor Roosevelt quoted in the *New York Times*, June 9, 1943, and again in a similar vein, June 30, 1943. CongresswomanRogers, along with Congresswomen Bolton and Luce, called for an investigation of the origin of the rumors in the *Washington Post*, June 4, 1943.

8. Cynthia Enloe holds that the very nature of the military ritualizes and institutionalizes misogyny; aggressiveness toward females is enshrined in the military vernacular, military training is couched in its opposition to "feminine" civilizing forces, and weapons become extensions of virility. See Cynthia Enloe, *Does Khaki Become You?: The Militarization of Women's Lives* (Boston: South End Press, 1983), 18–47. See also Susan Gubar, "'This Is My Rifle, This Is My Gun': World War II and the Blitz on Women," in Margaret Randolph Higonnet, et al., eds., *Behind the Lines: Gender and the Two World Wars* (New Haven, CT: Yale University Press, 1987), 227–59.

9. For more analysis of the smear campaign, see Mattie E. Treadwell, *The United States Army in World War II, Special Studies: The Women's Army Corps* (Washington, DC: Government Printing Office, 1954), 191–218.

10. Enloe, *Does Khaki Become You?*, 30; Karen Anderson, *Wartime Women: Sex Roles, Family Relations, and the Status of Women during World War II* (Westport, CT: Greenwood Press, 1981) 104–08.

11. See Margaret Chase Smith's newspaper column, "Washington and You," March 19, and March 26, 1941, MCSLC.

12. The May Act, which became Public Law 163 in July 1941, essentially reenacted Section 13 of the Draft Act of 1917, establishing moral zones free of alcohol and prostitution around military camps. See Bascom Johnson, director of the Division of Legal and Social Protection of the Federal Security Agency, "The Vice Problem and

Defense," *Survey Midmonthly*, May 1941, 141–43; U.S. House of Representatives, 77th Congress, 1st Session, Committee on Military Affairs, H.R. 2475, "Prohibition of Prostitution in Areas Adjacent to Military and/or Naval Establishments," Report No. 399, *Congressional Record*, April 21, 1941, 3206–07.

13. While this point hardly needs corroboration, it is discussed in Allan M. Brandt, *No Magic Bullet: A Social History of Venereal Disease in the United States since 1880* (New York: Oxford University Press, 1985), 54; Enloe, *Does Khaki Become You?*, 22.

14. Quote is from Irwin Ross, "Sex in the Army," *American Mercury*, December 1941, 668. Social Protection Director Bascom Johnson, too, publicly worried about the sexual needs of young men and called for more information about this "fundamental question." Johnson, "The Vice Problem and Defense," 143.

15. Irwin Ross, "Sex in the Boom Towns," *American Mercury*, November 1942, 606–13; Brandt, *No Magic Bullet*, 166.

16. The popular small magazine *American Mercury* carried a series of incendiary articles about the topic in the early 1940s. For example, see Ross, "Sex in the Army," 661–69; "Sex in the Boom Towns," 606–13; Lucius Beebe, "San Francisco: Boom Town De Luxe," January 1943, 66–74; and the one that seemed to launch the congested areas investigation, J. Blan Van Urk, "Norfolk—Our Worst War Town," February 1943, 144–51.

17. Francis Sill Wickware, "National Defense vs Venereal Disease: U.S. Government Fights to Protect Its New Soldiers," *Life*, October 13, 1941, 128–30.

18. Brandt holds that venereal disease during World War I cost the government almost $50 million. Brandt, *No Magic Bullet*, 111; "Army Cracks Down on Vice That Still Preys on Soldiers," *Newsweek*, August 31, 1942, 27–31.

19. The book also earned Parren a reprimand from FDR. An outspoken foe of venereal disease since taking over the Public Health Service, Parren in his efforts prompted the passage of the national Venereal Disease Control Act of 1937. Thomas Parren and R. A. Vonderlehr, *No. 1 Saboteur of Our Defense: Plain Words about Venereal Disease* (New York: Reynal & Hitchcock, 1941); review by Paul DeKruif, *New York Times Book Review*, November 23, 1941; discussion of this book and its consequences in Brandt, *No Magic Bullet*, 138–62.

20. Robert Moses was then director of the Port of New York. His report was so secret that the navy did not admit its existence until Knox brought it before the House Committee on Naval Affairs. I have been unable to obtain a copy of the original Moses Report despite a lengthy search through Army and Navy Archives, the National Archives, and the Moses Papers in New York City. A "Summary of Recommendations of Mr. Robert Moses' Covering Report of Surveys of Congested War Production Areas for the Army and Navy Munitions Board," March 2, 1943, was located in the National Archives, RG 212, Records of the Committee for Congested Production Areas, Entry 13: Records Relating to the Operation of the Area Offices, 1943–44; Folder: Portland, Maine, Moses Report. See *Portland Press Herald*, February 23, 1943 and March 5, 1943. For Smith's version of the subcommittee's genesis, see her speech to Portland Rotary Club, September 3, 1943, and Press Release, University of Maine Group, January 13, 1944; both in *Statements and Speeches*, vol. 2, 386, 415, MCSLC.

21. Harold Smith, "Memorandum for the President," April 6, 1943, in President's Official File: President's Committee on Congested Production Areas (hereinafter C.C.P.A.), OF 5298, Franklin D. Roosevelt Presidential Library, Hyde Park, NY.

(hereafter, FDRL); matter also discussed in Corrington Gill, *C.C.P.A.—Final Report*, 4, FDRL; *Portland Press Herald*, February 23, 1943, March 5, 1943.

22. The subcommittee operated under House Resolution 30, "A Resolution Authorizing and Directing an Investigation of the Progress of the War Effort," 78th Congress, 1st Session. This was part of a series of investigations, beginning in 1941, by both houses of Congress, into the nation's state of preparedness for war. The Senate Special Committee to Investigate the National Defense Program, called the Truman Committee after its chairman, was part of this effort.

23. See, for example, Francis Sill Wickware, "National Defense vs Venereal Disease," *Time*, March 20, 1942, 138, as cited in Costello, *Virtue under Fire*, 214; Van Urk, "Norfolk—Our Worst War Town," 144–51.

24. Portland, Maine, reported rates at about 36 per 1,000 and dropping. Newport, Rhode Island, admitted a rate of 3.7 per 1,000 among civilians; San Diego recorded a very low rate of 2 per 1,000. *I.C.A. Hearings*, Pt. 1, Hampton Roads, 79; Pt. 5, Portland, 1169; Pt. 4, Newport, 1122; Pt. 2, San Diego, 423. Later hearings in November 1943, in Los Angeles and the Columbia River, Oregon, area revealed rising rates, but by this time, no one seemed particularly excited about the matter. *I.C.A. Hearings*, Pt. 8, Los Angeles–Long Beach, 1917; Pt. 7, Columbia River Area, 1658, 1725.

25. Chief of Police H. D. Kimsey, "Monthly venereal-disease index of Seattle, Wash." *I.C.A. Hearings*, Pt. 6, Puget Sound, 1553.

26. Hot spots were discussed primarily in Virginia; see *I.C.A. Hearings*, Pt. 1, Hampton Roads, 24, 72, 344, and *I.C.A. Report* No. 66, Hampton Roads, 643, where they are described as "little more difficult to reach than the city's points of attraction."

27. These names, along with numerous others, were used in many press reports and by those testifying at the hearings. For example, see Albert Deutsch, "Danger! Venereal Disease!" *The Nation*, September 22, 1945, 284–85; "Army Cracks Down...," *Newsweek*, 28; *I.C.A. Hearings*, Pt. 1, Hampton Roads, 306; Pt. 6, Puget Sound, 1316; Pt. 3, San Francisco, 677.

28. See discussion between Smith and John J. Hurley, field representative for the social protection section of Virginia Health and Welfare Service, in *I.C.A. Hearings*, Pt. 1, Hampton Roads, 225–26.

29. Enloe, *Does Khaki Become You?*, 18–45. See also Brandt, *No Magic Bullet*, 72–77; Judith Walkowitz, *Prostitution and Victorian Society: Women, Class and the State* (Cambridge, England: Cambridge University Press, 1980), passim.

30. By and large, these curfew laws either did not apply to males or were, in practice, seldom so applied. See, for example, discussion in *I.C.A. Hearings*, Pt. 5, Portland, 1170–73.

31. Testimony of San Diego police chief Clifford E. Peterson, *I.C.A. Hearings*, Pt. 2, San Diego, 413-14; Pt. 3, San Francisco, 786; John J. Hurley, health and welfare service, *I.C.A. Hearings*, Pt. 1, Hampton Roads, 224.

32. In the interest of venereal disease control, the Maine state health code was changed to declare all venereal disease "contagious, infectious, communicable and dangerous to public health," giving health authorities the power to force examinations and subsequent treatment. For other testimony on the detention and treatment of infected women, see *I.C.A. Hearings*, Pt. 3, San Francisco, 692; Pt. 8, Los Angeles-Long Beach, 1920, 2010–11; Pt. 5, Portland, 1170–73, 1223, 1240.

33. The implication that young men, particularly in groups, were impossible to control when they wanted sex seemed to be conventional wisdom and was a recurring theme in the subcommittee hearings. Testimony of Chief J. F. Woods, *I.C.A. Hearings*, Pt. 1, Hampton Roads, 166.

34. Elisabeth May Craig, "Inside in Washington" column, *Portland Press Herald*, April 6, 1943; MCS Interview, January 18, 1989.

35. See the *San Diego Union*, April 9, 1943; Craig, "Inside in Washington," *Portland Press Herald*, April 30, 1943.

36. Craig, "Inside in Washington," *Portland Press Herald*, April 6, 1943; see also Robert H. Mason, "Girls Behind Norfolk Jail Bars Visited by Congresswoman; Cells Found Clean But Crowded," newspaper source unknown, and numerous other clippings in Scrapbook 28, MCSLC; MCS Interview, January 18, 1989. See also Smith press release, March 31, 1943, in *Statements and Speeches*, vol. 2, 360, MCSLC.

37. Mason, "Girls behind Norfolk Jail Bars. . . ."

38. Ibid.; press release, March 31, 1943, MCSLC; MCS Interview, January 18, 1989.

39. *I.C.A. Hearings*, Pt. 1, Hampton Roads, 22; Pt. 8, Los Angeles-Long Beach, 1950.

40. Women working in war industry typically made 3 to 4 times that amount. See Smith discussion with John J. Hurley, *I.C.A. Hearings*, Pt. 1 Hampton Roads, 225–26, 259; Mason, "Girls behind Norfolk Jail Bars. . . ;" press release, 31 March 1943, MCSLC; MCS Interview, January 18, 1989.

41. Mason, "Girls behind Norfolk Jail Bars. . . ," MCSLC.

42. Smith to Newport News city manager J. C. Biggins in *I.C.A. Hearings*, Pt. 5, Portland, 1194.

43. *I.C.A. Hearings*, Pt. 2, San Diego, 600; Pt. 5, Portland, 1242.

44. *I.C.A. Report* No. 113, Portland, 903; *I.C.A. Hearings*, Pt. 5, Portland, 1230; *I.C.A. Report* No. 96, San Francisco, 807; Testimony of Vallejo mayor John Stewart and Richmond City manager J. A. McVittie, *I.C.A. Hearings*, Pt. 3, San Francisco, 900–03, 836.

45. *I.C.A. Hearings*, Pt. 1, Hampton Roads, 294-96; Pt. 6, Puget Sound, 1351, 1367; Pt. 3, San Francisco, 684, 792, 977.

46. See *I.C.A. Hearings*, Pt. 1, Hampton Roads, 1, 8, 113–19; Pt. 5, Portland, 1215–17; Pt. 6, Puget Sound, 1345; Pt. 2, San Diego, 605; Pt. 3, San Francisco, 651.

47. This was a major theme of the hearings. *I.C.A. Report* No. 91, San Diego, 730; *I.C.A. Hearings*, Pt. 1, Hampton Roads, 212–19; Pt. 5, Portland, 1277; Pt. 2, San Diego, 487; Pt. 7, Columbia River, 1655.

48. *I.C.A. Hearings*, Pt. 1, Hampton Roads, 648.

49. Quote from report authored by Smith: *I.C.A. Report* No. 118, Portland, 959–60.

50. Hot beds were rented for 8–hour stretches; that is, three men would share a single bed in a 24-hour period. *I.C.A. Hearings*, Pt. 1, Hampton Roads, 97; *The Honolulu Advertiser*, March 16, 1945. Labor Secretary Frances Perkins referred to these hot beds in U.S. House of Representatives, 78th Congress, 1st Session, Committee on Naval Affairs, No. 51, Hearings on H.R. 1876, "A Bill to Require All Department of the Navy Contractors and Subcontractors to File Information with Respect to Absenteeism," March 3–12, 1943, 503.

51. From the Bethlehem concessionaire's ration allotment of 64 pounds of meat per day, he was expected to provide meals for 18,000 workers; had four ounces been allocated per person, he could feed only 256. See testimony of Thomas P. White, Western Workers Council, *I.C.A. Hearings*, Pt. 3, San Francisco, 895, 927; and his report in Appendix, xi.

52. *I.C.A. Report* No. 164, Puget Sound, 1219.

53. Although women were making more money than ever before, wage differentials actually widened during the war. See Ruth Milkman, "Organizing the Sexual Division of Labor," *Socialist Review* 49 (January–February 1980): 130–33; Alice Kessler-Harris, *Out to Work: A History of Wage-Earning Women in the United States* (New York: Oxford University Press, 1982), 289.

54. *I.C.A. Hearings*, Pt. 4, Newport, 1126–28; Campbell, *Women at War*, 117.

55. Of fifty-two skilled workers recruited for an important war plant, 51 quit and left because of lack of housing. See *Hearings on H.R. 1876*, 501–05, 558–59; *I.C.A. Report* No. 91, San Diego, 730. See also Gill, *C.C.P.A.-Final Report*, 2.

56. U.S. House of Representatives, 78th Congress, 1st Session, Committee on Naval Affairs, *Hearings on H.R. 1876*.

57. *Ibid.*, 280, 408, 498–507.

58. For Smith's comments on H.R. 1876, see Craig, "Inside in Washington," *Portland Press Herald*, March 21, 1943; Margaret Chase Smith, "Washington and You," March 17, 1943, April 7, 1943.

59. For example, Consolidated Vultee Aircraft Corporation in San Diego had 42 percent women employees and, as a consequence, a labor turnover rate of 88 percent, according to testimony of Employment Manager H. E. Pasek. Homer Ferguson, president of Newport News Shipbuilding and Dry Dock, complained that increasing women employees simply meant increasing rates of absenteeism. *I.C.A. Hearings*, Pt. 2, San Diego, 462; Pt. 1, Hampton Roads, 272–76.

60. Campaigns were coordinated by the Office of War Information, which provided guidelines and suggestions to the press, radio, and advertisers. Eleanor F. Straub, "United States Government Policy toward Civilian Women during World War II," *Prologue* (Winter 1973):240–54; "Women in the Civilian Labor Force," in Mabel D. Deutrich and Virginia C. Purdy, eds., *Clio Was a Woman: Studies in the History of American Women*, (Washington, DC: Howard University Press, 1980), 206–26; Maureen Honey, "Remembering Rosie: Advertising Images of Women in World War II," in this volume.

61. See Susan Estabrook Kennedy, *If All We Did Was to Weep at Home: A History of White Working-Class Women in America* (Bloomington: Indiana University Press, 1979), 201–09; Maureen Honey, *Creating Rosie the Riveter: Class, Gender and Propaganda during World War II* (Amherst: University of Massachusetts Press, 1984); Leila J. Rupp, *Mobilizing Women for War: German and American Propaganda 1939–1945* (Princeton: Princeton University Press, 1978); Anderson, *Wartime Women*, 28; Kessler-Harris, *Out to Work*, 287.

62. For examples, see *I.C. A. Hearings*, Pt. 2, San Diego, 540; Pt. 5, Portland, Maine, 1242; Campbell, *Women at War, 165*. Sonya Michel calls this manipulation of domestic ideology "the discourse of the democratic family," which not only reinforced traditional views about women but "invested the family with major political significance, thus making it more difficult for women to challenge the social division of labor without

appearing virtually treasonous." Sonya Michel, "American Women and the Discourse of the Democratic Family in World War II," in Higonnet *et al., Behind the Lines*, 154–67.

63. Straub, "Women in the Civilian Labor Force," 206–10; Rupp, *Mobilizing Women*, 87.

64. See Barbara J. Harris, *Beyond Her Sphere: Women and the Professions in American History* (Westport, CT: Greenwood Press, 1978) 153–55; Mary Heaton Vorse, "Women Don't Quit, If–," *Independent Woman*, January 1944, 191.

65. A number of progressive companies hired woman counsels to address problems of their female workers.   Susan Laughlin, quoted by Elizabeth Field in "Boom Town Girls," *Independent Woman*, October 1942, 297. See also Harris, *Beyond Her Sphere*, 153.

66. *I.C.A. Hearings*, Pt.5, Portland, 1230; Pt.3, San Francisco, 768; Pt.2, San Diego, 462.

67. See *I.C.A. Hearings*, Pt.2, San Diego, 556; Gill, *C.C.P.A. Final Report*, 2, FDRL; *I.C.A. Report* No.39, Pearl Harbor-Honolulu, 515; *I.C.A. Hearings*, Pt.3, San Francisco, 775.

68. Vorse, "Women Won't Quit, If–," 25.

69. *I.C.A. Hearings*, Pt. 2, San Diego, 462–66; Pt.1, Hampton Roads, 272–76.

70. There was considerable evidence of federal foot-dragging.   In one case, Portland, Maine, applied for Lanham funds for nurseries for working mothers four times without success, according to Superintendent Harrison Lyseth. *I.C.A. Hearings*, Pt.5, Portland, 1228.

71. Beal, not otherwise identified, addressed the subcommittee with J. Harold Webster, city manager of South Portland. *I.C.A. Hearings*, Pt.5, Portland, 1264.

72. Campbell argues, "The soaring marriage and birth rates during the war, accomplished without benefit of propaganda campaigns, strongly suggests that young women wanted more than anything else to be wives and mothers." Campbell, *Women at War*, 7, 95–96.

73. Michel, "Discourse of the Democratic Family," 156, 164.

74. For discussion of low participation rates, see *I.C.A. Hearings*, Pt.6, Puget Sound, 1605; Pt.8, Los Angeles-Long Beach, 1970; Summary Report No.272, 2495.

75. See *I.C.A. Hearings*, Pt.6, Puget Sound, 1304, 1443, 1460–62.

76. For example, see *I.C.A. Report* No. 66, Hampton Roads, 644–45; *Report* No. 118, Portland, 963. The quotation is from the Portland report.

77. *I.C.A. Reports*: Summary Report No. 144, 1109–10; Summary Report No. 272, 2504. Gill mentioned only two instances of aid for child care: area representatives helped a Mobile, Alabama, center in publicizing its services, aided acquisition of additional centers in San Diego, and devised acceptable standards of operation.   Gill, *C.C.P.A.-Final Report*, 19–20, FDRL.

78. See, for example, *I.C.A. Report* No. 91, San Diego, 733–34; No. 96, San Francisco, 811; No. 39, Pearl Harbor-Honolulu, 515; No. 164, Puget Sound, 1219; No. 272, Summary Report, 2504.

79. Documents relating to Executive Order 9327 "Providing for the More Effective Handling of Governmental Problems in Congested Production Areas in Order to Further the Successful Prosecution of the War Effort," forming the Executive Committee for Congested Production Areas (C.C.P.A.), signed by FDR, April 7, 1943, in President's Official File, OF 5298, FDRL.

80. The close cooperation between the two committees was noted in *I.C.A. Summary Report* No. 144, 1088; referred to in Gill, *C.C.P.A.-Final Report*, 24, FDRL. C.C.P.A. representatives testified in *I.C.A. Hearings*, Pt. 6, Puget Sound, 1388; Pt. 7, Columbia River, 1713–15. President Roosevelt expressed his appreciation for the remarks about "close teamwork" in letter to Carl Vinson, February 16, 1944, copy in Naval Affairs Committee file, MCSLC; copy also in President's Official File, FDRL.

81. *I.C.A. Summary Reports*: Report No. 144, October 1943, 1088; Report No. 272, November 1944, 2494. For the ice cream debate, see *I.C.A. Hearings*, Pt. 1, Hampton Roads, 34; Pt. 2, San Diego, 430, 589 and *I.C.A. Report* No. 91, San Diego, 733.

82. See *I.C.A. Hearings*, Pt.4, Newport, 1060; Pt.6, Puget Sound, 1453–55.

9

Did the "Good War" Make Good Workers?

John Modell

THE UNIVERSITY OF HARD KNOCKS

The "University of Hard Knocks, especially if it is war, is an expensive and dangerous way to obtain experience, but it does develop men." Men so developed, according to the president of the Scott Paper Company in 1943, constituted a manpower–training boon that alert employers would shortly reap.[1] Three years later, just after World War II ended, *The Personnel Journal* echoed the thesis that military experience was generically valuable, easily transferable to the civilian economy. "Training in the U.S. Army develops in each individual the following qualities: morale, discipline, health and endurance, technical proficiency, initiative, adaptability, leadership, teamwork, and tactical proficiency. . . . The veteran returned to civilian life after a successful period in the Army will be possessed of these qualities. The qualities desired by any personnel manager in an employee include most of those named above. Where else can he find men who have been so trained and proven?"[2]

The scene for the triumphant accession of war–tested men to the civilian labor force had been set by a decade and more of "human relations" emphasis in management theory. Well before the United States had to raise a mass army for the second time in a quarter century,[3] theorists who sought to provide guidance to employers had spoken with heightened reverence of the need for "leadership." Tight supervision of low–level employees had increasingly come to seem counterproductive and was slowly, then more rapidly, replaced by less hierarchical arrangements, especially where unionization was achieved or might be.[4] Workers must be led rather than driven to produce.

Characteristic of this emphasis was the brilliant work of Chester I. Barnard, telephone executive and informal colleague of Elton Mayo and the Harvard Pareto group. The ideas about organizational leadership enunciated in Barnard's 1938 *The Functions of the Executive*—which made an explicit analogy to the military—were explored at more length in a 1940 essay. Barnard noted here an increasing tendency for organizational leaders to be chosen exclusively from those who already possessed specific *technical capacity*, often understood to be indicated by credentials of formal education. Barnard argued that concrete situations of leadership, in fact, require certain capacities that are neither technical nor fundamentally intellectual—notably when the enterprise involves "great instability, uncertainty, speed, intense action, great risks, important stakes, life and death issues. Here leaders must have physical or moral courage, decisiveness, inventiveness, initiative, even audacity." These capacities, rarely instructed, are in fact probably developed and certainly revealed in practical situations of "general experience in leadership," but these were becoming rare within enterprise itself, as specialization increased. "The most 'natural' opportunities at present . . . are insufficient sources for the supply of general leaders. Hence, we need to develop the artificial methods of giving wide experience."[5]

Material incentives were played down in the human relations literature, thus heightening the analogy between business and military organizations. Douglas McGregor's human relations classic on the "Conditions of Effective Leadership in the Industrial Organization,"[6] published in 1944, focuses on the way that leaders structure the necessary dependence of their subordinates so that the state of dependence will be psychologically rewarding. *Security* is to be the chief reward, to be humanized by "an atmosphere of approval," knowledge of what is expected of the subordinate, and consistent, fair discipline.

When *The Infantry Journal* sounded off in 1945 on the question of the nature of military leadership (not command), it employed like ideas.[7] The leader, whether at the front or on the rear lines, "must know his men as individuals . . . . Every man needs to feel that his squad, section, platoon, and company leaders *know* him. . . . A most important part of leadership is the availability of the leader to his men. His door must be open. . . . Men of all units, wherever they may be serving, will do their jobs better if they know why they are doing what they are doing." Or, in the words of a young "instant Lieutenant," assigned to a replacement outfit: "Think of your platoon as fifty separate individuals, each one of whom must be known, evaluated, advised, inspected, trained, and equipped. . . . The great majority of men are all you could wish for and are begging for leadership. They are good soldiers."[8]

When the military set up job placement bureaus as demobilization began, it presumed that employers would want to learn of veterans' military achievements. The Soldier's Qualification Card that they designed included (along with background information on formal education and prewar occupations) soldiers' scores on tests taken in the military, their military specialty, learned skills, assignments, and attained rank. It also included a statement of "highest position of leadership (includes military)."[9]

Marine Corps officials concerned with the transition of their men into the postwar labor force hoped to capitalize on a diffusely positive view of military experience:

These men have been in positions of responsibility and authority and have developed accordingly. On the whole, it can be confidently asserted that real personal development has resulted from the experience of military leadership. . . . The training, supervision, and control of groups of men and the care and servicing of extremely important material is invariably involved. . . . The responsibility involved is not exclusively that of leading the men into battle. First they [a leader's subordinates] must be trained, which involves teaching of the most difficult kind on a great variety of subjects. Varied personnel problems, disciplinary in nature and otherwise must be solved. Each officer must make certain that his men are equipped and fed, that sanitary conditions are satisfactory, and that as far as possible, each man's wants are met. . . . It is extremely difficult to measure and earmark such experience. However, it can be confidently said that in many cases, it would not be duplicated in a lifetime of following a business or industrial career. With intelligent retraining in civilian skills, leadership of the finest kind is available.[10]

THE WAGES OF MILITARY EXPERIENCE

But how much difference did military service in World War II actually make in the occupational world? A special tabulation of the 1960 census allows us to make a general assessment at around the midpoint of veterans' occupational careers.[11] For men of the age group whose careers were most profoundly affected by wartime military service—those 20–29 at war's end—most differences in occupational concentration for men at given levels of educational attainment were quite modest.[12] This counts veteran mobility cautiously, since it, in effect, eliminates any indirect advantage in occupational mobility they may have enjoyed by way of additional postwar education. On balance, the World War II veterans, within educational groupings, did enjoy a small advantage in achieving white–collar status by 1960, especially among those whose formal education was at a level to which wartime military service could evidently provide a boost: notably, high school graduates and those with some college but no degree. Even in these groups, the overproportion in white-collar occupations (compared with the non–agriculturalist non–veterans of like age and education) was only about 5 percent. If we look at distribution by occupational type *within* the broad white–collar grouping, we find that there was a considerably stronger relative focus within the generally less prestigious and less well–remunerated white-collar classifications: clerical workers and, to a lesser extent, sales workers, rather than professionals, managers, or proprietors.

Among the less educated men and with regard to attaining the more remunerative and prestigious blue–collar occupations, that World War II military service seems, in fact, to have had its most pronounced effect. Craft status was appreciably more often attained by those with no college background (and especially by those with no high school education) if they had served in World War II; and veterans who had never graduated from high school had an advantage in entering operative jobs. Service in World War II, then, may have made men more desirable employees, up to a point, but veterans had no particular advantage in moving ahead into the sort of positions where "leadership" might come into play. In comparison to the impact of formal education on occupational placement by 1960, the university of hard knocks counted only slightly.

A unique longitudinal data set allows us to get somewhat closer to the wartime evolution and postwar evaluation of "leadership." The data pertain to members of the U.S. army who, in 1943, volunteered for training as air–crew officers: navigators, bombardiers, and pilots.[13] The data set includes information on personal background, scores on 20 tests (some school–like, others—including a number of apparatus tests designed to measure various psychomotor skills like hand–eye coordination—distinctly not),[14] information on postwar job histories, and one lone piece of information about their military experience: the highest rank that they attained.[15]

The volunteers were exceptionally competent men—often, but not always, from somewhat advantaged backgrounds—and as a group they made out quite well in the postwar labor market. Our approach here is to make comparisons *within* the sample, focusing on achievement of officer status and on first full–time postservice occupation.[16]

The data indicate an unmistakable tendency toward occupational inheritance. Sons of nonproprietary white-collar fathers were some 20 percent more likely than were all other airmen to be found in professional jobs in the 1950s. Sons of proprietors, on the other hand, were quite prominent among those who entered middle management positions after 1945 and extremely prominent among those who themselves entered small business. Farm owners' sons headed toward substantial blue–collar positions. Blue–collar sons moved, not surprisingly, into blue-collar work, but also into technical and low–paying white–collar jobs. The pattern that we have already noted, of wartime military service associated with limited movement into middling positions, is repeated here.

Occupational categories were reproduced intergenerationally through characteristic paths. Thus, sons of professionals and managers were usually able to attain educated professional positions, especially when they had entered the military directly from school, without having entered the labor force. Where they did not, they often moved into less-prestigious positions in middle management, clerical work, or even blue–collar employment. Conversely, sons of blue–collar fathers who stayed out of the labor force before their military service had an unusually good chance of entering the top of the occupational hierarchy, at the same time avoiding blue–collar postwar employment, which was a very likely outcome (along with technical jobs) for those who had earlier left school and entered work. Premilitary labor force entry, similarly, lessened the chances for sons of proprietors to move directly into small business after demobilization. It was those who were the least "marked" by preinduction gainful employment upon whom the military experience seems to have had the most impact in their subsequent civilian careers.

When we examine the impact of individual achievement within the military context (as indicated by whether or not the young man succeeded in becoming a pilot, navigator, or bombardier, thus becoming an officer),[17] we see that in a variety of ways, achieving officer status was a step on the way toward favorable postwar job placement. This was so even after we take into consideration the (more substantial) impact upon postwar job placement of parental class background and preinduction commitment to the civilian labor force.

At the same time, we must note that progress within the military, too, was, to a degree, a function of these same dimensions of civilian occupational placement. Even within this select group of volunteers, 69 percent of the sons of professionals and managers became officers, as compared with 59 per cent of the sons of blue collar workers, with young men from proprietary and farm backgrounds falling in between these two extremes. About 8 percent more of the young men who went directly into the military became officers than of those who entered the army from civilian jobs. These two dimensions were interactive, with preinduction employment considerably hindering the military achievement of men of white–collar origin, but not those whose fathers were workers or farmers.

Figure 8.1 indicates the proportionate boost[18] to entry into white-collar work and to three specific categories of such work that can be attributed to attaining officer status. These estimates are shown *within* paternal occupational classes and are net of the considerable impact of academic prowess (as self–assessed) while in high school. It would seem that especially meritorious military service—here, achievement of officer status—was a career contingency that mattered even among these young men, who as a group were the cream of the crop. To understand why this is so, we must look at the intervening role of formal education. For sons who had professional–managerial, proprietary, and farm-owner fathers and who had not had a full–time job before the war, those who served as officers eventually gained about half a year more of formal education than those of like background who served as enlisted men. Military achievement seems to have especially affected blue–collar sons. Achieving officer status among blue–collar sons with no preinduction jobs was associated with almost a full year's more formal education.[19] Much of the relationship of military service and military achievement to occupational mobility that can be seen in this data set was an outcome of the extended formal education that military service (and, even more, officer rank) encouraged.[20] Higher horizons seemingly were promoted by exposure to the world (and to relatively well-educated fellow servicemen), but soldiers apparently recognized that *formal* education, not the university of hard knocks, was the way to reach them.

Of course, if the same characteristics and qualities that typically made for success in formal education were demanded to just the same degree for progress in the military, wartime service would constitute merely a second chance to move along the same path to eventual placement in the civilian labor force. The test scores in this data set allow us to find out whether military service really *did* demand different qualities of a young man, altering, to that extent, the *composition* of the group most likely to succeed in the postwar labor market. The answer, as with virtually all the quantitative data bearing on our general topic, suggests that the military *did* recognize different qualities, but only marginally so.

We should, of course, not be surprised that the test results, in general, were better correlated with achieving officer status than with educational attainment, since the tests were administered as part of the process of qualifying young men for flight school, and it was mainly those who successfully completed flight school who became officers, but the tests were in no way connected administratively with the young men's further formal education.[21]   The differences in *pattern* that matter here. Put simply, most measured factors were substantially correlated with achieving officer status, including general intellectual, mathematical, spatial, mechanical, and psychomotor tests. But where intellectual and mathematical ability considerably outweighed spatial ability in closeness of correlation with *educational* attainment, and spatial ability outweighed mechanical knowledge and psychomotor skills, these differences among the relative importance of attributes were, by no means, so great when we examine them in connection with eventual *achievement of officer status*.

Where boys of blue-collar background (and to a lesser extent farm background, and to a still lesser extent, small-business background) scored far less well in general intellectual and mathematical tests than did the sons of professionals, class differences were considerably less pronounced on tests of mechanical knowledge and psychomotor skills. The military, then, was neither a pure aristocracy nor a pure meritocracy. Like the schools and like the occupational system the schools served, the military favored boys with attributes derived from having been brought up in the right families. But the military also favored boys with the "right stuff"—and the right stuff for the military was just a bit different from what schools demanded.[22] Military achievement, depending on a broader range of personal characteristics than did formal education, became an attribute in itself, referable by the young man himself in making his postwar educational choices, to the extent the relevant world shared his perspective.

But, once again, we must recall that war service produced a small deflection, not an overthrow, of career trajectories.

EVALUATING WAR'S TEACHING

Most business leaders initially viewed the return of the veterans not as a boon but as a burden. They obviously owed a debt of gratitude to those who had fought for their country. They had, moreover, a legal obligation to offer still-extant prewar jobs to those veterans who wished to return to them, an obligation that for many seemed to permit a reduced sense of what was morally owed to veterans. Many anticipated that the limited horizons associated with most veterans' depression-blighted preinduction jobs would prove intolerable to them now. Morris S. Viteles, a leading industrial psychologist, wrote in 1944 that many of the "men who have received technical training or whose war experience has been such as to create dissatisfaction with the jobs held before entering military service and an expectation of placement in better or more responsible jobs. . . . will expect industry at least to provide jobs on which they can use their newly acquired skills and experience."[23]

Both employers and unions anticipated a downturn in the economy like that following World War I, and together they sought seniority rules that would avoid the turmoil that would follow a sharp devaluation of wartime civilian labor experience.[24] They also anticipated an upsurge of labor unrest, already more than lightly foreshadowed despite wartime hindrances to its expression.[25] A 1944 article in *Personnel* worried that "the returning veteran is a hero. Movie stars have felt privileged to perform before him; tycoons have enjoyed serving him hot dogs and doughnuts and washing his dishes; he has been a welcome guest in many places inaccessible to him as a civilian. Even the best balanced serviceman has the right to the attitude that he is a special person."[26] *Fortune* reported in 1945 that corporate management talent scouts, looking to the postwar, were out again, but on the whole they were not approaching even such a likely group as army air force veterans, many of whom were officers and technically advanced.[27] Even though the National City Bank of New York, optimistically expanding in late 1946, took cognizance of "an important responsibility toward its own and other veteran employees in their rapid reestablishment," it chose to disregard military accomplishment at hiring time:

Insofar as an applicant's qualifications are concerned, importance is placed on evidences of the individual's interest in banking and assumption of responsibility in school, interim civilian occupations, and armed forces experience. However, such intangible qualities as character, personality, and perseverance are emphasized over armed forces accomplishments. In fact, earnest effort is made to de–emphasize service connections and achievements.[28]

In this atmosphere, an inane boosting tone, combined with what in fact was sound job analysis, did little to assist the veteran who sought to translate war experience into job qualifications:

And now a word to employers about the great assets this nation has in the returned veterans. Have you employers thought how profitable the skills our service men learned in wartime can be both to the new veterans and to you employers, now that peace is here? For example, aerial gunners work out as first rate repair men and mechanics. Camouflage experts become painters and decorators. Another good bet not to be overlooked is the men who have been in radar and electronics, a field that is now developing with the greatest rapidity. Remember, employers, the veterans are among our nation's greatest assets—both as men and women, and as possessors of greatly increased skills our industry must have to produce the goods needed for peace.[29]

How employers understood and evaluated job applicants was the focus of a fine empirical study, conducted in 1945–1946 in two cities. At the time of the survey, about four-fifths of its sample of employers in New Haven, Connecticut, and about 7 in 10 in Charlotte, North Carolina, said that they anticipated giving veterans hiring preference even beyond the legally enjoined rehiring requirement. These figures did not vary much according to whether the position hypothetically applied for was common laborer, production worker, service and maintenance, routine clerical, or administrative and managerial.[30]

There was generalized good will, then, or at least a sense of the social desirability of espousing such good will. How deep did it run? Employers were asked to tell which of a long list of qualifications they considered to be "of outstanding importance" at hiring time. In New Haven, veteran status was rather unimportant, slightly less important overall than was American citizenship or being a married man. Moreover, it mattered most commonly in the common labor and production jobs, rather than for managerial employees. Only 1 in 10 employers considered military service to be of "outstanding" importance in New Haven. Three months later, the proportion feeling even that ambivalently about military service was less than half this high in Charlotte, and once again its occasional relevance showed up mainly for manual jobs.

But military service mattered in a negative fashion when an applicant had received a less–than–honorable discharge. In both cities, such a discharge was just about as damning as having served a "term in a penal institution," and the dishonorable discharge was especially important for *managerial* employees. Meritorious military service, it seems, mainly vouchsafed a sound character that was assumed to be fairly general in the population, hence, significant mainly where demonstrably lacking. Failed military service was, by contrast, a morally significant distinction, one of the most important things one might wish to know about an employee, certainly one in a position of responsibility.

The uncertainty about how to respond to veterans that is reflected in the employers' statements sometimes was resolved into an unambivalent expression of anxiety. An IBM middle manager provides an instance, for even in late 1946 he was still worried that veterans had lived too long in an all–encompassing institution and had developed a sense of dependence that was too ingrained for the industrial setting:

Larabee said that the company could not fire them without a very good and legitimate reason and they were especially on the look–out to abide by this rule. He said, however, that the G.I.'s knew all this and as they were backed up by national legislation and as they knew all the wrinkles from the American Legion and V.F.W. and all these various organizations. . . . [The veteran believes he has] a certain amount of security, you might say, to go around and fuss to be promoted to this and that job that he would like.[31]

Many employers simply did not much accept the argument of Chester Barnard and others that formal education (or other characteristics closely related to social–class background) was overrated as a criterion for leadership and that education in the university of hard knocks correspondingly underrated. The personal traits at first understood to underlie leadership seemed increasingly not to matter anywhere near so much as did situation. One psychologist, engaged in a large leadership research project that for a decade would rely jointly on military and industrial sponsorship, argued in 1947:

A person does not become a leader by virtue of the possession of some combination of traits, but the pattern of personal characteristics of the leader must bear some relevant relationship to the characteristics, activities, and goals of the followers. . . . The persistence of individual patterns of human behavior in the face of constant situational change appears to be a primary obstacle encountered not only in the practice of leadership, but in the selection and placement of leaders. It is not especially difficult to find persons who are leaders. It is quite another matter to place these persons in different situations where they will be able to function as leaders.[32]

If leadership was a function neither of training nor of character, then prowess in war had no further practical implications.

Another study of the long-term economic returns to World War II military service asked about the occupational rewards 20 years later for military service in World War II, employing a representative national sample of white men who had been in their mid-20s in 1945. Once the impact of educational attainment, region of residence, non-military job training, job tenure, and father's occupational level were statistically controlled, the average positive impact of World War II military service on hourly pay rate in 1966, apart from job-specific vocational training received within the military, amounted to *only about six cents* (the overall hourly pay average was $3.32), a negligible and statistically insignificant sum.[33]

About 3 in 10 of the men in the sample, however, had had some vocational training while in the military. Among these, one-third reported that they were making current use of this training in their jobs. These men received about 20¢ more in hourly wages, after we have statistically accounted for the characteristics mentioned before, and also the small generic return to military service itself.[34]

Skills training paid off, where generic military experience did not, because many Americans did not believe that the military organization bore close analogy to anything in American civilian life, despite technological and strategic changes that made the World War II military considerably more like it than before.[35] Even in the mid-1950s, as Morris Janowitz observed, "many civilians still see the military profession as it existed in an earlier phase, when authoritarian domination was the typical mode of behavior."[36] That the hierarchy and discipline were tolerated only as long as there was a war to fight was made clear by the "mutiny" of 1946 in the army, which focused on the slow pace of demobilization.[37] Even as the war ended, officers were striving to fend off criticism of their leadership, desperately urging that, during the war, "on the forge of necessity and hard training," a special bond had been formed between the GIs and all but a few deficient officers. "At war's end, the words 'officer' and 'enlisted man' were merely categorical. Both had developed to a synonymous term, that of 'soldier.'" This had been proven in "the final test, . . . combat," where "the bonds of discipline, common danger, and mutual respect, cemented once, and for all, the relationship of officer and man—and the name was 'soldier' for all who could qualify."[38]

In mid-1946, the Secretary of War's Board on Officer-Enlisted Man Relationships, born in response to popular resentment and headed by Air Corps Lieutenant General James H. ("Jimmy") Doolittle, and including both enlisted men and enlisted men risen to officer rank, issued its startling report:

Americans look with disfavor upon any system which grants unearned privileges to a particular class of individuals and find distasteful any tendency to make arbitrary social distinctions between two parts of the Army. . . . There is need for a new philosophy in the military order, a policy of treatment of men, especially in the 'ranks,' in terms of advanced concepts in social thinking. The present system does not permit full recognition of the dignities of man. . . . Under the present system enlisted men are dependent for the satisfaction of many of their needs upon the behavior and attitudes of their officers, but are denied a feeling of security and opportunities for development and self–realization.[39]

"Human relations" concepts are again promoted here but are now said to have been conspicuously ignored in the army.

Among its recommendations, the Board included more thoughtful promotion and training practices, the former explicitly (and the latter implicitly) "based upon the most advanced practices in personnel selection found in industry, business, government, and those developed in the Army," including a mandatory one–year stint in the enlisted ranks for all officers except for a few technicians and other exceptions. The Board also suggested that separate quarters and chow provision for officers and enlisted men be abolished and that a single uniform be issued (although anyone might purchase supplementary clothing "provided that whatever is purchased conforms in texture and cut"). Off-base and off-duty behavior (including saluting etiquette) should now conform to "normal social patterns comparable to our democratic way of life." If these recommendations appear to suggest that the Doolittle Board wanted to abolish the officer vs. enlisted man distinction, that is pretty near to the case, at least on the symbolic level. They even recommended "that necessary steps be taken to eliminate the terms and concepts, 'enlisted men' and 'officer,' that suitable substitutes be employed (e.g., members of noncommissioned corps, members of commissioned corps, etc.), and that all military personnel be referred to as 'soldiers.'"

Thus, as demobilized soldiers were still finding their way back into the civilian labor force, the honorific assumptions connected with having achieved formal leadership were, at best, attenuated and at worst entirely reversed less than a year after the war had ended.

REFLECTIONS

The United States wages war with exalted purpose, and its citizens, in some part, evaluate its warriors accordingly. The word "veteran" is a heavily freighted category, with heavy moral implications. War is an enterprise of the state, and the state in war and peacetime maintains a regular interest in providing its citizens with a particular view of such salient categories as "veteran." But examination of the historical record indicates that the lofty virtues that wartime service *might* have communicated were only barely ascribed to veterans' occupational capabilities. The government conceived of the job of helping its soldiers make the transition into the civilian labor force to be an essentially technical one, of matching explicit skills to explicit job demands, and leery employers and unionists did the rest.[40]

One cannot appreciate the ideological basis of the way Americans engaged in World War II without recalling the enormous resonance of the idea of "democracy." The notion provided a basis for evaluating friend and enemy, for subverting some of the organizational prescriptions of the peacetime military, and, it seems, for muting in peacetime most of the content of individual military achievement.

On the whole, military service in World War II ascribed to those performing it a clean bill of health in adult competence in daily affairs, and just a bit more. The most expansive notion that might have translated military accomplishment into civilian terms—"leadership"—did not win much acceptance. Employers were unanimous in saying veterans deserved jobs (back) because they had sacrificed years of their civilian careers, but they were less at ease in characterizing the positive content of their military careers in civilian terms. Institutions of formal education, for which the returning soldiers constituted customers rather than labor pool, proved more welcoming.[41] As things worked out, the larger part of the eventual occupational advantage veterans achieved was, in fact, brought about by postwar formal education, coin with which employers were already familiar.

Military service drew on a somewhat different and perhaps wider range of abilities than was emphasized in most highly rewarded civilian jobs, and the military recognized achievement in these lines no matter what personal basis it rested upon. These newly exercised and recognized capabilities provided part of the sense of self-worth with which veterans addressed the postwar world—both the world of work and (perhaps to a lesser degree) the ordinarily class-bound world of formal education.[42]

Surprisingly often, although most GIs saw but little reflective of their military accomplishments in their subsequent occupational careers, military service affected a long-term improvement in the life chances of many disadvantaged persons.[43] The mechanism by which this was accomplished is often understood as "maturing," "training in teamwork and self-discipline," "making a man out of a boy," or—as characterized by our most thoughtful academic analysis[44]—the "knifing off" of a troubled, insecure past. Whatever the precise imagery, changes are understood to have occurred *within* the soldier: social categories stand still, while those who march to their call change within themselves. The military phase, according to this interpretation, is *remedial*.

Yet, to place the process of change entirely within the soldier is to oversimplify a complex situation, in which the (at least temporary) effacement of social markers is dialectically related to psychological change in the individual. I conclude these reflections with an appropriately ambiguous account, reported by Eli Ginzberg, of a "shy and self-conscious" high school dropout who, once in the Army, claimed to have been a teacher in civilian life. "Many of his fellow soldiers believed him and by the time the division left for Hawaii in 1944 he had established himself as a leader of malcontents in the outfit. His advice on methods of outwitting the officers was frequently sought and he found this very satisfying." Demobilized, he shortly sought "to obtain more education in the hope that he could attain the feeling of satisfaction he had experienced in the Army when he was known as an educated man, a school teacher." In this, he succeeded well, and by 1953 he had obtained an M.Ed. degree and was employed as a principal "and doing very well at it."

Graph 1

Role of Officer Status as a Determinant of
White-Collar Status, by Father's Occupation

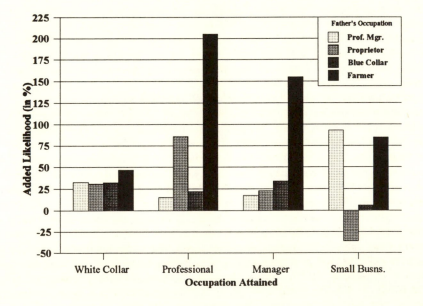

NOTES

1. Thomas B. McCabe, "Post-War Executive Talent," *Advanced Management* 8 (1943): 134-35.

2. George E. Tucker, "Veterans in Industry," *Personnel Journal* 24 (1946): 334-337 at 335.

3. On the practical incompatibility of coercive discipline and a mass conscript Army in World War I, see Jennifer Diane Keene, "Civilians in Uniform: Building an American Mass Army for the Great War," unpublished Ph.D. dissertation, Department of History, Carnegie Mellon University, 1991.

4. Sanford M. Jacoby, *Employing Bureaucracy: Managers, Unions, and the Transformation of Work in American Industry*. New York: Columbia University Press, 1985.

5. Chester I. Barnard, *The Functions of the Executive* (Cambridge: Harvard University Press, 1938); Barnard, "The Nature of Leadership," in *Human Factors in Management*, ed. Schuyler Dean Hoslett (Parkville, MO: Park College Press, 1946): 13-38.

6. *Leadership and Motivation.* (Cambridge: MIT Press, 1966 [1944]): 49-65.

7. Editorial, "It Takes a Man," *Infantry Journal* 56 (May, 1945): 6-7.

8. J. M. Culligan, "Package Commander," *Infantry Journal* 56 (Feb. 1945): 40-41 at 41. For a statement by a sociologist who served as a naval officer, see George Homans, "The Small Warship," *American Sociological Review* 11 (1946): 294-300.

9. A photograph of the Soldier's Qualification Card is reproduced in Carroll A. Shartle, *Occupational Information. Its Development and Application* (New York: Prentice-Hall, 1946): 215-216. At IBM, the "Application for Employment" form that was in effect in 1947 asked men to state whether they had served in World War I or World War II (it was uninterested in peacetime service), their branch, and highest attained rank. A copy of the application is in Box 67, Folder 12, Technology and Society Collection, Yale University Library Special Collections.

10. USMC Rehabilitation Division, Special Services Branch, Personnel Dept., "A Consideration of the Young Officer Problem," mimeographed, April, 1945, in National Archives, Record Group 2444—Retraining and Employment Administration General Files, Series 1, Box 56, folder 10-13, "Rehabilitation." And see the parallel case by a manager concerned with personnel at Standard Oil of California: Kenneth H. Shaffer, "Discovering and Developing Leadership Abilities in Management Personnel," *Advanced Management* 13 (1948): 84-87.

11. U.S. House, Committee on Veterans' Affairs, *Veterans in the United States--1960* (House Committee Report No. 17; 90th Cong. 1st Sess., 1967): 20-23. One must compare these data, foolishly pertaining *only* to veterans and categorized somewhat idiosyncratically, to total–population data in U.S. Bureau of the Census, *United States Census of Population: 1960. Subject Reports. Occupational Characteristics* (Final Report PC(2)-7A. USGPO, 1963): 144-173. I exclude from the base of the tabulations presented here those in agriculture, who were in fact far more common among the nonveterans, because agricultural employment was an extremely common basis for military deferment in World War II.

12. The findings I report for 1960 are largely consistent with what Michael Neiberg and I have so far discovered in a study of veterans' employment patterns in 1950, based on the public–use microdata sample for that year, which allow for more detailed analysis.

See Inter–University Consortium for Political and Social Research, *Census of Population, 1950 [United States]: Public Use Microdata Sample* (Ann Arbor, MI: The Consortium, 1984).

13. Of the records of approximately 75,000 men who were tested at three sites between July and December, 1943, the occupational psychologists Robert L. Thorndike and Elizabeth Hagen took a one-in-five sample in the early 1950s, seeking to trace them down to find out what civilian jobs they in fact had come to occupy, so they might relate occupations to occupational aptitudes. Their assiduous search located about four in five of the men sampled, to whom they administered a small additional questionnaire, mainly about occupational history. Some of these cases were then lost, but data for nearly 9000 survived another decade and a half, to arouse the curiosity of economists Paul J. Taubman and Terence Wales, who traced and re-interviewed 5085 of them, focusing upon occupational and particularly earnings histories, although with considerable focus on work–related values and on family. Professor Taubman was most generous in providing me with a data tape and codebook. Robert L. Thorndike and Elizabeth Hagen, *Ten Thousand Careers* (New York: John Wiley, 1959); Paul Taubman and Terence Wales, *Higher Education and Earnings* (New York: McGraw–Hill, 1974).

14. The tests are described briefly in Thorndike and Hagen, *Ten Thousand Careers*, pp. 9-13. Beyond making some fairly heroic assumptions about the relevance of college education to performance as officers, the American military in World War II sought to use "objective" individual–level measures to match man and military job, most prominently in the Army Air Forces. Lyle H. Lanier, "Army Air Forces Aviation Psychology Program Research Reports," *Psychological Bulletin* 46 (1949): 499-528; U. S. Bureau of Naval Personnel, *Personnel Research and Test Development in the Bureau of Naval Personnel* (Dewey B. Stuit, ed.) (Princeton: Princeton University Press, 1947); *Review of Educational Research* 18 no. 6 (December, 1948; special number on psychological research in the Armed Forces).

15. Longitudinal studies rarely take up military service as a career contingency. When they do, they typically omit consideration both of the attainment process within the military, and of the articulation of that institution with the stratification system of the society as a whole. *The American Soldier* (the first two volumes of Samuel A. Stouffer *et al., Studies in Social Psychology in World War II* [Princeton: Princeton University Press, 1949; 4 volumes]), however, shrewdly develops the point that men carried their prior, class–based experiences and expectations into the military, and responded to the fact of having been denied entrance to officer's candidate school or of being promoted through the non-commissioned ranks slowly according to their civilian mobility expectations. See also Carl C. Seltzer and Seymour Jablon, "Army Rank and Subsequent Mortality by Cause: 23–Year Follow–Up," *American Journal of Epidemiology* 105 (1977): 559-566.

16. The findings are virtually unchanged if we examine occupation as of 1968, when the veterans were in mid-career.

17. Flight officers, who commanded planes but were not made officers, are here treated as enlisted men, treating their rank rather than their function, thus, as it is theoretically relevant to the argument of this essay.

18. With dichotomous dependent variables, logistic regression was the technique of choice.

19. For those young men who held full–time jobs before entering the military, the additional formal education associated with having attained officer status ranged from about one–tenth of a year to not quite half a year.

20. Stouffer's Army Research Branch asked enlisted men and officers in a large number of postings in mid-1944 an intentionally permissive opening question about their postwar educational plans: "Do you feel that you have had as much school or college as you want, or would you like to go back to school or college after the war?" If we compare enlisted men to officers at given age groups and levels of pre–war education, so chosen as to exclude men whose ongoing education was *directly* interrupted by the war, we consistently find a somewhat higher proportion of officers than of enlisted men would "like" to return to school. For instance, among men who by 25-29 had completed high school but had not begun college, 65% of officers as compared to 56% of enlisted men said they would like postwar schooling. (I omit those offering no response.) Corresponding proportions for those who had begun but not completed college were 74% of officers and 72% of enlisted men. The data from these studies, discussed only briefly in the four published volumes of Stouffer *et al., Studies in Social Psychology in World War II*, are available from the Electronic Data Division, National Archives. I combined three studies of white enlisted men (S–106EE, S–106EH, and S–106EU) and three of white officers (S–106OE, S–106OH, and S–106OU). Together, the samples include 19,356 enlisted men and 4840 officers. On the situational quality of these attitudes, see John Adam Clausen, "Soldiers' Plans and the Prediction of Post-War Activities of Veterans," unpublished Ph.D. dissertation, Department of Sociology, University of Chicago, 1949.

21. In calculating the factor scores for individual airmen in my sample, I employed composite scales identified empirically by Taubman and Wales (*Higher Education and Earnings*) and by Thorndike and Hagen *(Ten Thousand Careers)*.

22. Remember that Tom Wolfe's *The Right Stuff* (New York: Farrar, Straus, and Giroux, 1979), examines *military* test pilots. And see Robert C. Stone, "Status and Leadership in a Combat Fighter Squadron," *American Journal of Sociology* 31 (1946): 388–394.

23. "Planning for Postwar Placement," *Management Review* 33 (1944): 85–86. For evidence that at least some veterans had developed such attitudes, see Erwin O. Smigel, "Unemployed Veterans in New York City," unpublished Ph.D. dissertation, Department of Sociology, New York University, 1948.

24. Women, a very sizable component in the wartime civilian labor force were, of course, treated in exactly this way. Ruth Milkman, *Gender at Work: the Dynamics of Job Segregation by Sex During World War II* (Urbana: University of Illinois Press, 1987).

25. Conveying very well this whole range of concerns is the speech and question-and-answer session at The Conference Board in May, 1944, by the head of the Veterans Personnel Division of the Selective Service System. Benjamin M. Golder, "Reemployment of Veterans," *Management Record* 6 (1944): 179–185.

26. David C. Post, "The Veterans' Problem–a Challenge and an Opportunity," *Personnel* 21 (1944): 126-130 at 127.

27. "The Next Business Generation," *Fortune* 32 (August, 1945): 150-191.

28. "Training Future Executives," *Management Review* 35 (1946): 462-464.

29. Excerpt from the script of a radio show ("The American Dairy Program," February 10, 1946), included with letter of Major General G. B. Erskine to an executive of The Advertising Council, March 18, 1946. Erskine characterized this as "a fine, public–spirited announcement" of the sort that should be continued. National Archives, Record Group 244—Retraining and Employment Administration General Files, Series 2, Box 125, folder "Veterans—Employment Feb.-March."

30. E. William Noland and E. Wight Bakke, *Workers Wanted* ("Yale Labor and Management Center Series"; New York: Harper and Brothers, 1949): 176–177, 182–183, 206–207.

31. Interview with Mr. Larabee Oct 24–25, 1946. Yale University Technology and Society Collection, Yale University Libraries, Box 67, Folder 20. Used by permission.

32. Ralph M. Stogdill, "Personal Factors Associated with Leadership: a Survey of the Literature," *Journal of Psychology* 25 (1948): 35–71 at 64–65; and see W. O. Jenkins "Review of Leadership Studies with Particular Reference to Military Problems," *Psychological Bulletin* 44 (1947): 54–79.

33. John Eric Fredlund and Roger D. Little, "Long–Term Returns to Vocational Training: Evidence from Military Sources," *Journal of Human Resources* 15 (1980): 49–66.

34. It was *not* service training courses in manual skills that earned some veterans higher pay, but rather personnel and resources–management training, which the authors speculate was taught to those being groomed for field leadership.

35. Harold Wool, *The Military Specialist* (Baltimore: The Johns Hopkins Press, 1968); Allan R. Millett, "The United States Armed Forces in the Second World War," in Allan R. Millett and Williamson Murray, *Military Effectiveness, Volume III: the Second World War* ("Mershon Center, Series on Defense and Foreign Policy"; Boston: Allen & Unwin, 1988): 45–89.

36. Morris Janowitz, *The Professional Soldier* (Glencoe, IL: The Free Press, 1960): 51.

37. R. Alton Lee, "The Army 'Mutiny' of 1946," *The Journal of American History* 53 (1966): 555-571.

38. "We Can't Lose It," *The Reserve Officer* 23 (March, 1946): 16. The extent to which enlisted men pressured for this understanding of military order is a brilliantly–handled theme in volume I of Stouffer *et al., Studies in Social Psychology in World War II.*

39. U.S., Secretary of War's Board on Officer–Enlisted Man Relationships, *Officer-Enlisted Man Relationships, Report* (May 27, 1946) (Senate Document 196; 79th Cong, 2nd Sess, 1946).

40. Carroll L. Shartle, "Occupational and Vocational Counseling of Military and Civilian Personnel During the Period of Post–War Demobilization and the Years Immediately Thereafter," *Psychological Bulletin* 41 (1944): 697-705; Colonel George R. Evans, "The Army Separation Classification and Vocational Counseling Program," *Occupations* 23 (1944): 69-74; U. S., War Manpower Commission, Bureau of Manpower Utilization, *Special Aids for Placing Military Personnel in Civilian Jobs (Enlisted Army Personnel)* (Washington: USGPO, 1944; revised edition, 1946); U. S., War Manpower Commission, Bureau of Manpower Utilization, *Special Aids for Placing Naval Personnel in Civilian Jobs* (Washington: USGPO, 1945).

41. An American Council on Education "Conference on Emergency Problems in Higher Education" in mid-1946, for instance, characterized the moment as "the greatest project in the history of higher education—a project which shines forth in the dark aftermath of world strife with glorious promise for the era to come." The educators resolved to evaluate military experience favorably: "in passing upon the admission of veterans to institutions of higher education, full consideration should be given to the veteran's aptitude, ability and maturity to undertake college work successfully, as evidenced by his previous academic records, by appropriate examinations, by performance in the service, and by other prognostic factors." The assembled college educators even went so far (albeit beyond their purview) as to recommend "that high schools should consider whether on the basis of the above enumerated favors a diploma should be awarded." American Council on Education, *Bulletin* No. 102, July 18, 1946. American Council on Education, Commission on Accreditation of Service Experiences, *A Guide to the Evaluation of Educational Experiences in the Armed Forces* (Washington: The Council, 1946).

42. Norman Fredericksen and H. B. Schrader, *Adjustment to College* (Princeton: Educational Testing Service, 1951).

43. John Modell, Marc Goulden, and Sigurdur Magnusson, "World War II in the Lives of Black Americans: Some Findings and an Interpretation," *Journal of American History* 77 (1990): 838–848; Louis A. Lurie and Florence M. Rosenthal, "Military Adjustment of Former Problem Boys," *American Journal of Orthopsychiatry* 14 (1944): 400–405; D. Dressler, "Men on Parole as Soldiers in World War II," *Social Service Review* 20 (1946): 537–550; Hans W. Mattick, "Parolees in the Army during World War II," *Federal Probation* 24 no. 3 (September, 1960): 49–55; Eli Ginzberg and Douglas W. Bray, *The Uneducated* (NY: Columbia University Press, 1953). This point can be overstated. The services discharged over 5 percent of its enlisted personnel for ineffectiveness during the course of World War II, men judged to be on balance of no use and in some cases a detriment to the military effort. Eli Ginzberg *et al., The Lost Divisions* ("The Ineffective Soldier," volume 1; New York: Columbia University Press, 1959): 58–87.

44. Glen H. Elder, Jr., "Military Times and Turning Points in Men's Lives," *Developmental Psychology* 22 (1986): 233–245; Elder, "War Mobilization and the Life Course: a Cohort of World War II Veterans," *Sociological Forum* 2 (1987): 449–72; Elder and S. Bailey, "The Timing of Military Service in Men's Lives," in Joan Aldous and David Klein, eds., *Social Stress and Family Development* (New York: Guilford, 1988); Elder and Elizabeth C. Clipp, "Wartime Losses and Social Bonding: Influences Across 40 Years in Men's Lives," *Psychiatry* 51 (1988): 177–198; Elder and Clipp, "Combat Experience and Emotional Health: Impairment and Resilience in Later Life," *Journal of Personality* 57 (1989): 311–339; Elder and Avshalom Caspi, "Studying Lives in a Changing Society," in A. I. Rabin *et al.*, eds., *Studying Persons and Lives* (New York: Springer, 1990): 201–247; Elder, Cynthia Gimbel, and Rachel Ivie, "Turning Points in Life: The Case of Military Service and War," *Military Psychology* 3 (1991): 215–232.

10

Bad News from the Good War: Democracy at Home During World War II

Roger Daniels

Writing in 1975, the British military historian, Michael Howard, gave a concise analysis of the effects of World War II on the American people:

For most of the American people the Second World War was not seen as a time of suffering in any way comparable to the Great Depression ten years earlier. The unemployed got jobs and business boomed. Only a small minority considered either at that time or in retrospect that America had been mistaken in getting involved in the war; the mistake had been, by ignoring the world outside, to allow it to happen at all.

Howard went on to argue that, as a major consequence, Americans became aware of themselves as a military nation, had fully professional military heroes—specifically George Patton and Douglas MacArthur—and that World War II had been for the United States what 1871 had been for Germany, "not an end but a beginning." Finally, according to Howard, American leadership felt that "the American century had . . . now truly begun."[1]

However satisfactory such an analysis may be for one oriented to military and international affairs, social historians have a different agenda, ask other sorts of questions, and examine another order of evidence. Such historians focus on the domestic, rather than the international, aspects of war, on its social, rather than its military, effects.[2]

My particular focus is on a paradox: what I call the bad news from the "good war." The paradox is simply this: although the United States entered and fought World War II for lofty aims at home and abroad—the four freedoms and an economic bill of rights—the means used to fight the war were often undemocratic. The war greatly enhanced the power of the federal government—particularly the executive branch—and increased its contact with the lives of ordinary Americans. Although the United States was opposed to international racism, it fought the war with a Jim Crow military establishment and denied justice to members of more than one minority group. Yet, as is so often the case, within the story of bad news there will be some good news as well. One piece of good news—and something that Americans simply take for granted—is that the political process went on, that in the midst of the greatest war in history the United States, alone of the democracies fighting the war, held a national election. Political democracy flourished during the war, although many politicians resisted—with some success—efforts to make it easier for those in uniform to vote.[3]

Social historians have often been concerned with war as a generator of social change. Such a view, of course, has become almost a cliché, but even clichés need explication and analysis. The contemporary historian who has written most widely—and, I think, astutely—about the impact of war upon modern society is the Englishman Arthur Marwick, who argues:

War can be broken down into four dimensions. . . . First is the immediate obvious *destructive* and *disruptive* dimension of war: capital is destroyed, peacetime processes are disrupted, people are projected into new situations. Second is the *test* dimension. War brings new stresses, offers new challenges, and imposes new necessities. Institutions adapt; or they may even collapse.
. . . . In meeting the test of war societies will be forced to change, not necessarily in a positive direction. Third is the *participation* dimension. . . . As wars more and more involve the participation of hitherto underprivileged groups in the community . . . those groups tend to benefit from such participation. Finally there is the *psychological* dimension. War . . . is an enormous emotional and psychological experience comparable with the great revolutions in history.[4]

But before I discuss these crucial home-front matters, there is a different aspect of the war about which we must remind ourselves: the casualties, what military men sometimes call the butcher's bill, because if we forget that war is, in the final analysis, butchery, we will not understand anything about it. American participation in the military was relatively high. Total military forces as a function of total population ran at 11.2 percent for World War II, as opposed to 4.6 percent in World War I, 4.5 percent during Vietnam, and 3.8 percent in Korea.[5] Over 400,000 young Americans were killed in the armed services between Pearl Harbor and V-J Day, and another 670,000 were wounded; the total military casualty list was nearly 1.1 million persons.

On the other hand, although on a global basis many more civilians than soldiers were killed, very few American civilians became casualties. A few dozen were killed at Pearl Harbor, as were six persons in Oregon who picked up a Japanese balloon bomb. Other American civilians came in harm's way overseas and were killed, wounded, or taken prisoner, but they numbered only a few thousand persons. Although the price America paid in blood for victory in World War II was great and is surpassed only by its losses in the Civil War, these losses were but a tiny fraction of the direct human cost of World War II, which, by one estimate, involved the deaths of 45 million human beings. If one adds to that the deaths caused indirectly by the war from such things as famines in Bengal and in China, the total runs above 60 million. How, then, can this be called the "good war"?

Let me assure you that no one called it that at the time, nor did the term come into use immediately afterward. The phrase was popularized by Studs Terkel's charming but often misleading book, The *"Good War,"* published in

1984;[6] it was possible to use that term only after Korea,—often called the "wrong war," and particularly after Vietnam, almost universally perceived as the "bad war." World War II was, as Michael Howard noted, a war that united, rather than divided, the American people; a war that ended the worst depression in our history; a war that set off a decades-long boom that transformed the economic and social life of the American people; a war that made the United States clearly and unmistakably the most powerful nation on earth. It reinforced Americans' notions about themselves as a "can do" people who could solve almost any problem. So, it is no wonder that, in retrospect, a kind of nostalgia has allowed Americans to think of it as the "good war."

In addition, many historians have celebrated the way in which the war was conducted at home and compared the disgraceful violations of civil liberty during World War I with the much-improved record in World War II. A favorite index of this improvement was a comparison of the number of indictments under federal security statutes. World War II, although more than twice as long, generated about 1 percent of the number of such indictments during World War I: 26 as opposed to more than 2,500. To be sure, historians often noted, almost in passing, that there was, as Harold M. Hyman put it in 1959, a "major blot" on this improved record: the incarceration of more than 120,000 Japanese Americans. But even this "sorry event," he noted with approval, "was handled by officials rather than vigilantes. Loyalty-testing in World War II remained . . . in the hands of the executive departments of the federal government."[7]

Half a century after the events a different perspective seems appropriate. Now, World War II can be seen not as a final product but rather as a phase in an ongoing process. What the federal government did during World War II has been crucial to what happened during the cold war, and, until 1993, the United States was governed by presidents who, in one way or another, were shaped by their experiences in, or resulting from, the 1939–1945 conflict. To describe even a major fraction of important home-front events and trends would exceed by far the space allotted here.[8] My strategy, therefore, is two-fold: first of all, I survey governmental restrictions on liberty during World War II and then examine in greater detail two executive orders which exemplify the paradox to which I alluded: Executive Order 8802, which established the Fair Employment Practices Committee and Executive Order 9066 which resulted in the incarceration of two distinct ethnic groups. My stress is on race and ethnicity; that I largely ignore gender and class is due to limitations of space.[9]

The wartime enhancement of the powers of the federal government began almost immediately after war broke out in Europe. On September 8, 1939, Franklin Roosevelt proclaimed a limited national emergency; two days previously he had publicly placed the Federal Bureau of Investigation (FBI) in charge "of investigative work in matters relating to espionage, counterespionage, sabotage, and violations of the neutrality regulations," and on May 21, 1940, he privately authorized the FBI to conduct wiretapping "of persons suspected of subversive activities." At that time he instructed Attorney General Robert Jackson to make only limited use of the authority and to restrict wiretaps "insofar as possible to aliens."[10] Roosevelt, as part of his ongoing reorganization of the executive branch, had just moved the Immigration and Naturalization Service from the Department of Labor to the Department of Justice, from an agency that viewed its functions as protective to one that viewed its functions as prosecutorial.[11]

After the fall of France, as the United States entered the period long ago labeled "the undeclared war," the government became concerned about sabotage and about a largely mythical fifth column and took a number of potentially repressive actions. Chief of these was an Alien Registration Act, which, for the first time, required all aliens, regardless of age or gender, to register and be fingerprinted. Thus all aliens, even those who had lived in the United States for decades, were required to have—but not to carry—an internal passport. Although not reflected in its title, this statute, popularly known as the Smith Act, was also a peacetime sedition law and expanded significantly the grounds for deportation.[12] FDR, in a public statement, claimed that the registration program was designed "not only for the protection of the country but also for the protection of the loyal aliens who are its guests." He did not mention either the sedition or deportation provisions of the new law.[13] The purposes of the registration were not primarily protective: its twofold purpose was to provide some element of control over aliens and to ensure that alien control be exclusively federal. Department of Justice officials and others remembered all too clearly the lawlessness with which state and local officials treated aliens during World War I, and Roosevelt stressed federal control in his message, a theme on which later historians of liberty have rung changes. The sedition law was used only twice during World War II: indictments were brought in against some Minneapolis Trotskyists and twenty-six American "fascists," including the two Geralds—Winrod and L. K. Smith—and Elizabeth Dilling. The Trotskyists were convicted, much to the satisfaction of American Communists; charges against the "fascists" were dropped after more than two years and a mistrial.[14] During the cold war, of course, the Smith Act was used to send many of the leaders of the American Communist Party to jail.

The federal government sought to curb free expression by use of other statutes, and militant liberals often led the way. Aubrey Williams, for example, wrote Franklin Roosevelt in early 1942: "The right of *free speech* carries with it the *obligation* not to use it to aid the enemy. The Russians have set a damn good example there."[15] But, it must be emphasized, there was relatively little interference with speech, thanks, in part, to the Supreme Court. In 1943, the Court reversed the conviction of George Sylvester Viereck for not fully revealing his activities as a propaganda agent of the German government *before* Germany declared war on the United States, although those two supposed paladins of liberalism, Hugo Black and William O. Douglas, voted to sustain it; the next year the Court unanimously reversed the denaturalization of a German-born citizen because it had not been demonstrated that his 1932 naturalization oath was fraudulent, and five justices reversed the conviction of a vicious anti-Semitic and pro-Nazi publicist, holding that, even in time of war or national emergency, "an American citizen has the right to discuss these matters either by temperate reasoning or by immoderate and vicious invective." Finally, in 1945, the justices reversed the convictions of leaders of the German American Bund who had been charged with counseling resistance to the Selective Service Act of 1940.

That act, of course, affected the "liberty" of more Americans than any other law of the period, but it has been little examined by historians.[16] Few are aware, for example, that it contained antidiscrimination provisions:

In classifying a registrant there shall be no discrimination for or against him because of his race, creed or color, because of his membership or activity in any labor, political, religious or other organization. Each registrant shall receive equal and fair justice.

Similar language appears in dozens, perhaps hundreds, of wartime statutes, and anyone foolish enough to write a history of the war years based solely on the language in laws passed by Congress would have to conclude that the home front was marked by a high degree of racial, ethnic, and class egalitarianism. Nothing, of course, could be further from the truth, but it is significant, I think, that the language was there, even though it was ignored. The military, the selective service system, the Department of Justice, and President Roosevelt himself all conspired to violate the law. In addition, the racial, ethnic, and class biases of the thousands of groups of "friends and neighbors" who made up local draft boards accurately reflected the biases of the middle classes from which almost all of them came. The nation's 6,442 local draft boards had a total of only 250 black members, with very few of those in the South, where most blacks still lived.[17]

The one aspect of selective service that has been studied in any depth at all is conscientious objection. As was the case with civil liberties, the government's performance was much improved over its sorry record during World War I. But promise was better than performance. The law stated that no man would be forced to be a combatant if he "by reason of religious training and belief, is conscientiously opposed to participation in war in any form." Those who received conscientious objector status could be given noncombatant service in the military—many served as medical corps personnel—or, if they objected to any kind of military service, they could perform "work of national importance under civilian direction." No one, however, was exempted from the obligation to register for the draft, and the act did not define "religious belief" or provide any ground rules for alternative national service.

The first director of selective service, the civilian Clarence A. Dykstra, President of the University of Wisconsin, took a broad view and held that "religious belief" might merely involve moral or ethical considerations, but his successor, Major General Lewis B. Hershey, not usually thought of as a theologian or moral philosopher, ruled in March 1942, that "religious belief" could not be merely ethical but had to involve "recognition of some source of all existence, which, whatever the type of conception, is Divine because it is the Source of all things."

Dykstra had originally favored a scheme, proposed by some church leaders, by which objectors would be paid basic military wages and receive board and clothing in work camps run by the government à la the Civilian Conservation Corps (CCC). But according to the historians of conscientious objection,

Franklin Roosevelt objected vehemently to any government money being given to those who refused military service.[18] Some churches therefore agreed to organize and finance the camps, and under a system set up in early 1941 the conscientious objectors received no pay whatsoever for their labor. Most American liberals, however, congratulated themselves on how much better things were for conscientious objectors than in the bad old days of World War I. It took a Norman Thomas to tell FDR, without noticeable effect, that "for the government to require unrequited service smacks of slavery to the state and is a bad precedent in these times."[19]

Most conscientious objectors were members of one of the three largest traditional peace churches, the Society of Friends, the Mennonites, and the Church of the Brethren. But large numbers of their eligible members were willing to enter military service; perhaps three Quakers in four, for example, did not apply for conscientious objector status, including, of course, Richard M. Nixon. About 25,000 persons accepted military service as conscientious objectors, and, after 1943, all were assigned to the medical corps. About half that number refused to wear a uniform and went to the unpaid service camps, where they did CCC-type work. About 500 objectors volunteered as guinea pigs for military medical research, mostly directed toward treating malaria and typhus.

But there was no protection at all for those who refused even to register for the draft. Almost every history textbook now has a line or two about the Jehovah's Witness cases, celebrating the reversal of the *Gobitis* decision of 1940 by the *Barnette* decision of 1943. In *Gobitis* that naturalized patriot Felix Frankfurter held that schoolchildren had to salute the flag because "national unity is the basis of national security." In *Barnette* Hugo Black, for a six-to-three majority, held more sensibly that "neither our domestic tranquility in peace nor our martial effort in war depend on compelling little children to participate in a ceremony which ends in nothing for them but a fear of spiritual condemnation."[20]

But no textbook that I have seen even mentions the problems that Jehovah's Witnesses had with the draft. The crux of the problem was that the Witnesses do not reject the use of force in all situations but are waiting to join in the battle of Armageddon, which they believe may occur at any time. Some Witnesses refused even to register for the draft; others refused to serve even when denied conscientious objector status or status as a minister. (The Witnesses regard all of their members as ministers.) All told, between 5,000 and 6,000 men went to federal penitentiaries for draft violations during World War II. Almost all were draft resisters, not draft evaders, and three-quarters of them were Witnesses. To put effective conscientious objection into numerical perspective, fewer than 50,000 persons, all told, either received such status or went to jail for their beliefs; more than 15 million men and women served in the armed forces.

Because there was such great wartime unity, much government control was exercised by consent. A few days after Pearl Harbor, the United States set up an Office of Censorship, and, shrewdly, Roosevelt chose a working newspaperman, Byron Price, an editor for the Associated Press, to head it. Most of the censorship as applied to American media was self-censorship. A

Code of Wartime Practices was issued and almost universally adhered to. Much of it was reasonable—military information and weather reports were restricted—but some of it was simply silly. Because of the fifth-column phobia certain kinds of radio broadcasts—so-called "man-on-the-street" interviews, musical request shows and lost and found notices—were forbidden because it was feared that they could contain coded messages. According to Richard Polenberg, one cautious official believed that even "the Star Spangled Banner can be played in a manner to convey a message from someone in Kansas City to someone in Mexico."[21] The most effective example of censorship that I know of concerns the Japanese balloon bombs, almost 300 of which actually reached North America, started many fires, and killed at least six people.[22] Not a word about them was published or aired during the war, and Japanese authorities, assuming that they were not arriving, dropped the project. There is no time here to discuss the successive wartime propaganda agencies—the Office of Government Reports, the Office of Facts and Figures, and the Office of War Information (OWI)—but it should be noted that another of the great improvements over the World War I performance was the separation of propaganda and censorship during World War II.[23]

The war years also spawned the loyalty-security programs that are usually associated with the cold war. The Hatch Act of August, 1939—its title was "An Act to Prevent Pernicious Political Activities"—was essentially an anti-New Deal measure designed to curb real or imagined political activity by government employees and Work Progress Administration (WPA) workers, but it also contained provisions barring the federal employment of any member of an organization advocating the overthrow of the government.[24] In 1943, Franklin Roosevelt created the Interdepartmental Committee on Employee Investigations, which supplemented loyalty investigations normally conducted by the Civil Service Commission. Although it could fire no one—it was empowered only to make recommendations to the appropriate government departments or independent agencies—and caused little stir, it began practices that became all too familiar, including investigations of so-called "fellow travelers" and placing on the employee or job applicant the burden of proof to show that any past membership in "disloyal" organizations had been repudiated. On the other hand, the wartime committee did insist on standards that were later lowered: any charges had to be in writing, and accused persons were given adequate time to prepare defenses and might be represented by counsel.

It is now time to discuss the two executive orders and the wartime experiences of two minority groups, African Americans and Japanese Americans. I do not discuss the wartime history of Mexican Americans, Native American, Italian and German Americans, refugees, and other groups, not because the experiences of these groups are unimportant (they are not) but, again, simply because of space constraints.[25]

Wars often have social effects undreamed of by those who direct them. Just as the American Civil War, despite Abraham Lincoln's initial indifference, eventually became "a war to make men free," the war that began at Pearl Harbor unleashed forces that *eventually* transformed American theory and practice about civil rights; these years were what Richard Dalfiume has called "the forgotten years of the civil rights revolution," forgotten, I would suggest, because so little positive and permanent change was accomplished.[26] Despite the exceptions discussed later, the federal government contributed to a continuation of discrimination throughout the war. Good examples are the assumptions governing the way in which it assigned jobs and housing at its own facility, the purpose-built atomic town at Oak Ridge, Tennessee. First-class jobs—and the housing that went with them—were for white males. Blacks and women, whatever their qualifications, were simply not thought of as prime providers of skilled labor.[27]

The wartime struggle for black economic rights began, like the rest of our story, during the undeclared war. By June 1941, the defense program was already beginning to transform the economic face of America, although unemployment that year still averaged 9.9 percent of the labor force. Black Americans quickly perceived that defense employment was not benefiting them very much. Today it is difficult for anyone who was not alive before 1954 to realize how thoroughly segregated American society was: not just southern society but all American society. One black leader, A. Philip Randolph, conceived of a mass demonstration—what he called the "March on Washington Movement"—to protest the discrimination and the inferior position of black people in American life generally and to demand that blacks receive a more equitable share of the federally financed defense jobs that were being created. Roosevelt would have been embarrassed by even a small march, and Randolph knew it. After all, in his January 1941 annual message to Congress, FDR had proclaimed American war aims and listed the "Four Freedoms," which he hoped the postwar world would be based on: "freedom of speech and expression," "freedom . . . to worship," "freedom from want," and "freedom from fear." Each of these freedoms was to be enjoyed "everywhere in the world."[28] Randolph was thus, I believe, the first minority group leader to exploit successfully the desire of American statesmen for moral leadership abroad and to force them to take strides—or at least baby steps—toward freedom at home. (The first significant liberalization of American immigration law since 1924—the 1943 repeal of Chinese Exclusion—was another example of this phenomenon.)[29]

Through intermediaries, the president negotiated with the civil rights leader, and a compromise was reached. FDR would issue an executive order outlawing discrimination in government employment, and Randolph would call off his march.[30] There was no discussion of getting civil rights legislation through Congress—both sides knew that no such bills could pass—and we should note that FDR had just been elected to a third term so that certain political risks were minimized. FDR's Executive Order 8802, dated June 25, 1941, is an important landmark in the social history of World War II. In it, for the first time, the U.S. government enunciated a policy of nondiscrimination in employment. The words were noble:

whereas it is the policy of the United States to encourage full participation in the national defense program by all citizens . . . regardless of race, creed, color or national origin, in the firm belief that the democratic way of life within the Nation can be defended successfully only with the help and support of all national groups within its borders; and whereas there is evidence that available and needed workers have been barred from employment solely because of race, creed, color and national origin, to the detriment of workers' morale and of national unity.[31]

The executive order declared it the duty of employers and labor organizations not to discriminate, ordered that all future defense contracts contain nondiscrimination clauses, and established a Fair Employment Practices Committee (FEPC) to receive and investigate complaints and to take appropriate steps to redress grievances that it found valid. But the Committee could only make recommendations and issue directives; it could not order anyone to do anything nor send anyone to jail, nor impose fines. It was an agency of moral suasion only. It clearly had some positive results, but large numbers of defense employers, trade unions, and American workers themselves resisted even the slightest job integration. In my home city of Cincinnati, for example, white workers at the large Curtiss-Wright engine factory walked off the job when a few blacks were upgraded to skill levels that were traditionally for whites only. Eventually, at the urging of the Civil Rights Division of the Department of Justice, Cincinnati set up one of the first local committees to combat discrimination, the "Mayor's Friendly Committee," which, like the national FEPC, had no teeth at all. Clearly, some advances in employment were achieved by blacks and other minority groups, particularly Mexican Americans, but more often than not desegregation, when it occurred, was of a token variety. Clete Daniel has provided a nice epitaph for the wartime FEPC:

The FEPC's inability to guarantee equal employment opportunity to the nation's minorities was a function of the majority's unwillingness to honor at home the democratic and egalitarian ideals for which Americans . . . were dying abroad. Simply put, it was the FEPC's unhappy fate to champion an idea whose time was yet to come in America. Still, even as it fell far short of fulfilling the hopes that it inspired among millions of minority workers, the FEPC forced the American people to glimpse, if not to comprehend and accept, the . . . future that lay before them.[32]

In addition, of course, most of the millions of black Americans who served, and fought, and died during World War II, did so in segregated units. The black press considered it a great victory when two all-black air force units were set up by a decidedly reluctant War Department, largely due to pressures from black leaders, the urgings of the White House in general, and Eleanor Roosevelt in particular. The generals and their civilian superiors, such as War Secretary Henry L. Stimson, were genuinely surprised when these black aviators compiled an excellent record in combat.[33] General segregation in the armed forces did not end until well into the Korean War of the 1950s.

Despite these and other gains, many articulate blacks spoke of a "Double V" campaign—V for victory not only abroad but also at home.[34] It would be nice to say that they won both fights, but that would be a vast overstatement. We can see, in retrospect, that important gains were made, but as World War II came to an end, it would have been difficult to make that argument with any conviction to a black audience. Not only had little real progress been made, but the war years at home had witnessed a number of race riots, most seriously in New York City, Detroit, and Los Angeles that we can now see were harbingers of the long hot summers of the 1960s.[35]

When war itself came suddenly on December 7, 1941, and, almost incomprehensibly to most Americans, Japan was worsting the United States, there was set in train the worst single governmental violation of civil rights in modern times. The removal of the Japanese-American people from the West Coast and their subsequent incarceration in concentration camps, in some cases for nearly four years, involved more than 120,000 persons, more than two-thirds of them native-born American citizens. Although the incarceration of the Japanese Americans drew enthusiastic support from the Congress, like the FEPC, it was triggered by an executive order, in this case Executive Order 9066, dated February 19, 1942. It is difficult to improve on the summary by the presidential Commission on the Wartime Internment and Relocation of Civilians (CWIRC) which judged, in 1982:

The promulgation of Executive Order 9066 was not justified by military necessity, and the decisions which followed from it—detention, ending detention and ending exclusion—were not driven by analysis of military conditions. The broad historical causes which shaped these decisions were race prejudice, war hysteria and a failure of political leadership. Widespread ignorance of Japanese Americans contributed to a policy conceived in haste and executed in an atmosphere of fear and anger at Japan. A grave injustice was done to American citizens and resident aliens of Japanese ancestry who, without individual review or any probative evidence against them, were excluded, removed and detained by the United States during World War II.[36]

The injustices done to the Japanese Americans are too well known to detain us long here. But getting rid of Japanese Americans was not the only use to which Executive Order 9066 was put even though, at the time it was drafted, it was applied only to them. Vaguely worded, it could have been used against any group and was used to bar some Italian and German enemy aliens from certain sensitive West Coast areas.[37] Power once used tends to be reused, and Japan's invasion of the Aleutian Islands in June 1942—done largely to mask the Imperial Japanese navy's main thrust at Midway—put more than 800 American citizens, Aleut residents of those barren islands, in harm's way, and the army evacuated them. Then, although there were no doubts about their loyalty, Executive Order 9066 was invoked to effect their incarceration. They were kept under unspeakable conditions in abandoned canning factories and mining camps in southern Alaska, in some cases for nearly three years.

A medical officer of the Territorial Board of Health inspected one such facility in 1943 and officially reported:

As we entered the first bunkhouse the odor of human excreta and waste was so pungent that I could hardly make the grade. . . . The buildings were in total darkness except for a few candles here and there [which] I considered distinct fire hazards. [A] mother and as many as three to four children were found in several beds and two or three children in one bunk. . . . The garbage cans were overflowing, human excreta was found next to the doors of the cabins and the drainage boxes into which dishwater and kitchen waste was to be placed were filthy beyond description. . . . I realize that . . . we saw the community at its worst. I know that there were very few adults who were well. . . . The water supply is discolored, contaminated and unattractive . . . [F]acilities for boiling and cooling the water are not readily available. . . . It is strange that they could have reverted from a state of thrift and cleanliness on the Islands to the present state. . . . With proper facilities for leadership, guidance and stimulation . . . the situation could have been quite different.[38]

Some 10 percent of the Aleuts died in their confinement, and many of the survivors were in poor health. Tuberculosis was particularly rampant. The CWIRC's judgment—"The standard of care which the government owes to those in its care was clearly violated by this treatment" is a decided understatement.[39]

What does this brief survey tell us about civil liberties and ethnocultural democracy on the American home front? First of all, things were neither as good as generally depicted nor as bad as they could have been. But second, it is clear that events on the home front during World War II must not be taken in isolation but considered as part of a continuum. Take the matter of race. The "March on Washington" that Phil Randolph conceived never took place, and no similar march would occur until 1963, when, under circumstances that would have been hard to imagine in 1941, Dr. Martin Luther King, with the support of the federal government, gave his "I have a dream" speech to perhaps half a million people. By that time segregation in the armed forces had ended, and the civil rights revolution was in full swing. It is possible, but not very fruitful, to view the ethnocultural history of the United States since the "good war" as a steady progression toward a truly multicultural society.

No such Whiggish view is possible in terms of general civil liberties. It should be clear that the growth of executive power has greatly diminished civil liberty in a number of ways since 1945, ways that largely build on wartime precedents. The wartime sanctioning of wiretapping allowed J. Edgar Hoover, abetted by a chain of supine, often intimidated and sometimes felonious attorneys general, to compile the incredible dossiers about everyone from prominent politicians to the Beatles and beauty queens that have since become notorious. The use of the Smith Act to prosecute the Communist Party leaders, and the creation of list upon list of subversive individuals and organizations are other parts of our legacy from World War II. The excesses of the cold war were not solely the product of that era; all can be found during the WW II era, and some of them, of course, antedate it. Leo Ribuffo has written perceptively about a "brown scare" that preceded and set precedents for the "red scares" of our time.[40]

Finally, most historians have cut off their analysis of what William Leuchtenburg rightly called "the Roosevelt reconstruction" too soon. Most, perhaps, have been seduced by the great charmer himself, who assured reporters in the middle of the war that his persona of "Dr. New Deal" had been replaced by "Dr. Win the War." But just a glance at his 1944 State of the Union message—which Samuel Rosenman titles "Unless There Is Security Here at Home, There Cannot Be Lasting Peace in the World"—shows that Dr. New Deal had not given up his practice even if he was no longer making house calls.

In that speech FDR called for "a second Bill of Rights" and laid out a social agenda that the nation has not yet achieved.[41] The occasion of the 50th anniversary of the war has produced numerous conferences, exhibits, and publications that will provide all of us with new insights into the war period, and that is, of course, all to the good. But the primary task of the historians of the World War II home front is not just to examine what happened during the war but to relate those events more closely to what had gone before and to what has followed. By the end of the present decade, we ought to have a new perspective, not just on the war years but on the entire "age of Roosevelt." Any evaluation of the changes wrought by Roosevelt made without taking into account the wartime years of his presidency is, at best, incomplete. What this brief survey of bad news from the good war suggests is that not all of those changes were positive.

NOTES

1. Michael Howard, "Total War in the Twentieth Century," in B. Bond and I. Roy, ed., *War and Society: A Yearbook of Military History* (New York: Holmes & Meier, 1975), 224-25.

2. For a recent reexamination of the important wartime rhetoric of sacrifice, see Mark H. Leff, "The Politics of Sacrifice on the American Home Front in WW II," *Journal of American History* 77 (1991):1296-1318.

3. Michael J. Anderson, "The Presidential Election of 1944," (Ph.D. diss., University of Cincinnati, 1990), elaborates on these and other aspects of that little-examined election. This work should see print soon.

4. Arthur Marwick, "Problems and Consequences of Organizing Society for Total War," in N.F. Dreisziger, ed., *Mobilization for Total War: The Canadian, American and British Experience, 1914-1918, 1939-1945* (Waterloo, Canada: Wilfred Laurier Press, 1981), 3-4. Previously, the British social critic Richard Titmuss had observed that wartime social policy was largely determined by "how far the co-operation of the masses is essential to the successful prosecution of the war." See Richard Titmuss, "War and Social Policy" *Essays on "the Welfare State"* (London: Allen and Unwin, 1958). Cf. Arthur A. Stein, *The Nation at War* (Baltimore: The Johns Hopkins University Press, 1980).

5. From Stein, *Nation at War*, p. 35, Table 4-2.

6. *The "Good War": An Oral History of World War Two* (New York: Pantheon, 1984). Terkel says that *New York Times* staffer Herbert Mitgang suggested the title.

7. Harold M. Hyman, *To Try Men's Souls: Loyalty Tests in American History* (Berkeley: University of California Press, 1959), 329.

8. Among the important topics not considered here or elsewhere in this volume is civilian defense. Robert E. Miller, "The War that Never Came: Civilian Defense, Mobilization, and Morale during World War II," (Ph.D. diss., University of Cincinnati, 1991), should see print soon.

9. Historians have paid a good deal of attention to unionized workers—especially those in the Congress of Industrial Organizations—but little has been written about either American Federation of Labor workers, who were a majority of organized workers, or

the unorganized majority. For the CIO, or some of it, see Nelson Lichtenstein, *Labor's War at Home: The CIO in World War II* (New York: Cambridge University Press, 1982) and Steven Fraser, *Labor Will Rule: Sidney Hillman and the Rise of American Labor* (New York: Free Press, 1991).

10. Samuel I. Rosenman, comp., *The Public Papers and Addresses of Franklin D. Roosevelt, 1928-1945* (New York: Macmillan and Random House, 1938-1950), 1939 volume, 488-89 and 478-79, hereafter cited as Rosenman, *FDR Papers*; Athan Theoharis, *Spying on Americans: Political Surveillance from Hoover to the Huston Plan* (Philadelphia: Temple University Press, 1978), 99-100. Theoharis so concentrates on unconsummated government operations that he makes no connection, in a chapter on "Emergency Detention Programs," 40-64, between such programs and the incarceration of Japanese Americans. For an analysis of the most obvious connection, see Roger Daniels, *The Decision to Relocate the Japanese Americans* (Philadelphia: Lippincott, 1975), 57.

11. "Reorganization Plan No. V," *Federal Register* 5 (June 1940):2223.

12. 54 *Stat.* 670. Title I was "Interference with the Military or Naval Forces of the United States"; Title II was "Additional Deportable Classes of Aliens"; and only Title III dealt with the "Registration and Fingerprinting" of aliens. For an illuminating discussion of Titles II and III, see Richard W. Steele, "The War on Intolerance: The Reformulation of American Nationalism, 1939-1943," *Journal of American Ethnic History* 9 (Fall 1989):9-35.

13. Rosenman, *FDR Papers*, 1940 vol. 274-75.

14. The most sophisticated account of these trials is in Leo Ribuffo, *The Old Christian Right: The Protestant Far Right from the Great Depression to the Cold War* (Philadelphia: Temple University Press, 1983). See also note 38. For brilliant essays on cold war justice, see Stanley I. Kutler, *The American Inquisition: Justice and Injustice in the Cold War* (New York: Hill and Wang, 1982).

15. Letter to Franklin Roosevelt, February 17, 1942, Aubrey Williams Mss., Franklin D. Roosevelt Library, as cited by Richard Polenberg, *War and Society: The United States, 1941-1945* (Philadelphia: Lippincott, 1972), 46. Polenberg's book is the pioneering survey of the home front. See his essay, "World War II and the Bill of Rights," in this volume and his "The Good War? A Reappraisal of How World War II Affected American Society," *Virginia Magazine of History and Biography* 100(July 1992):295-322. Also Allan M. Winkler, *Homefront U.S.A.: America during World War II.* (Harlan Davidson: Arlington Heights, IL, 1986).

16. The best work has been done by the system itself in a series of monographs published between 1949 and 1953. See, for example, U. S. Selective Service System, *Special Monograph 10, Special Groups*, 2 vols. (Washington, DC: Government Printing Offoce, 1953).

17. George Q. Flynn, *Lewis B. Hershey: Mr. Selective Service* (Chapel Hill: University of North Carolina Press, 1985), 118-26, documents some aspects of selective service racism but ignores the special case of Japanese Americans. See Roger Daniels, *Asian America: Chinese and Japanese in the United States since 1850* (Seattle: University of Washington Press, 1988), 248-54, 269, and the volumes cited in the previous note.

18. Mulford Q. Sibley and Philip E. Jacob, *Conscription of Conscience* (Ithaca, NY: Cornell University Press, 1952), 112-21 and passim. This is the source of the statistical data used later. See also Mitchell L. Robinson, "Civilian Public Service during World War II: The Dilemmas of Conscience and Conscription in a Free Society," (Ph.D. diss.,

Cornell University, 1991), and Cynthia Eller, *Conscientious Objectors and the Second World War: Moral and Religious Arguments in Support of Pacifism* (New York: Praeger, 1992). Cf. Flynn, *Lewis B. Hershey*, 126-34.

19. Letter, Norman Thomas to FDR, May 5, 1943, as cited in Polenberg, *War and Society*, 56. Thomas, almost alone among American political leaders, also opposed the incarceration of Japanese Americans.

20. *Minersville School District v. Gobitis*, 310 U.S. 586 (1940), and *West Virginia State Board of Education v. Barnette*, 319 U.S. 624 (1943).

21. Polenberg, *War and Society*, 51.

22. Robert C. Mikesh, *Japan's World War II Balloon Bomb Attacks on North America*, (Washington, DC: Smithsonian, 1973).

23. For the OWI, see Allan M. Winkler, *The Politics of Propaganda: The Office of War Information, 1942-1945* (New Haven, CT: Yale University Press, 1978). Richard W. Steele, *Propaganda in an Open Society: The Roosevelt Administration and the Media, 1933-1941* (Westport, CT: Greenwood, 1985), covers the pre-OWI years.

24. FDR's message on the Hatch Act ignores the loyalty aspects of the measure; see Rosenman, *FDR Papers*, 1939 vol., 410-5.

25. Because the burgeoning Chicano scholarship has focused largely on community studies, there exists no sophisticated overall account of the impact of the war on Mexican Americans, although there is much wisdom in Mario Garcia, *Mexican Americans: Leadership, Ideology and Identity, 1930-1960* (New Haven, CT: Yale University Press, 1990). There is a large literature on the bracero program and Raul Morin, *Among the Valiant: Mexican Americans in World War II and Korea* (Alhambra, CA: Borden, 1966), shows that Chicanos were greatly overrepresented in the armed services. For Indians, see Alison R. Bernstein, *American Indians and World War II: Toward a New Era in Indian Affairs* (Norman: University of Oklahoma Press, 1991). Frederick C. Luebke makes some astute and comparative comments about German Americans during the war in *Germans in the New World: Essays in the History of Immigration* (Urbana: University of Illinois Press, 1990), 72-73 and passim. For Italians, see the late George Pozzetta's chapter in this book.

26. Richard M. Dalfiume, "The 'Forgotten Years' of the Negro Revolution," *Journal of American History* 55 (1968):90-106 and *Desegregation of the United States Armed Forces: Fighting on Two Fronts, 1939-1953* (Columbia: University of Missouri Press, 1969).

27. See Charles W. Johnson and Charles O. Jackson, *City Behind a Fence: Oak Ridge, Tennessee, 1942-1946* (Knoxville: University of Tennessee Press, 1981), passim.

28. Rosenman, *FDR Papers*, 1940 [*sic*] vol., 672.

29. See the account in Daniels, *Asian America*, 191-98, and passim.

30. The literature on the "March on Washington Movement" is quite large. The most recent biography of Randolph is Paula F. Pfeffer, *A. Philip Randolph* (Baton Rouge: Louisiana State University Press, 1990). For a recent reexamination by two leading scholars, see John H. Bracey and August Meier, "Allies or Adversaries?: The NAACP, A. Philip Randolph and the 1941 March on Washington," *Georgia Historical Quarterly* 75 (Spring 1991):1-17.

31. Executive Order 8802, June 25, 1941 in Rosenman, *FDR Papers*, 1941 vol., 233-37. See also FDR's memorandum of June 12, 1941, to William S. Knudsen and Sidney Hillman, ibid., 215-7.

32. Clete Daniel, *Chicano Workers and the Politics of Fairness: The FEPC in the Southwest, 1941-1945* (Austin: University of Texas Press, 1991), 188-89. See also Merl E. Reed, *Seedtime for the Modern Civil Rights Movement: The President's Committee on Fair Employment Practice, 1941-1946* (Baton Rouge: Louisiana State University Press, 1991). Andrew E. Kersten, a doctoral student at the University of Cincinnati, is investigating the FEPC successes and failures in the Midwest and will soon publish an essay about its frustrations in Cincinnati.

33. Robert J. Jakeman, *The Divided Skies: Establishing Segregated Flight Training at Tuskegee, Alabama, 1934-1942* (University: University of Alabama Press, 1992).

34. Byron R. Skinner, "The Double 'V': The Impact of World War II on Black America" (Ph.D. diss., University of California, Berkeley, 1978).

35. Dominic J. Capeci, *The Harlem Riot of 1943* (Philadelphia: Temple University Press, 1977) and *Race Relations in Wartime Detroit: The Sojourner Truth Housing Controversy of 1942* (Temple University Press, 1984); Dominic J. Capeci and Martha Wilkerson, *Layered Violence: The Detroit Rioters of 1943* (Jackson: University of Mississippi Press, 1992); Cheryl Greenberg, "The Politics of Disorder: Reexamining Harlem's Riots of 1935-1943," *Journal of Urban History* 18 (August 1992):395-441; Mauricio Mazon, *The Zoot Suit Riots: The Psychology of Symbolic Annihilation* (Austin: University of Texas Press, 1984).

36. Commission on Wartime Internment and Relocation of Civilians, (CWIRC) *Personal Justice Denied: Report of the Commission on Wartime Relocation and Internment of Civilians* (Washington, DC: Government Printing Office, 1982), 18. For the most recent synthesis see Roger Daniels, *Prisoners without Trial: Japanese Americans in World War II* (New York: Hill and Wang, 1993).

37. Stephen C. Fox, ed., *The Unknown Internment: An Oral History of the Relocation of Italian-Americans during World War II* (Boston: Twayne, 1990) is a pioneering but impressionistic treatment. See also Rose D. Scherini, "Executive Order 9066 and Italian Americans: The San Francisco Story," *California History* 70 (Winter 1991):366-77, 422-4.

38. CWRIC, *Personal Justice Denied*, 20-22. For details, see John C. Kirtland and David F. Coffin, Jr., *The Relocation and Internment of the Aleuts during World War II*, (Anchorage: Aleutian/Pribilof Islands Association, 1981), and eight reels of microfilm with the same authors and title; Ryan Madden, "The Forgotten People: The Relocation and Internment of Aleuts during World War II," *American Indian Culture and Research Journal* 16:4 (1992):55-76.

39. CWIRC, *Personal Justice Denied*, 21.

40. "The right-wing political activism begun during the Depression prompted a militant counterattack—what I call the Brown Scare. To a left horrified by Hitler and Mussolini, figures like Pelley, Winrod, and Smith seemed to foreshadow an analogous fascist threat to the United States. Liberals and radicals, often cast as heroes in books about the 1930s, certainly deserved praise for their early opposition to tyranny abroad and bigotry at home. Yet their campaign against what they regarded as native fascism should not be taken at face value. Rather, their tracts warning against incipient dictatorship, no less than publications of the far right, reveal the era's hopes, anxieties, and ambiguities. Even more important, from the mid-1930s through World War II, fear of the far right undermined the left's commitment to civil liberties. Diverse liberals and radicals favored restrictions on the right of native 'fascist' agitators to speak, publish and assemble. In 1944, the Roosevelt administration used the Smith Act to prosecute thirty

assorted Nazi propagandists and far right agitators, including Pelley and Winrod. This conspiracy case, *United States v. McWilliams*, received almost unanimous approval from the left, but, like the Brown Scare in general, set precedents for suppression that liberals and radicals would later regret during the Cold War." Leo Ribuffo, *The Old Christian Right*, xiii.

41. Rosenman, *FDR Papers*, 1944-5 Vol., 41.

Bibliography

Several excellent, general historiographical essays on World War II already exist. The most recent and comprehensive can be found in Michael C. C. Adams's *The Best War Ever* (1993), an up-to-date, well-balanced, and judicious introduction to the war's literature. Rather than duplicate Adams, the following bibliography offers comprehensive coverage of the recent and rapidly growing literature of the home-front war. No such bibliography has previously been published.

This compilation identifies more than 500 items written in the past 10 years that examine various aspects of the American home front during World War II. The entries have been divided into five categories: Economics and Politics, Localities and Regions, Racial and Ethnic Groups, Society and Culture, and Women. But, in order to provide as useful and full coverage of the home-front war as possible, we have omitted the many biographies of the powerful and important, the rich literature on diplomatic history, and most of the large number of pieces on the military experiences of America's women and minorities.

Categorization within a large bibliography is obviously a matter of judgment. In this compilation, "who" took precedence over "what" or "where." Articles that focus on a particular group are found in either "Women" or "Racial and Ethnic Groups," even when the piece concentrates on the group's economic or political experience. In addition, the small literature on American conscientious objection, since this was a political decision, has been assigned to "Politics and Economics." The more extensive literature on enemy prisoners of war (POWs) has been placed in "Regions and Localities." In the end, the reader may need to look in more than one place for all the pieces on a particular subject.

Almost a half century after the war's end, a good deal remains to be done. The particularities of experience still need to be defined with much greater precision. We are just beginning, for example, to learn about the specific experiences of localities, and even there, a chapter of the story has been missing. An important part of the home-front war was the creation of thousands of local war councils, initiated by the federal government and coordinated by state agencies to organize local communities for the war effort. The range of their activities was extraordinary, encompassing almost every aspect of the war-related activity: labor relations, transportation, civilian protection, and civil mobilization, which included rationing programs, scrap drives, and milkweed collections. Yet, there is little mention of these political organizations in the historical literature. In short, we need many more local and regional studies that will unveil the particularities of experience, as they were defined by the complex interactions of region, race, ethnicity, age, class, and gender. Only then will we be able to recapture the home-front war in all its variety, the way it was actually waged in American communities.

ECONOMICS AND POLITICS

Abrahamson, James L. *The American Home Front*. Washington, DC: National Defense University Press, 1983.

Adams, David P. "Wartime Bureaucracy and Penicillin Allocation: The Committee on Chemotherapeutic and Other Agents, 1942–44." *Journal of the History of Medicine and Allied Sciences* 44 (1989): 196–217.

Adams, Michael C. C. *The Best War Ever: America and World War II*. Baltimore: Johns Hopkins University Press, 1994.

Adler, Sy. "The Transformation of the Pacific Electric Railway: Bradford Snell, Roger Rabbit, and the Politics of Transportation in Los Angeles." *Urban Affairs Quarterly* 27 (1991): 51–86.

Alexander, Thomas G. "Utah War Industry during World War II: A Human Impact Analysis." *Utah History Quarterly* 51 (1983): 72–92.

Aruga, Natsuki. "'An' Finish School': Child Labor during World War II." *Labor History* 29 (1988): 498–530.

Bauer, K. Jack. "Inland Seas and Overseas: Shipbuilding on the Great Lakes during World War II." *Inland Seas* 38 (1982): 84–94, 165–70.

Beck, Warren A., and Susanne T. Gaskins. "Henry J. Kaiser—Entrepreneur of the American West." *Journal of the West* 25 (1986): 64–72.

Boyden, Richard. "'Where Outsized Paychecks Grow on Trees': War Workers in San Francisco Shipyards." *Prologue* 23 (1991): 253–59.

Brinkley, David. *Washington Goes to War*. New York: A. A. Knopf, 1988.

Burk, James. "Debating the Draft in America." *Armed Forces & Society* 15 (1989): 431–48.

Burke, Robert E. "A Friendship in Adversity: Burton K. Wheeler and Hiram W. Johnson." *Montana* 36 (1986): 12–25.

Burrowes, John H. "Civilian Public Service, Camp #19, Buck Creek, North Carolina." *Southern Friend* 14 (1992): 22–31.

Cain, Louis, and George Neumann. "Planning for Peace: The Surplus Property Act of 1944." *Journal of Economic History* 41 (1981): 129–37.

Capeci, Dominic J., Jr. "Fiorello H. LaGuardia and Employment Discrimination, 1941–1943." *Italian American* 7 (1983): 49–67.

―――. "Wartime Fair Employment Practice Committees: The Governor's Committee and the First FEPC in New York City, 1941–1943." *Afro-Americans in New York Life and History* 9 (1985): 45–63.

Carter, Kent. "Total War: The Federal Government and the Home Front." *Prologue* 23 (1991): 224–29.

Cuff, Robert D. "Organizational Capabilities and U.S. War Production: The Controlled Materials Plan of World War II." *Business and Economic History* 19 (1990): 103–12.

―――. "United States Mobilization and Railroad Transportation: Lessons in Coordination and Control, 1917–1945." *Journal of Military History* 53 (1989): 33–50.

Dalton, Glen P. "GE: More Than Light Bulbs." *Naval History* 4 (1990): 44–47.

Daniel, Clete. *Chicano Workers and the Politics of Fairness: The FEPC in the Southwest, 1941–1945.* Austin: University of Texas Press, 1991.

Dasenbrock, J. Henry. "In the Blue Ridge Mountains of Virginny—Some Personal Memories of Civilian Public Service." *Southern Friend* 14 (1992): 5–10.

Davidson, Joel. "Building for World War II: The Aerospace Industry." *Blueprints* 11 (1993): 2–8.

Dawley, Alan. "Total War and Class Conflict: American Labor in the 1940's." *Bulletin of the Society for the Study of Labour History* (Great Britain) 49 (1984): 77–81.

Dembo, Jonathan. "Washington State Labor Politics during World War II, 1942–1945." *Journal of the West* 25 (1986): 44–58.

Denfeld, D. Colt. "How World War II Bases Were Built Fast—and Good!" *Periodical: Journal of the Council on America's Military Past* 18 (1991): 24–31.

Devany, John. *America Goes to War, 1941.* New York: Walker, 1991.

Dorn, David R. "Ships for Victory." *U.S. Naval Institute Proceedings* 111 (1985): 68–75.

Eller, Cynthia. *Conscientious Objectors and the Second World War: Moral and Religious Arguments in Support of Pacifism.* New York: Praeger, 1992.

―――. "Oral History as Moral Discourse: Conscientious Objectors and the Second World War." *Oral History Review* 18 (1990): 45–75.

Evans, Paul. "The Effects of General Price Controls in the United States during World War II." *Journal of Political Economics* 90 (1983): 944–66.

Fagerberg, Dixon, Jr. "A World War II Cost Accounting Assignment." Accounting Historians Journal 17 (1990): 81–88.

Feagin, Joe R., and Kelly Riddell. "The State, Capitalism and World War II: The U.S. Case." *Armed Forces and Society* 17 (fall 1990): 53–79.

Feagins, Mary E. Brown. "Alternative Service." *Southern Friend* 14 (1992): 27–37.

Flynn, George Q. "American Medicine and Selective Service in World War II." *Journal of the History of Sciences* 42 (1987): 305–26.

———. "Lewis Hershey and the Conscientious Objector: The World War II Experience." *Military Affairs* 47 (1983): 1–6.

Fones-Wolf, Elizabeth. "Industrial Recreation, the Second World War, and the Revival of Welfare Capitalism, 1934–1960." *Business History Review* 60 (1986): 232–57.

George, James H., Jr. "Another Chance: Herbert Hoover and World War II Relief." *Diplomatic History* 16 (1992): 389–407.

Gersuny, Carl, and Gladis Kaufman. "Seniority and the Moral Economy of U.S. Automobile Workers, 1934–1946." *Journal of Social History* 18 (1985): 463–75.

Gleason, Philip. "Pluralism, Democracy, and Catholicism in the Era of World War II." *Review of Politics* 49 (1987): 208–30.

Goossen, Rachel Waltner. "The 'Second Sex' and the 'Second Milers': Mennonite Women and Civilian Public Service." *Mennonite Quarterly Review* 66 (1992): 525–38.

Greene, Thomas R. "Catholic Thought and World War II Labor Legislation." *Records of the American Catholic Historical Society of Philadelphia* 95 (1984): 37–55.

Harris, William H. "Federal Intervention in Union Discrimination: FEPC and West Coast Shipyards during World War II." *Labor History* 22 (1981): 325–47.

Harrison, Mark. "Resource Mobilization for World War II: The U.S.A., U.K., U.S.S.R. and Germany, 1938–1945." *Economic History Review* 41 (1988): 171–92.

Harrison, Robert. "The Breakup of the Roosevelt Supreme Court: The Contribution of History and Biography." *Law and History Review* 2 (1984): 165–222.

Heinrichs, Waldo. *Threshold of War: Franklin D. Roosevelt and American Entry into World War II.* New York: Oxford University Press, 1988.

Heitmann, John A. "Demagogue and Industrialist: Andrew Jackson Higgins and Higgins Industries." *Gulf Coast Historical Review* 5 (1990): 152–62.

———. "The Man Who Won the War: Andrew Jackson Higgins." *Louisiana History* 34 (1993):35–50.

Higgs, Robert. "Wartime Prosperity? A Reassessment of the U.S. Economy in the 1940's." *Journal of Economic History* 52 (1992): 41–60.

Hooks, Gregory. "From an Autonomous to a Captured State Agency: The Decline of the New Deal in Agriculture." *American Sociological Review* 55 (1990): 29–43.

———. *The Military Industrial Complex: World War II's Battle of the Potomac.* Urbana: University of Illinois Press, 1991.

————. "The Weakness of Strong Theories: The U.S. State's Dominance of the World War II Investment Process." *American Sociological Review* 58 (1993): 37–53.

————, and Leonard E. Bloomquist. "The Legacy of World War II for Regional Growth and Decline: The Cumulative Effects of Wartime Investments on U.S. Manufacturing, 1947–1972." *Social Forces* 71 (1992): 303–7.

Horwich, George, and David J. Bjornstad. "Spending and Manpower in Four U.S. Mobilizations: A Macro/Policy Perspective." *Journal of Policy History* 3 (1991): 173–202.

Hurwitz, Ariel. "The Struggle over the Creation of the War Refugee Board (WRB)." *Holocaust and Genocide Studies* 6 (1991): 17–31.

Jackson, Peter. "Vito Marcantonio and Ethnic Politics in New York." *Ethnic and Racial Studies* 6 (1983): 50–71.

James, D. Clayton, and Anne Sharp Wells. *A Time for Giants: Politics of the American High Command in World War II.* New York: Watts, 1987.

Jeffries, John W. "The 'New' New Deal: FDR and American Liberalism, 1937–1945." *Political Science Quarterly* 3 (1990): 397–418.

Jones, Carolyn C. "Split Income and Separate Spheres: Tax Law and Gender Roles in the 1940s." *Law and History Review* 6 (1988): 259–310.

Justice, Joyce. "World War II Civilian Public Service: Conscientious Objector Camps in Oregon." *Prologue* 23 (1991): 266–78.

Kaplan, Fred. "Scientists at War: The Birth of the Rand Corporation." *American Heritage* 34 (1983): 49–64.

Keehn, Richard H., and Gene Smiley. "Small Business Reactions to World War II Government Controls." *Essays in Economic and Business History* 8 (1990): 303–16.

Keim, Albert N. "Mennonites and Selective Service in World War II: An Ambiguous Relationship." *Mennonite Quarterly Review* 66 (1992): 508–24.

Kidwell, Peggy. "Harvard Astronomers in the Second World War." *Journal for the History of Astronomy* 21 (1990): 105–6.

Kimball, Warren F. *The Juggler: Franklin Roosevelt as Wartime Statesman.* Princeton: Princeton University Press, 1991.

Kimeldorf, Howard. "World War II and the Deradicalization of American Labor: The ILWU as a Deviant Case." *Labor History* 33 (1992): 248–78.

Krammer, Arnold. "Hitler's Legions in America." *American History Illustrated* 18 (1983): 54–64.

————. "In Splendid Isolation: Enemy Diplomats in World War II." *Prologue* 17 (1985): 25–43.

Launius, Roger D. "'Never Was Life More Interesting': The National Advisory Committee for Aeronautics, 1936–1945." *Prologue* 24 (1992): 361–73.

Lees, Lorraine M. "National Security and Ethnicity: Contrasting Views during World War II." *Diplomatic History* 11 (1987): 113–25.

Leff, Mark H. "The Politics of Sacrifice on the American Home Front in World War II." *Journal of American History* 77 (1991): 1296–1318.

Lemke-Santangelo, Gretchen. "The Radical Conscientious Objectors of World War II: Wartime Experiences and Postwar Activism." *Radical History Review* 45 (1989): 5–29.

Lewandowski, Michael J. "Democracy in the Workplace: Working Women in Midwestern Unions, 1943–1945." *Prologue* 25 (1993): 157–69.

Lichtenstein, Nelson. *Labor's War at Home: The CIO in World War II.* New York: Cambridge University Press, 1982.

———. "The Making of the Postwar Working Class: Cultural Pluralism and Social Structure in World War II." *Historian* 51 (1988): 42–63.

Maines, Rachel. "Wartime Allocation of Textiles and Apparel Resources: Emergency Policy in the Twentieth Century." *Public Historian* 7 (1985): 29–51.

Maney, Patrick J. *The Roosevelt Presence: A Biography of Franklin Delano Roosevelt.* New York: Twayne, 1992.

Mills, Geofrey, and Hugh Rockoff. "Compliance with Price Controls in the United States and the United Kingdom during World War II." *Journal of Economic History* 47 (1987): 197–213.

Nash, Gerald D. *The Crucial Era: The Great Depression and World War II, 1929–1945.* 2d ed. New York: St. Martin's Press, 1992.

Naske, Claus M. "Governor Gruening and the Alaska War Council: The Battle for Civilian Control of Alaska during World War II." *Alaska Journal* 16 (1986): 48–54.

Olinger, John C. "They Called It Camp Downey." *Idaho Yesterdays* 31 (1988): 15–23.

O'Neill, William L. *A Democracy at War: America's Fight at Home and Abroad in World War II.* New York: Free Press, 1993.

Ourada, Patricia K. "Reluctant Servants: Conscientious Objectors in Idaho during World War II." *Idaho Yesterdays* 31 (1988): 2–14.

Pessen, Edward. "A Young Industrial Worker in Early World War II in New York City." *Labor History* 22 (1981): 269–81.

Phillips, William H. "Southern Textile Mill Villages on the Eve of World War II: The Courtenay Mill of South Carolina." *Journal of Economic History* 45 (1985): 269–75.

Rakes, Paul H. "Casualties on the Homefront: Scotts Run Mining Diasters during World War II." *West Virginia History* 53 (1994): 95–118.

Ranki, György. "Economy and the Second World War: A Few Comparative Issues." *Journal of European Economic History* 17 (1988): 303–47.

Raymond, Raymond James. "American Public Opinion and Irish Neutrality, 1939–1945." *Èire-Ireland* 18 (1983): 20–45.

Reagan, Patrick D. "The Withholding Tax, Beardsley Ruml, and Modern American Public Policy." *Prologue* 24 (1992): 19–31.

Rennick, Robert M. "On the Success of Efforts to Retain the Names of Several American Communities in the Two World Wars." *Names* 32 (1984): 26–32.

Renshaw, P. "Organized Labor and the United States War Economy." *Journal of Contemporary History* 21 (1986): 3–22.

Rhodes, Richard. *The Making of the Atomic Bomb.* New York: Simon & Schuster, 1986.

Rockoff, Hugh. "The Response of the Giant Corporations to Wage and Price Controls in World War II." *Journal of Economic History* 41 (1981): 123–28.

Romer, Christina D. "What Ended the Great Depression?" *Journal of Economic History* 52 (1992): 757–84.

Rumbarger, John J. "The War Production Board and Historical Research: Some Observations on Writing Public History." *Public Historian* 6 (1984): 5–19.

Sawrey, Robert D. "Who Will Run the Machines? An American Business, the Arsenal of Democracy, and the Realities of World War II Production." *Journal of the West Virginia Historical Association* 9 (1985): 53–57.

Saxton, Alexander. "World War II: Opening the Home Front." *Reviews in American History* 8 (1980): 393–97.

Schomer, Howard. "From 'Just War' to 'Just Peace': CPS and War Resistance among Congregationalists." *Mennonite Quarterly Review* 66 (1992): 598–614.

Sirgiovanni, George. *An Undercurrent of Suspicion: Anti-Communism in America during World War II.* New Brunswick, NJ: Transaction, 1990.

Sprunger, Keith L., and John D. Thiesen. "Mennonite Military Service in World War II: An Oral History Approach." *Mennonite Quarterly Review* 66 (1992): 481–91.

Stafford, William. "Selections from 'Down in My Heart.'" *Georgia Review* 38 (1984): 836–52.

Steele, Richard W. "The Great Debate: Roosevelt, the Media, and the Coming of the War, 1940–1941." *Journal of American History* 71 (1984): 69–92.

Stuhler, Barbara. "A Minnesota Footnote to the 1944 Presidential Election." *Minnesota History* 52 (1990): 27–34.

Torigan, Michael. "National Unity on the Waterfront: Communist Politics and the ILWU during the Second World War." *Labor History* 30 (1989): 409–32.

Tuttle, William M., Jr. "The Birth of an Industry: The Synthetic Rubber 'Mess' in World War II." *Technology and Culture* 22 (1981): 35–67.

VanDyck, Harry R. *Exercises of Conscience: A WWII Objector Remembers.* Buffalo, NY: Prometheus Books, 1990.

Vatter, Howard. *The U.S. Economy in World War II.* New York: Columbia University Press, 1985.

Walker, Henry, Jr. "Beyond the Call of Duty: Representative John Sparkman of Alabama and World War II, 1939–1945." *Southern Historian* 11 (1988): 24–42.

Warnes, Kathleen. "The Submarines for World War II." *Inland Seas* 42 (1986): 12–23.

Washburn, Patrick S. "The Office of Censorship's Attempt to Control Press Coverage of the Atomic Bomb during World War II." *Journalism Monographs* 120 (1990): 1–43.

Westbrook, Robert. "Horrors—Theirs and Ours: The Politics Circle and the Good War." *Radical History Review* 36 (1986): 9–25.

White, Steven Jay. "Quakers, Conscientious Objectors, the Friends' Civilian Public Service Corps, and World War Two." *Southern Friend* 14 (spring 1992): 5–21.

Woodruff, Nan Elizabeth, and Harold D. Woodman. "Pick or Fight: The Emergency Farm Labor Program in the Arkansas and Mississippi Deltas during World War II." *Agricultural History* 64 (1990): 74–85, 115–21.

Wynne, Lewis N., and Carolyn J. Barnes. "They Still Sail: Shipbuilding in Tampa during World War II." *Gulf Coast Historical Review* 5 (1990): 179–91.

Zeitzer, Glen, and Charles F. Howlett. "Political versus Religious Pacifism: The Peace Now Movement of 1943." *Historian* 48 (1986): 375–93.

LOCAL AND REGIONAL HISTORY

Adams, Gerald M. "The Casper Army Air Force Field in World War II." *Wyoming Annals* 64 (1992): 6–23.

Adams, Patricia L. "Fighting for Democracy in St. Louis: Civil Rights during World War II." *Missouri Historical Review* 80 (1985): 58–75.

Allen, Ann. "The News Media and the Women's Army Auxiliary Corps: Protagonists for a Cause." *Military Affairs* 50 (1986): 77–83.

Althoff, William F. "NAS Lakehurst—The War Years: Photographic History." *American Aviation Historical Society Journal* 30 (1985): 140–51.

Andrews, Clarence. "Sheldon, Iowa during WWII." *Palimpsest* 70 (1989): 146–55.

Arendale, Marirose, and Frances Bishop. "Chattanooga Schools Go to War: 1941–1945." *Tennessee Historical Quarterly* 49 (1989): 46–53.

Arnow, H. S. "Detroit during World War II." *Michigan Quarterly Review* 25 (1986): 292–95.

Baxter, Robert L, Jr., and J. L. Wagoner. "Higher Education Goes to War: The University of Virginia's Response to World War II." *Virginia Magazine of History and Biography* 100 (1992): 399–428.

Bergh, Helen J. "Troop Trains and Pheasant Sandwiches: The Aberdeen Canteen in World War II." *South Dakota History* 23 (1993): 133–41.

Bertelsen, Lance. "How Texas Won the Second World War." *Southwest Review* 76 (1991): 309–35.

Billinger, Robert, Jr. "Behind the Wire: German Prisoners of War at Camp Sutton, 1944–1946." *North Carolina Historical Review* 61 (1984): 481–509.

Boardman, Edna. "Winning World War II: How a North Dakota Farm Child Did Her Part for the War Effort." *Heritage Review* 22 (1992): 3–5.

Boney, F. N. "G.I. Georgia: The Army in the State during World War II." *Georgia Historical Quarterly* 71 (1987): 297–308.

———, and Gary L Doster. "A University Goes to War: The Navy at the University of Georgia during World War II." *Georgia Historical Quarterly* 76 (1992): 115–27.

Braatz, Werner E., and Virginia G. Crane. "Ordinary People in Oshkosh, Wisconsin: Videotaped Interviews and the Study of World War II." *Midwest Review* 13 (1991): 54–61.

Brown, DeSoto. *Hawaii Goes to War: Life in Hawaii from Pearl Harbor to Peace.* Honolulu: Ed. Limited, 1989.

Buecker, Thomas R. "Mules, Horses and Dogs: Fort Robinson in World War II." *Journal of the Council on America's Military Past* 16 (1989): 34–49.

———. "Nazi Influence at the Fort Robinson Prisoner of War Camp during World War II." *Nebraska History* 73 (1992): 32–41.

Clive, Alan. *State of War: Michigan in World War II.* Ann Arbor: University of Michigan Press, 1979.

Coates, Kenneth, and Judith Powell. "Whitehorse and the Building of the Alaska Highway, 1942–1946." *Alaska History* 4 (1989): 1–26.

Coker, Kathy Roe. "World War II Prisoners of War in Georgia: German Memories of Camp Gordon, 1943–1945." *Georgia Historical Quarterly* 19 (1992): 837–61.

Cole, Merle T. "The Special Military Police at Morgantown Bridge, 1942–1943." *Military Affairs* 52 (1988): 18–22.

Colwell, James L. "Hell from Heaven! Midland Army Air Field in World War II." Parts I, II, III. *Permian Historical Annual* 25 (1985): 11–42; 26 (1986): 51–90; 27 (1987): 95–128.

———. "Wings over West Texas: Pecos Army Air Field in World War II." *West Texas Historical Association Yearbook* 63 (1987): 42–62.

Corbett, William P. "'They Hired Every Farmer in the Country': Establishing the Prisoner of War Camp at Tonkawa." *Chronicles of Oklahoma* 69 (1991–1992): 368–91.

Cox, Lori. "What Did You Do in the War?" *Nebraska History* 72 (1991): 158–256.

Cox, Thomas F., Jr. "Fort Myers during World War II." *Tampa Bay History* 11 (1989): 22–40.

Curtis, Peter H. "A Place of Peace in a World of War: The Scattergood Refugee Hostel, 1939 to 1943." *Palimpsest* 65 (1984): 42–52.

Daniel, Pete. "Going among Strangers: Southern Reactions to World War II." *Journal of American History* 77 (1990): 886–911.

Dooley, Patricia L. "Gopher Ordinance Works: Condemnation, Construction and Community Response." *Minnesota History* 49 (1985): 214–28.

Doyle, Susan Badger. "German and Italian Prisoners of War in Albuquerque, 1943–1946." *New Mexican Historical Review* 66 (1991): 327–40.

Dwyer, Margaret Clifford. "The U.S. Naval Reserve Midshipmen School, Northampton, 1942 to 1945." *Historical Journal of Massachusetts* 22 (1994): 34–50.

Dyke, Samuel E. "War Production at Armstrong Cork Company: 1940–1945." *Journal of the Lancaster County Historical Society* 85 (1981): 30–46.

Edwards, G. Thomas. "The Oregon Coast and Three of Its Guerrilla Organizations, 1942." *Journal of the West* 25 (1986): 20–34.

Egerton, John. "Days of Hope and Horror: Atlanta after World War II." *Georgia Historical Quarterly* 78 (1994): 281-305.

Everett, Dianna, comp. "Photo Essay: The Texas Panhandle during World War II." *Panhandle-Plains Historical Review* 62 (1989): 1–18.

Fagan, Michele L. "Kennedy General Hospital: The War Years, 1941–1945." *Tennessee Historical Quarterly* 51 (1992): 51–67.

———. "Nebraska Nursing Education during World War II." *Nebraska History* 73 (1992): 126–37.

Fickle, James E., and Donald W. Ellis. "POWs in the Piney Woods: German Prisoners of War in the Southern Lumber Industry, 1943–1945." *Journal of Southern History* 4 (1990): 695–724.

Fisher, Charles R. "The Maryland State Guard in World War II." *Military Affairs* 47 (1987): 11–14.

Folsom, Carlton. "Centenary at War: 1941–1945." *Northern Louisiana Historical Association Journal* 19 (1988): 133–42.

"German Prisoners of War in Alaska: The POW Camp at Excursion Inlet." *Alaska Journal* 14 (1984): 16–20.

Goodstein, Phil. "The Day the Army Invaded Montgomery Ward." *Colorado Heritage* (1991): 40–47.

Gordon, Susan L. "Home Front Tennessee: The World War II Experience." *Tennessee Historical Quarterly* 51 (1992): 3–18.

Hall, Clarence. "The Pocatello Car Department during World War II." *Rendezvous* 22 (1987): 52–55.

Hanson, David E. "National Education Policy and the Primacy of Local Interests: Portland, Oregon Schools in World War II." *Journal of the West* 25 (1986): 59–63.

Harms, Richard H. "In the Mood: Grand Rapids during World War II." *Michigan History* 74 (1990): 25–29.

Hartzell, Karl D. "New York State and World War II: Preserving the Record." Edited by Daniel Linke. *New York History* 73 (1992): 321–36.

Hays, Otis E., Jr. "The Silent Years in Alaska: The Military Blackout during World War II." *Alaska Journal* 16 (1986): 40–47.

———. "When War Came to Seward." *Alaska Journal* 13 (1983): 107–14.

Holl, Richard E. "Axis Prisoners of War in the Free State, 1943–1946." *Maryland Historical Magazine* 83 (1988): 142–56.

Holzimmer, Kevin C. "Wake Up Detroit!" *Michigan History* 74 (1990): 38–45.

Howard, Patricia Brake. "Tennessee in War and Peace: The Impact of World War II on State Economic Trends." *Tennessee Historical Quarterly* 51 (1992): 51–70.

Huss, Stephen F. "Milkweed, Machine Guns and Cows: Jefferson County Farmers in World War II." *Missouri Historical Review* 86 (1992): 265–81.

Jepson, Daniel A. "Camp Carson, Colorado: European Prisoners of War in the American West during World War II." *Midwest Review* 13 (1991): 32–53.

Joachim, George. *Iron Fleet: The Great Lakes in World War II.* Detroit: Wayne State University Press, 1994.

Johnson, Charles W. "V for Virginia: The Commonwealth Goes to War." *Virginia Magazine of History and Biography* 100 (1992): 365–98.

Johnson, Judith R. "Patriotic Prisoners and National Defense: Penitentiaries of the Far Southwest in World War II." *Nevada Historical Society Quarterly* 33 (1990): 208–18.

Johnson, Marliynn S. "Urban Arsenals: War Housing and Social Change in Richmond and Oakland, California, 1941–1945." *Pacific Historical Review* 60 (1991): 283–308.

———. "War as Watershed: The East Bay and World War II." *Pacific Historical Review* 63 (1994): 315–41.

"Kansas at War." *Kansas History* 15 (1992): 36–43, 116–25.

Karolevitz, Robert F. "Life on the Home Front: South Dakota in WWII." *South Dakota History* 19 (1989): 392–423.

Keefer, Louis E. "Enemies Turned Allies: Italian POWs in Ohio." *Timeline* 10 (1993): 46–54.

———. "Fliers on the Homefront: Virginia's Civil Air Patrol in World War II." *Virginia Cavalcade* 41 (1992): 112–23.

———. "From Captive to Ally: Italian Prisoners of War in Virginia 1943–45." *Virginia Cavalcade* 39 (1990): 182–91.

———. "Little Hunks of Home: The School for Morale and Washington and Lee University, 1942–1946." *Virginia Cavalcade* 43 (1993): 24–35.

———. "Students, Soldiers, Sailors: Trainees on Virginia College Campuses during World War II." *Virginia Cavalcade* 39 (1989): 22–35.

Keen, Richard. "Recreational and Morale Activities in the Hereford Prisoner of War Camp, 1943–1946." *Permian Historical Annual* 29 (1989): 89–108.

Larson, George A. "Nebraska's World War II Bomber Plant: The Glenn L. Martin-Nebraska Company." *Nebraska History* 74 (1993): 32–43.

Launius, Roger D. "World War II Military Aviation in the Rockies: From Natural to National Resource." *Journal of the West* 32 (1993): 86–93.

Lee, James Ward, Carolyn N. Barnes, and Kent A. Bowman, eds. *1941: Texas Goes to War*. Denton: Center for Texas Studies Book, with the University of North Texas Press, 1991.

Leonard, Stephen J. "Denver at War: The Home Front in World War II." *Colorado Heritage* (1987): 30–39.

Leonhirth, Janene. "Tennessee's Experiment: Women as Military Flight Instructors." *Tennessee Historical Quarterly* 51 (1992): 170–78.

Lobdell, George H. "A Tale of Two Christmases at the Algona Prisoner of War Camp." *Palimpsest* 73 (winter 1992): 178–79.

Lotchin, Roger W. "California Cities and the Hurricane of Change: World War II in the San Francisco, Los Angeles, and San Diego Metropolitan Areas." *Pacific Historical Review* 63 (1994): 393-420.

———. *Fortress California, 1919–1961: From Warfare to Welfare*. New York: Oxford University Press, 1992.

Lovett, Christopher C. "Don't You Know That There's a War On ? A History of the Kansas State Guard in World War II." *Kansas History* 8 (1985–1986): 226–35.

Lowenstein, Sharon. *Token Refuge: The Story of the Jewish Refugee Shelter at Oswego, 1944–1946*. Bloomington: Indiana University Press, 1986.

McConaghy, Lorraine. "Wartime Boomtown: Kirkland, Washington, A Small Town during World War II." *Pacific Northwest Quarterly* 80 (1989): 42–51.

McDaniel, George William. "World War II Comes to Davenport." *Palimpsest* 73 (1992): 89–96.

"Michigan Goes to War." *Michigan History* 78 (1994): 33–35.

"Michigan Goes to War: World War II Memories." *Michigan History* 77 (1993): 42–45.

Mihelich, Dennis N. "The Lincoln Urban League: The Travail of Depression and War." *Nebraska History* 70 (1989): 303–16.

Miller, Duane Ernest. "Barbed-Wire Farm Laborers: Michigan's Prisoners of War Experience during World War II." *Michigan History* 73 (1989): 12–17.

Miller, Marc. *The Irony of Victory: World War II and Lowell, Massachusetts*. Urbana: University of Illinois Press, 1988.

Miller, Robert Ernest. "The War That Never Came: Civilian Defense in Cincinnati, Ohio, during World War II." *Queen City Heritage* 49 (1991): 3–22.

Miner, Curtis. "'Hi Butch': The WWII Letters of Everett Johns." *Pittsburgh History* 72 (1989): 178–91.

Moehring, Eugene P. "Las Vegas and the Second World War." *Nevada Historical Society Quarterly* 29 (1986): 1–30.

Moore, John Hammond. "No Room, No Rice, No Grits: Charleston's Time of Trouble, 1942–1944." *South Atlantic Quarterly* 85 (1986): 23–31.

Morris, Cynthia. "Arkansas' Reaction to the Men Who Said 'No' to WWII." *Arkansas Historical Quarterly* 43 (1984): 153–77.

Myers, James. "The Army Comes to Abilene." *West Texas Historical Association Year Book* 65 (1989):101–10.

———. "Prisoners of War at Camp Barkeley." *West Texas Historical Association Year Book* 61 (1985): 134–40.

Nash, Gerald D. *The American West Transformed: The Impact of the Second World War.* Bloomington: University of Indiana Press, 1985.

———. "Planning for the Postwar City: The Urban West in World War II." *Arizona and the West* 27 (1985): 99–112.

———. "The West and the Military-Industrial Complex." *Montana* 39 (1989): 72–75.

———. *World War II and the West: Reshaping the Economy.* Lincoln: University of Nebraska Press, 1990.

Noble, Antonette Chambers. "Utah's Defense Industries and Workers in World War II." *Utah Historical Quarterly* 59 (1991): 365–79.

O'Brien, Patrick G., Thomas D. Isern, and Daniel R. Lumley. "Stalag Sunflower: German Prisoners of War in Kansas." *Kansas History* 7 (1984): 182–98.

Otey, George N. "New Deal for Oklahoma's Children: Federal Day Care Centers, 1933–1946." *Chronicles of Oklahoma* 62 (1984): 296–312.

Parson, Don. "Los Angeles' 'Headline Happy Public Housing War.'" *Southern California Quarterly* 65 (1983): 251–85.

Paulette, Irene. "Odessa during the War Years, 1941–1945: A Microcosm of the Nation." *Permian History Annual* 22 (1982): 15–33.

Petersen, Todd. "Kearney, Nebraska, and the Kearney Army Air Field in World War II." *Nebraska History* 3 (1991): 118–26.

———. "Nazi Influence at the Fort Robinson Prisoner of War Camp during World War II." *Nebraska History* 73 (1992): 32–41.

Pfaff, Christine. "Bullets for the Yanks: Colorado's World War II Ammunition Factory." *Colorado Heritage* (1992): 33–45.

Pfluger, James R. "Fuel for Victory: Texas Panhandle Petroleum, 1941–1945." *Panhandle-Plains Historical Review* 62 (1989): 19–56.

Politzer, Geneva B. "Rising Sun over Alaska." *American History Illustrated* 25 (1990): 36–39.

Powell, Allan Kent. *Splinters of a Nation: German Prisoners of War in Utah.* Salt Lake City: University of Utah Press, 1989.

Quillman, Catherine. "No Summer Solstice: War Stories of the Home Front Survivors." *Pennsylvania Heritage* 19 (1993): 4–11.

Reid, Robert L. "Extra! Extra!: World War II Hits the Streets of El Paso." *Password* 34 (1989): 127–34.

Robbins, William G. "Timber and War: An Oral History of Coos Bay, Oregon, 1940–1945." *Journal of the West* 25 (1986): 35–43.

Rogers, Joe D. "Camp Hereford: Italian Prisoners of War on the Texas Plains, 1942–1945." *Panhandle-Plains Historical Review* 62 (1989): 57–110.

Sanger, S. L. *Hanford and the Bomb: An Oral History of World War II.* Seattle: Living History, 1989.

Sanson, Jerry Purvis. "Louisiana Reaction to the Beginning of World War II." *Journal of Southern History* 7 (1986): 31–39.

Scheiber, Harry N., and Jane L. "Constitutional Liberty in World War II: Army Rule and Martial Law in Hawaii, 1941–46." *Western Legal History* 3 (1990): 341–78.

Schott, Matthew J. "Camp Ruston POWs: Notes and Documents, 1984." *North Louisiana Historical Association Journal* 15 (1984): 78–85.

Schwantes, Carlos A. "The Pacific Northwest in World War II." *Journal of the West* 25 (1984): 4–19.

Schwieder, Dorothy. "The Iowa State College Cooperative Extension Service through Two World Wars." Commentary by Allan G. Bogue. *Agricultural History* 64 (1990): 219–30.

Shea, William L., and Merrill R. Prichett. "The Wehrmacht in Louisiana." *Louisiana History* 23 (1982): 5–19.

Shragge, Abraham. "'A New Federal City': San Diego during World War II." *Pacific Historical Review* 63 (1994): 333–61.

Simmons, Jerold. "Public Leadership in a World War II Boom Town: Bellevue, Nebraska." *Nebraska History* 65 (1984): 484–99.

Sloan, Charles William, Jr., ed. "The Newsletters: E. Gail Carpenter Describes Life on the Homefront." *Kansas History* 11 (1988): 54–72, 123–42, 150–70, 243–59.

Smith, C. Calvin. *War and Wartime Changes: The Transformation of Arkansas, 1940–1945.* Fayetteville: University of Arkansas Press, 1986.

Sneddeker, Duane R. "St. Louis on the Home Front: Photographs from World War II." *Gateway Heritage* 13 (1992): 34–45.

Spude, Robert L. S., and Sandra McDermott Faulkner. "World War II at Dutch Harbor: Preserving the Record." *Alaska History* 2 (1986–1987): 57–65.

Stahnke, Herbert H. "Ministry to German POWs at Fort Sill 1943–1946." *Concordia Historical Institute Quarterly* 62 (1989): 119–24.

Strong, Lester. "When 'Toyko Rose' Came to Albuquerque." *New Mexican Historical Review* 66 (1990): 70–92.

Swanson, Merwin R. "A Community at War: Pocatello Idaho and World War II." *Rendezvous* 22 (1987): 1–13.

Swisher, Perry. "World War II and Pocatello." *Rendezvous* 22 (1987): 91–95.

Thomas, Mary Martha. "The Mobile Homefront during the Second World War." *Gulf Coast Historical Review* 1 (1986): 55–75.

Thompson, Erwin N. "North Star Defense: Alaska World War II Military Bases, Part I." *Periodical: Journal of the Council on America's Military Past* 14 (1986): 26–44.

Toplovich, Ann. "The Tennessean's War: Life on the Home Front." *Tennessee Historical Quarterly* 51 (1992): 19–50.

Unsworth, Michael E. "Floating Vengeance: Japanese Balloon Attacks on Michigan." *Michigan History* 71 (1987): 8–14.

Urwin, Cathy Kunzinger. "The Coal Strikes of 1943." *West Virginia History* 45 (1984): 91–107.

Verge, Arthur C. "The Impact of the Second World War on Los Angeles." *Pacific Historical Review* 63 (1994): 289–314.

Volpenhein, Mark. "The Construction of Greater Cincinnati Airport: The Impact of World War II." *Queen City Heritage* 44 (1986): 39–48.

Wages, Hazel. "The Memphis Armed Service Forces Depot Prisoner of War Camp." *Tennessee Historical Quarterly* 52 (1993): 19–32.

Walker, Chip. "German Creative Activities in Camp Aliceville, 1943–1946." *Alabama Review* 38 (1985): 19–37.

Walker, Richard P. "The Swastika and the Lone Star: Nazi Activity in Texas POW Camps." *Military History of the Southwest* 19 (1989): 39–70.

Warner, Richard S. "Barbed Wire and Nazilagers: POW Camps in Oklahoma." *Chronicles of Oklahoma* 64 (1986): 36–67.

Welsh, Carol H. "Back the Attack: The Sale of War Bonds in Oklahoma." *Chronicles of Oklahoma* 61 (1983): 226–45.

———. "Some Thoughts on Prisoners of War in Iowa, 1943 to 1946." *Palimpsest* 65 (1984): 68–80.

Werts, Russell. "German Prisoners of War in Alaska: The POW Camp at Excursion Inlet." *Alaska Journal* 14 (1984): 16–20.

Whiting, Cécile. "American Heroes and Invading Barbarians: The Regionalist Response to Fascism." *Prospects* 13 (1988): 295–324.

Winkler, Allan M. "The Queen City and World War II." *Queen City Heritage* 49 (1991): 3–20.

Wit, Tracy Lyn. "The Social and Economic Impact of WWII Munitions Manufacture on Grand Island, Nebraska." *Nebraska History* 71 (1990): 151–63.

Wollenberg, Charles. *Marinship at War: Shipbuilding and Social Change in Wartime Sausalito.* Berkeley, CA: Western Heritage, 1990.

Worrall, Janet E. "Prisoners on the Home Front: Community Reactions to German and Italian POWs in Northern Colorado, 1943–1946." *Colorado Heritage* (1990): 32–47.

Wynne, Lewis N., and Carolyn J. Barnes. "They Still Sail: Shipbuilding in Tampa during World War II." *Gulf Coast Historical Review* 5 (1990): 179–91.

Yost, Harry. "Building the Alaska Highway: Snapshots from a Soldier's Scrapbook." *Alaska Journal* 15 (1985): 23–27.

RACE AND ETHNICITY

Allen, Robert L. "The Port Chicago Disaster and Its Aftermath." *Black Scholar* 13 (1982): 2–29.

Bailey, Beth, and David Farber. "The 'Double-V' Campaign in World War II Hawaii: African-Americans, Racial Ideology, and Federal Power." *Journal of Social History* 26 (1993): 286–309.

———. *The First Strange Place: Race and Sex in World War II Hawaii.* Baltimore: Johns Hopkins University Press, 1992.

Barbeau, Arthur E. "Civilian Internment in World War II." *Journal of the West Virginia Historical Association* 11 (1987): 1–19.

Baron, Lawrence. "Haven from the Holocaust: Oswego, New York, 1944–1946." *New York History* 64 (1983): 5–34.

Baumel, Judith Tydor. "The Transfer and Resettlement in the United States of Young Jewish Refugees from Nazism, 1934–1945." *American Jewish History* 77 (1988): 413–36.

Bearden, Russell. "Life inside Arkansas's Japanese-American Relocation Centers." *Arkansas Historical Quarterly* 48 (1989): 169–96.

Beardsley, Richard K. "Ethnic Solidarity Turned to New Activism in a California Enclave: The Japanese Americans of 'Delta.'" *California History* 68 (1989): 100–115.

Bernstein, Alison. *American Indians and World War II: Toward a New Era in Indian Affairs.* Norman: University of Oklahoma Press, 1991.

Bitner, Eric. "'Loyalty Is a Covenant': Japanese American Internees and the Selective Service Act." *Prologue* 23 (1991): 248–52.

Bracey, John H. and August Meier. "Allies or Adversaries?: The NAACP, A. Philip Randolph and the 1941 March on Washington," *Georgia Historical Quarterly* 75 (1991): 1–17.

Brcak, Nancy and John R. Pavia. "Racism in Japanese and U.S. Wartime Propaganda." *Historian* 56 (1994): 671–84.

Broussard, Albert S. "Strange Territory, Familiar Leadership: The Impact of World War II on San Francisco's Black Community." *California History* 65 (1986): 18–25, 71–73.

Capeci, Dominic J., Jr. "The Lynching of Cleo Wright: Federal Protection of Constitutional Rights during WW II." *Journal of American History* 72 (1986): 859–87.

———. *Race Relations in Wartime Detroit: The Sojourner Truth Housing Controversy of 1942.* Philadelphia: Temple University Press, 1984.

———, and Martha Wilkerson. *Layered Violence: The Detroit Rioters of 1943.* Jackson: University of Mississippi Press, 1991.

Chiasson, Lloyd. "Japanese-American Relocation during World War II: A Study of California Editorial Reactions." *Journalism Quarterly* 68 (1991): 263–68.

Christgau, John. "Collins versus the World: The Fight to Restore Citizenship to Japanese American Renunciants of World War II." *Pacific Historical Review* 54 (1985): 1–32.

———. *"Enemies": World War II Alien Internment.* Ames: Iowa State University Press, 1985.

Conroy, Hilary, and Sharlie Conroy Ushioda. "A Review of Scholarly Literature on the Internment of Japanese Americans during World War II: Toward a Quaker Perspective." *Quaker History* 83 (1994): 48–52.

Coser, Lewis A. "Refugee Intellectuals." *Society* 22 (1984): 61–68.

Cosgrove, Stuart. "The Zoot-Suit and Style Warfare." *Radical America* 18 (1984): 39–50.

Culley, John J. "Trouble at the Lordsburg Internment Camp." *New Mexico Historical Quarterly* 60 (1985): 225–48.

Daniels, Roger, ed. *American Concentration Camps: A Documentary Heritage of the Relocation and Incarceration of Japanese Americans, 1941–1945.* 9 vols. New York: Garland, 1989.

———. *Asian America: Chinese and Japanese in the United States since 1850.* Seattle: University of Washington Press, 1988.

———. "Japanese Relocation and Redress in North America." *Pacific Historian* 26 (1982): 2–13.

———. *Prisoners without Trial: Japanese Americans in World War II.* New York: Hill and Wang, 1993.

———, Sandra C. Taylor, and Harry H. L. Kitano. *Japanese Americans: From Relocation to Redress.* Salt Lake City: University of Utah Press, 1986.

Davidson, Sue. "Aki Kato Kurose: Portrait of an Activist." *Frontiers* 7 (1983): 91–97.

Dinnerstein, Leonard. "What Should American Jews Have Done to Rescue Their European Brethren?" *Simon Wiesenthal Center Annual* 3 (1986): 277–87.

Dower, John W. *War without Mercy: Race and Power in the Pacific War.* New York: Pantheon Books, 1986.

Drinnon, Richard. *Keeper of Concentration Camps: Dillon S. Myer and American Racism.* Berkeley: University of California Press, 1987.

Eagles, Charles W. "Two 'Double V's': Jonathan Daniels, FDR, and Race Relations during World War II." *North Carolina Historical Review* 59 (1982): 252–70.

Embrey, Sue Kunitomi, Arthur A. Hansen, and Betty Kulberg Mitson, comps. *Manzanar Martyr: An Interview with Harry Y. Ueno.* Fullerton: California State University at Fullerton, Fullerton Oral History Program, 1986.

Fairclough, Adam. "Racial Repression in World War Two: The New Iberia Incident." *Louisiana History* 32 (1991): 183–207.

Feingold, Henry L. "'Courage First and Intelligence Second': The American Jewish Secular Elite, Roosevelt and the Failure to Rescue." *American Jewish History* 72 (1983): 424–60.

Flynn, George Q. "Selective Service and American Blacks during World War II." *Journal of Negro History* 69 (1984): 14–25.

Fox, Stephen. "General John DeWitt and the Proposed Internment of German and Italian Aliens during World War II." *Pacific Historical Review* 57 (1988): 407–38.

———, ed. *The Unknown Internment: An Oral History of the Relocation of Italian Americans during World War II.* Boston: Twayne, 1990.

Franco, Jeré. "Bringing Them in Alive: Selective Service and Native Americans." *Journal of Ethnic Studies* 18 (1990): 1–27.

Friedlander, E. J. "Freedom of Press behind Barbed Wire: Paul Yokota and the Jerome Relocation Center Newspaper." *Arkansas Historical Quarterly* 44 (1985): 303–13.

———. "Journalism behind Barbed Wire, 1942–1944: An Arkansas Relocation Center Newspaper." *Journalism Quarterly* 62 (1985): 243–46, 271.

Gamboa, Erasmo. "Braceros in the Pacific Northwest: Laborers on the Domestic Front, 1942–1947." *Pacific Historical Review* 56 (1987): 378–98.

———. *Mexican Labor and World War II: Braceros in the Pacific Northwest, 1942–1947.* Austin: University of Texas Press, 1990.

Garcia, Mario T. *Mexican Americans: Leadership, Ideology and Identity, 1930–1960.* New Haven: Yale University Press, 1990.

———. "Americans All: The Mexican American Generation and the Politics of Wartime Los Angeles, 1941–45." *Social Science Quarterly* 65 (1984): 278–89.

Gentile, Nancy J. "Survival behind the Barbed Wire: The Impact of Imprisonment on Japanese–American Culture during World War II." *Maryland Historian* (1988): 15–31.

Gesensway, Deborah, and Mindy Roseman. *Beyond Words: Images from America's Concentration Camps.* Ithaca: Cornell University Press, 1987.

Greenberg, Cheryl. "The Politics of Disorder: Reexamining Harlem's Riots of 1935-1943." Journal of Urban History 18 (1992): 395-441.

Greenberg, Karen J. "A Missed Chance: Reassessing the Fort Ontario Emergency Refugee Shelter." *Hudson Valley Regional Review* 9 (1992): 129–36.

Gruber, Ruth. *Haven: The Unknown Story of 1,000 World War II Refugees.* New York: Coward, McCann, Geoghehan, 1983.

Hale, Duane K. "Uncle Sam's Warriors: American Indians in World War II." *Chronicles of Oklahoma* 69 (1991–1992): 408–29.

Hansen, Arthur A. "Cultural Politics in the Gila River Relocation Center, 1942–1943." *Arizona and the West* 27 (1985): 327–62.

————. ed. *Japanese American World War II Evacuation Oral History Project. Part I: Internees.* Westport, CT: Meckler, 1991.

————. "Representations of An Imprisoned Poston Past." *Journal of Orange County Studies* 3-4 (1989-1990): 102-8.

Hewitt, William. "Mexican Workers in Wyoming during WWII: Necessity, Discrimination, and Protest." *Annals of Wyoming* 54 (1982): 20-33.

Holm, Tom. "Fighting a White Man's War: The Extent and Legacy of American Indian Participation in World War II." *Journal of Ethnic Studies* 9 (1981): 69-81.

Hosokawa, Bill. "When Seattle's Japanese Vanished." *Annals of the Chinese Historical Society of the Pacific Northwest* (1984): 90-94.

Hughes, C. Alvin. "Let Us Do Our Part: The New York City Based Negro Labor Victory Committee, 1941-1945." *Afro-Americans in New York Life and History* 10 (1986): 19-29.

————. "We Demand Our Rights: The Southern Negro Youth Congress, 1937-1949." *Phylon* 48 (1987): 38-50.

Ichioka, Yuji. "A Study in Dualism: James Yoshinori Sakamoto and the Japanese American Courier, 1928-1942." *Amerasia Journal* 13 (1986-1987): 49-81.

Inouye, Ronald K. "Harry Sotaro Kawabe: Issei Businessman of Seward and Seattle." *Alaska History* 5 (1990): 34-43.

Irons, Peter H. *Justice at War.* New York: Oxford University Press, 1983.

————. "Race and the Constitution: The Case of the Japanese American Interment." *This Constitution* 13 (1986): 18-26.

Jakeman, Robert J. *The Divided Skies: Establishing Segregated Flight Training at Tuskegee, Alabama, 1934-1942.* University: University of Alabama Press: 1992.

James, Thomas. "The Education of Japanese Americans at Tule Lake, 1942-1946." *Pacific Historical Review* 56 (1987): 25-58.

————. *Exile Within: The Schooling of Japanese Americans, 1942-1945.* Cambridge: Harvard University Press, 1987.

————. "Life Begins with Freedom: The College Nisei, 1942-1945." *History of Education Quarterly* 25 (1985): 155-74.

Johnson, Melyn. "At Home in Amache: A Japanese-American Relocation Camp in Colorado." *Colorado Heritage* 1 (1989): 2-11.

Kelly, Thomas O., II. "Race and Racism in the American World War II Film: The Negro, the Nazi, and the 'Jap' in *Bataan* and *Sahara.*" *Michigan Academician* 24 (1992): 571-83.

Kessler, Lauren. "Fettered Freedoms: The Journalism of World War II Japanese Internment Camps." *Journalism History* 15 (1988): 70-79.

Kranzler, David. *Thy Brother's Blood: The Orthodox Jewish Response during the Holocaust.* Brooklyn, NY: Mesorah, 1987.

Langlois, Janet L. "The Belle Isle Bridge Incident: Legend Dialectic and Semiotic Systems in the 1943 Detroit Race Riots." *Journal of American Folklore* 96 (1983): 183–99.

Lees, Lorraine. "National Security and Ethnicity: Contrasting Views during World War II." *Diplomatic History* 11 (1987): 114–25.

Leonard, Kevin Allen. "Is That What We Fought For? Japanese Americans and Racism in California: The Impact of World War II." *Western Historical Quarterly* 21 (1990): 463–82.

Linehan, Thomas M. "Japanese American Resettlement in Cleveland during and after World War II." *Journal of Urban History* 20 (1993): 54–80.

Lookstein, Haskell. *Were We Our Brother's Keepers? The Public Response of American Jews to the Holocaust, 1939–1944.* New York: Hartmore House, 1985.

Macmillan, Michael E. "Unwanted Allies: Koreans as Enemy Aliens in World War II." *Hawaiian Journal of History* 19 (1985): 179–203.

Madden, Ryan. "The Forgotten People: The Relocation and Internment of Aleuts during World War II." *American Indian Culture and Research Journal* 6 (1991): 55–76.

Mazon, Mauricio. *The Zoot Suit Riots: The Psychology of Symbolic Annihilation.* Austin: University of Texas Press, 1984.

McAfee, Ward M. "America's Two Japanese-American Policies during World War II." *Southern California Quarterly* 69 (1987): 151–64.

McGuire, Philip. "Desegregation of the Armed Forces: Black Leadership, Protest and World War II." *Journal of Negro History* 68 (1983): 147–58.

———. *He Too, Spoke for Democracy: Judge Hastie, World War II, and the Black Soldier.* Westport, CT: Greenwood Press, 1988.

———. *Taps for a Jim Crow Army.* Santa Barbara, CA: ABC-Clio Press, 1983.

Michael, Robert. "America and the Holocaust." *Midstream* 31 (1985): 13–16.

"Michigan Goes to War: Detroit's 1943 Race Riot." *Michigan History* 77 (1993): 34–39.

Modell, John, Marc Goulden, and Sigurder Magnusson. "World War II in the Lives of Black Americans: Some Findings and an Interpretation." *Journal of American History* 76 (1989): 838–48.

Mormino, Gary R. "GI Joe Meets Jim Crow: Racial Violence and Reform in World War II." *Florida Historical Quarterly* 73 (1994): 23–42.

Morse, Arthur D. *While Six Million Died: A Chronicle of American Apathy.* Woodstock, NY: Overlook Press, 1983.

Murray, Paul T. "Who Is an Indian? Who Is a Negro? Virginia Indians in the World War II Draft." *Virginia Magazine of History and Biography* 95 (1987): 215–31.

Nagata, Donna K. "The Japanese-American Internment: Perceptions of Moral Community, Fairness, and Redress." *Journal of Social Issues* 46 (1990): 133–46.

Nash, Philip Tajitsu. "A More Perfect Union: Japanese Americans and the Constitution." *Radical History Review* 45 (1989): 139–42.

Naske, Clause-M. "The Relocation of Alaska's Japanese Residents." *Pacific Northwest Quarterly* 74 (1983): 124–32.

Noel, Cynthia. "Camp Haan—Only Ghosts Remain." *Periodical: Journal of the Council on America's Military Past* 16 (1989): 14–23.

Okihiro, Gary Y. *Cane Fires: The Anti-Japanese Movement in Hawaii, 1865–1945.* Philadelphia: Temple University Press, 1991.

———. "The Press, Japanese Americans, and the Concentration Camps." *Phylon* 44 (1983): 66–83.

———. "Religion and Resistance in America's Concentration Camps." *Phylon* 45 (1984): 220–33.

Olinger, John C. "They Called It Camp Downey." *Idaho Yesterdays* 31 (1988): 15–23.

Olmstead, Timothy. "Nikkei Internment: The Perspective of Two Oregon Weekly Newspapers." *Oregon Historical Quarterly* 85 (1984): 5–32.

Orbach, Barbara, and Nicholas Natanson. "The Mirror Image: Black Washington in World War II-Era Federal Photography." *Washington History* 4 (1992): 4–25, 92–93.

O'Reilly, Kenneth. "The Roosevelt Administration and Black America: Federal Surveillance Policy and Civil Rights during the New Deal and World War II Years." *Phylon* 48 (1987): 12–25.

Panayi, Panikos. "National and Racial Minorities in Total War." *Immigrants & Minorities* 2 (1990): 178–94.

Phan, Peter. "Familiar Strangers: The Fourteenth Air Service Group Case Study of Chinese American Identity during World War II." In Colleen Fong, ed., *Chinese America: History and Perspectives, 1993* San Francisco: Chinese Historical Society of America, 1993, 75–107.

Phenix, William. "Eagles Unsung: The Tuskegee Airmen in World War II." *Michigan History* 71 (1987): 24–30.

Reed, Marl E. "Black Workers, Defense Industries, and Federal Agencies in Pennsylvania, 1941–1945." *Labor History* 27 (summer 1986): 356–84.

———. "The Nashville Convention of the Southern Conference for Human Welfare, 1942." *Alabama Review* 37 (1984): 52–59.

Reese, Joan. "Two Enemies to Fight: Blacks Battle for Equality in Two World Wars." *Colorado Heritage* 1 (1990): 2–17.

Russell, Andrew. "A Fortunate Few: Japanese Americans in Southern Nevada, 1905–1945." *Nevada Historical Society Quarterly* 31 (1988): 32–52.

Sawada, Mitziko. "After the Camps: Seabrook Farms, New Jersey, and the Resettlement of Japanese Americans, 1944–1947." *Amerasia Journal* 13 (1986–1987): 117–36.

Schonberger, Howard. "Dilemmas of Loyalty: Japanese Americans and the Psychological Warfare Campaigns of the Office of Strategic Services, 1943–1945." *Amerasia Journal* 16 (1990): 20–38.

Schwartz, Joel. "The Consolidated Tenants League of Harlem: Black Self-Help vs. White Liberal Intervention in Ghetto Housing, 1939-1944." *Afro-Americans in New York Life and History* 10 (1986): 31-51.

Schweik, Susan. "The Pre-Poetics of Internment: The Example of Toyo Suyemoto." *American Literary History* 1 (1989): 89-109.

Shapiro, Edward S. "World War II and American Jewish Identity." *Modern Judaism* 10 (1990): 65-84.

Sperling, Paul. "Jews of Early Los Alamos: A Memoir." *Western States Jewish History* 18 (1986): 355-61.

Spickard, Paul R. "Injustice Compounded: Amerasians and Non-Japanese Americans in World War II Concentration Camps." *Journal of American Ethnic History* 5 (1986): 5-22.

―――. "The Nisei Assume Power: The Japanese American Citizens League, 1941-1942." *Pacific Historical Review* 52 (1983): 147-74.

Spinney, Rob. "The Jewish Community in Nashville, 1939-1949." *Tennessee Historical Quarterly* 52 (1993): 225-41.

Strum, Harvey. "Fort Ontario Refugee Shelter, 1944-1946." *American Jewish History* 73 (1984): 398-421.

―――. "Jewish Internees in the American South, 1942-1945." *American Jewish Archives* 42 (1990): 27-48.

Sundquist, Eric J. "The Japanese-American Internment: A Reappraisal." *American Scholar* 57 (1988): 529-47.

Tamura, Linda. "The Hood River Issei: Oral History and the Japanese Settlement in Hood River, Oregon." *International Journal of Oral History* 9 (1988): 221-26.

Tateishi, John, ed. *And Justice for All: An Oral History of the Japanese-American Detention Camp.* New York: Random House, 1984.

Taylor, Sandra C. "The Federal Reserve Bank and the Relocation of the Japanese in 1942." *Public Historian* 5 (1983): 9-30.

―――. "Interned at Topaz: Age, Gender and Family in the Relocation Experience." *Utah Historical Quarterly* 59 (1991): 380-94.

―――. "Japanese Americans and Keetley Farms: Utah's Relocation Colony." *Utah Historical Quarterly* 54 (1986): 328-44.

―――. *Jewel of the Desert: Japanese American Internment at Topaz.* Berkeley: University of California Press, 1993.

―――. "Leaving the Concentration Camps: Japanese American Resettlement in Utah and the Intermountain West." *Pacific Historical Review* 60 (1991): 169-94.

Tobler, Douglas F. "The Jews, the Mormons, and the Holocaust." *Journal of Mormon History* 18 (1992): 59-92.

Toelken, Barre. "Cultural Maintenance and Ethnic Intensification in Two Japanese-American World War II Internment Camps." *Oriens Extremus* 33 (1990): 69-94.

Tucker, Barbara M. "Agricultural Workers in World War II: The Reserve Army of Children, Black Americans and Jamaicans." *Agricultural History* 68 (1994): 54–73.

Turner, Stanton B. "Japanese-American Internment at Tule Lake, 1942–1946." *Journal of the Shaw Historical Library* 2 (1987): 1–34.

Tyler, Bruce. "The Black Double V Campaign for Racial Democracy during World War II." *Journal of Kentucky Studies* 8 (1991): 79–108.

———. "Black Jive and White Repression." *Journal of Ethnic Studies* 16 (1989): 31–66.

"Uprooted: A Portfolio of Japanese-Americans in World War II." *Colorado Heritage* (1989): 12–27.

Venturini, Nadia. "Italian American Leadership, 1943–1948." *Storia Nordamericana* 2 (1985): 35–62.

Walter, John C. "Frank R. Crosswaith and Labor Unionization in Harlem, 1939–1945." *Afro-Americans in New York Life and History* 7 (1983): 47–58.

Washburn, Patrick S. "J. Edgar Hoover and the Black Press in World War II." *Journalism History* 13 (1986): 26–33.

———. "The Pittsburgh Courier and Black Workers in 1942." *Western Journal of Black Studies* 10 (1986): 109–18.

———. *A Question of Sedition: The Federal Government's Investigation of the Black Press during World War II.* New York: Oxford University Press, 1986.

———, and Mary Alice Sentman. "How Excess Profits Tax Brought Ads to a Black Newspaper in World War II." *Journalism History* 64 (1987): 769–74.

Wax, Rosalie H. "In and out of the Tule Lake Segregation Center: Japanese Internment in the West, 1942–1945." *Montana* 37 (1987): 12–25.

Woods, Randall Bennett. "Uprooted: A Portfolio of Japanese-Americans in World War II." *Colorado Heritage* 1 (1989): 12–27.

Wyman, David S. *The Abandonment of the Jews: America and the Holocaust, 1941–1945.* New York: Pantheon Books, 1984.

SOCIETY AND CULTURE

Allen, Ann. "The News Media and the Woman's Army Auxiliary Corps: Protagonists for a Cause." *Military Affairs* 50 (1986): 77–83.

Altherr, Thomas L. "'Mallards and Messerschmitts': American Hunting Magazines and the Image of American Hunting during World War II." *Journal of Sport History* 14 (1987): 151–63.

Barkin, Steve M. "Fighting the Cartoon War: Information Strategies in World War II." *Journal of American Culture* 7 (1984): 113–17.

Barnes, Kenneth C. "The Missouri Synod and Hitler's Germany." *Yearbook of German-American Studies* 24 (1989): 131–47.

Basinger, Jeanine. *The World War II Combat Film: Anatomy of a Genre.* New York: Columbia University Press, 1986.

Bérubé, Allan. *Coming Out Under Fire: The History of Gay Men and Women in World War Two.* New York: Free Press, 1990.

Blum, John Morton. "United Against: American Culture and Society during World War." *Harmon Memorial Lectures in Military History* 25 (1983): 1–12.

Bradbury, Malcolm. "American Literature and the Coming of World War II." *European Contributions to American Studies* 18 (1990): 8–21.

Broekel, Ray. "Land of the Candy Bar." *American Heritage* 37 (1986): 74–80.

Brown, Sheldon. "The Depression and World War II as Seen through Country Music." *Social Education* 49 (1985): 588–95.

Brown, William R. "The American Girl and the Christmas Tree: World War II Soldier Poets Look at What the G.I.s Were Fighting For." *Journal of American Culture* 8 (1985): 25–30.

Burch, Robert. *Homefront Heroes.* New York: Puffin, 1992.

Casdorph, Paul D. *Let the Good Times Roll: Life at Home in America during World War II.* New York: Paragon House, 1989.

Chibnall, Steve. "Whistle and Zoot: The Changing Meaning of a Suit of Clothes." *History Workshop Journal* 20 (1985): 56–81.

Cosgrove, Stuart. "The Zoot-Suit and Style Warfare." *Radical America* 18 (1984): 39–50.

Costello, John. *Virtue under Fire: How World War II Changed Our Social and Sexual Attitudes.* Boston: Little, Brown, 1985.

Cowdrey, Albert E. *Fighting for Life: American Military Medicine in World War II.* New York: Simon & Schuster, 1994.

Cripps, Thomas. "Movies, Race and World War II: *Tennessee Johnson* as an Anticipation of Strategies of the Civil Rights Movement." *Prologue* 14 (1982): 49–67.

Degler, Carl. "World War II in the History and Memory of Carl Degler." *History Teacher* 3 (1990): 319–33.

Dick, Bernard F. *The Star-Spangled Screen: The American World War II Film.* Lexington: University of Kentucky, 1985.

Dolan, Edward F. *America in World War II: 1943.* Brookfield, CT: Millbrook Press, 1992.

Duis, Perry R. "Soldiers without Guns." *Chicago History* 16 (1987–1988): 28–63.

Elder, Glen H., Jr. "Military Times and Turning Points in Men's Lives." *Developmental Psychology* 22 (1986): 233–45.

———. "War Mobilization and the Life Course: A Cohort of World War II Veterans." *Sociological Forum* 2 (1987): 449–73.

Erenberg, Lewis A. "Introduction: World War II and American Culture." *Mid–America* 75 (1994): 81–94.

Farmer, Patrick A. "Moss Hart and Winged Victory: The Mind of 1943 America." *Southern Speech Communication Journal* 49 (1984): 187–97.

Fox, Richard Wightman, ed. "A Round Table: The Living and Reliving of World War II." *Journal of American History* 77 (1990): 553–93.

Fussell, Paul. *Wartime: Understanding and Behavior in the Second World War.* New York: Oxford University Press, 1989.

Garrett, Betty. "A Date with a Bombing." *American Heritage* 42 (1991): 36–40.

Garza, Hedda. "Bring the Boys Home!" *American History Illustrated* 20 (1985): 36–41.

Gerber, David. "Anger and Affability: The Rise and Representation of a Repertory of Self-Presentation Skills in a World War II Disabled Veteran." *Journal of Social History* 27 (1993): 5–28.

German, Kathleen M. "Frank Capra's 'Why We Fight' Series and the American Audience." *Western Journal of Speech Communication* 54 (1990): 237–48.

Gleason, Philip. "Americans All: World War II and the Shaping of Identity." *Review of Politics* 43 (1981): 483–518.

———. "World War II and the Development of American Studies." *American Quarterly* 36 (1984): 343–58.

Graebner, William. "The Apple Boy: Individual and Community in the Era of the Second World War." *New York Folklore* 10 (1984): 77–87.

Greenberg, Gershon. "America's Catholics during the Holocaust." *Simon Wiesenthal Center Annual* 19 (1987): 39–70.

Gregory, Ross. *America 1941: A Nation at the Crossroads.* New York: Free Press, 1989.

Grob, Gerald N. "World War II and American Psychiatry." *Psychohistory Review* 19 (1990): 41–69.

Hammon, Stratton. "The Impact of World War II on a Citizen Soldier." *Filson Club History Quarterly* 59 (1985): 40–53.

Hanson, Sam. "The Making of a Newspaper Man: A Kaleidoscope of Memories from the World War II Era." *Rendezvous* 22 (1987): 57–71.

Harris, Jonathan, Franklin D. Mitchell, and Steven J. Schechter, eds. *The Homefront: America during World War II.* New York: Putnam's, 1984.

Hoddeson, Lillian. "The Discovery of Spontaneous Fission in Plutonium during World War II." *Historical Studies in the Physical and Biological Sciences* 23 (1993): 279–300.

Holsinger, M. Paul, and Mary Anne Schofield, eds. *Visions of War: World War II in Popular Literature and Culture.* Bowling Green: Bowling Green State University Press, 1992.

Houston, Jeanne W., and James D. Houston. "No More Farewells: An Interview with Jeanne and James Houston." Interviewed by Anthony Friedson. *Biography* 7 (1984): 50–73.

"Inspired by Design: World War II Posters and the Virginia Home Front." *Virginia Cavalcade* 37 (1987): 68–73.

Jaunal, Jack W. "Those War Films—Fact, Fiction, Impact." *Periodical: Journal of the Council on America's Military Past* 16 (1989): 24–35.

Jones, David Lloyd. "Measuring and Mobilizing the Media, 1939–1945." *Midwest Quarterly* 26 (1984): 35–43.

Kay, Lily E. "Selling Pure Science in Wartime: The Biochemical Genetics of G. W. Beadle." *Journal of the History of Biology* 22 (1989): 73–101.

Kee, Robert. *The World We Fought For*. Boston: Little, Brown, 1985.

Keefer, Louis E. "Exceptional Young Americans: Soldiers and Sailors on College Campuses in World War II." *Prologue* 24 (1992): 375–83.

Kennett, Lee. *For the Duration: The U. S. Goes to War, Pearl Harbor–1942*. New York: Scribner's, 1985.

Ketchum, Richard M. *The Borrowed Years, 1938–1941: America on the Way to War*. New York: Random House, 1989.

Kidwell, Peggy. "Harvard Astronomers in the Second World War." *Journal for the History of Astronomy* 21 (1990): 105–6.

Klingaman, William K. *1941: Our Lives in a World on the Edge*. New York: Harper and Row, 1988.

Koppes, Clayton R., and Gregory D. Black. "Blacks, Loyalty and Motion Picture Propaganda in World War II." *Journal of American History* 73 (1986): 383–406.

———. *Hollywood Goes to War: How Politics, Profits and Propaganda Shaped World War II Movies*. New York: Free Press, 1987.

Kornweibel, Theodore, Jr. "Humphrey Bogart's *Sahara*: Propaganda, Cinema and the American Character in World War II." *American Studies* 22 (1981): 5–19.

Kozloff, Max. "Photographers at War." *Art in America* 73 (1985): 74–83.

Leiter, Samuel L. "Theater on the Home Front: World War II on New York's Stages, 1941–1945." *Journal of American Drama and Theatre* 5 (1993): 47–85.

Leslie, Paul, and James K. Skipper. "Big Bands and Big Band Music: Embedded Popular Culture." *Popular Music and Society* 17 (1993): 23–36.

Lincove, David A. "Activists for Internationalism: ALA Responds to World War II and British Requests for Aid, 1939–1941." *Libraries & Culture* 26 (1991): 487–510.

Lochtin, Roger W., ed. *The Martial Metropolis: U.S. Cities in War and Peace*. New York: Praeger, 1984.

Lott, Eric. "Double V, Double Time: Bebop's Politics of Style." *Callaloo* 11 (1988): 597–605.

Lundberg, David. "The American Literature of War: The Civil War, World War I, and World War II." *American Quarterly* 36 (1984): 373–88.

Mabee, Carlton. "Margaret Mead and Behavioral Scientists in World War II: Problems of Responsibility, Truth, and Effectiveness." *Journal of the History of the Behavioral Sciences* 23 (1987): 3–13.

Maslowski, Peter. *Armed with Cameras: The American Military Photographers of World War II*. New York: Maxwell Macmillan International, 1993.

McClintock, William R. "Clio Mobilizes: Naval Reserve Historians during the Second World War." *Public Historian* 13 (1991): 25–46.

McMillan, James E. "McFarland and the Movies: The 1941 Senate Motion Picture Hearings." *Journal of Arizona History* 29 (1988): 277–302.

Miner, Curtis, ed. "'Hi Butch': The World II Letters of Everett Johns." *Pittsburgh History* 72 (1989): 178–91.

Modell, John, and Duane Steffey. "Waging War and Marriage: Military Service and Family Formation 1940–1950." *Journal of Family History* 13 (1988): 195–218.

Molson, Francis J. "Film, Funnies and Fighting the War: Whitman's Children's Books in the 1940s." *Journal of Popular Culture* 17 (1984): 147–54.

Montgomery, M. R. *Saying Goodbye: A Memoir for Two Fathers*. New York: Knopf, 1989.

Nagy, Alex. "Word Wars at Home: U.S. Response to World War II Propaganda." *Journalism Quarterly* 67 (1990): 207–13.

Parrish, Robert. "Fact Meets Fiction in a World War II Celluloid Face-Off." *Smithsonian* 16 (1986): 164–68.

Pavalko, Eliza, and Glen Elder. "WWII and Divorce: A Life-Course Perspective." *American Journal of Sociology* 95 (1990): 1213–34.

Polan, Dana B. *Power and Paranoia: History, Narrative, and the American Cinema, 1940–1950*. New York: Columbia University Press, 1986.

Polenberg, Richard, ed. "The Good War? A Reappraisal of How World War II Affected American Society." *Virginia Magazine of History and Biography* 100 (1992): 295–322.

———. *War and Society: The United States, 1941–1945*. Philadelphia: J. B. Lippincott, 1972.

Rider, Mary M. "Images of Propaganda: World War I and World War II Posters." *Queen City Heritage* 41 (1983): 31–36.

Roeder, George H., Jr. *The Censored War: American Visual Experience during World War II*. New Haven, CT: Yale University Press, 1993.

———. "Censoring Disorder: American Visual Imagery of World War Two." *Mid-America* 75 (1993): 245–68.

———. "A Note on U.S. Photo Censorship in WW II." *Historical Journal of Film, Radio and Television* 5 (1985): 191–98.

Rooker, Oliver E. "Supplying the Civilians: A Photo Essay of World War II Ration Stamps." *Chronicles of Oklahoma* 69 (1991–1992): 430–41.

Saunders, Paul H. "My Most Valued Christmas Gift: A World War II Reminiscence." *Utah Historical Quarterly* 59 (1991): 361–64.

Schneider, James G. *The Navy V-12 Program: Leadership for a Lifetime*. Boston: Houghton Mifflin, 1987.

Segal, David R. *Recruiting for Uncle Sam: Citizenship and Military Manpower Policy*. Lawrence: University of Kansas Press, 1989.

Short, K.R.M., ed. *Film and Radio Propaganda in World War II*. London: Croom Helm, 1983.

———. "Washington's Information Manual for Hollywood, 1942." *Historical Journal of Film, Radio and Television* 3 (1983): 171–80.

Shulman, Holly C. *The Voice of America: Propaganda and Democracy, 1941–1945*. Madison: University of Wisconsin Press, 1990.

Siegel, Marcia B. "American Dance and World War II." *Southern Humanities Review* 27 (1993): 219–30.

Sloan, Charles William, Jr., ed. "The Newelletters: E. Gail Carpenter Describes Life on the Home Front." *Kansas History* 11 (1988): 54–72, 123–42, 150–70, 243–59.

Sorel, Edward. "Casablanca." *American Heritage* 42 (1991): 92–98.

Steele, Richard W. "News of the 'Good War': World War II News Management." *Journalism Quarterly* 62 (1985): 707–76.

———. "'No Radicals': Discrimination Against Ethnics in American Defense Industry, 1940–1942." *Labor History* 32 (1991): 66–90.

———. *Propaganda in an Open Society: The Roosevelt Administration and the Media*. Westport, CT: Greenwood Press, 1985.

Stoler, Mark A. "U.S. Civil-Military Relations in World War II." *Parameters* 21 (1991): 35–50.

Stout, Robert Joe. "Lend Him a Hand!" *Southwest Review* 69 (1984): 262–64.

Taylor, Barbara Wooddall, and Charles E. Taylor. *Miss You: The World War II Letters of Barbara Wooddall Taylor and Charles E. Taylor*. Edited by Judy Barrett Litoff and David C. Smith. Athens: University of Georgia Press, 1990.

Terkel, Studs. *"The Good War": An Oral History of World War Two*. New York: Pantheon Books, 1984.

Tuttle, William M. *Daddy's Gone to War: The Second World War in the Lives of America's Children*. New York: Oxford University Press, 1993.

Voss, Frederick S. *Reporting the War: The Journalistic Coverage of World War II*. Washington, DC: Smithsonian Institution, 1994.

Westbrook, Brett. "Fighting for What's Good: Strategies of Propaganda in Lillian Hellman's 'Negro Picture' and *The North Star*." *Film History* 4 (1990): 165–78.

Westbrook, Robert B. "'I Want a Girl Just like the Girl That Married Harry James': American Women and the Problem of Political Obligation in World War II." *American Quarterly* 42 (1990): 587–614.

Winkler, Allan M. *Homefront U.S.A.: America during World War II*. Arlington Heights, IL: Harlan Davidson, 1986.

Winks, Robin. *Cloak and Gown: Scholars in the Secret War, 1939–1961*. New York: Quill, 1988.

Yarrington, Gary. "World War II: Personal Accounts—Pearl Harbor to V-J Day." *Prologue* 25 (1993): 78–87.

Zimmerman, Robert W. "How We Won the War (with Tools Commonly Found in the Shop): The Model Aircraft Project." *Journal of American Culture* 8 (1985): 51–58.

WOMEN

Aldrich, Mark. "The Gender Gap in Earnings during World War II: New Evidence." *Industrial and Labor Relations Review* 42 (1989): 415–29.

Allen, Susan L. "Preparing Women for the National Crisis: The Role of Oklahoma A. and M. College." *Chronicles of Oklahoma* 69 (1991–1992): 392–407.

Anderson, Karen. "Last Hired, First Fired: The Black Women Workers during World War II." *Journal of American History* 69 (1982): 82–97.

———. *Wartime Women: Sex Roles, Family Relations, and the Status of Women during World War II.* Westport, CT: Greenwood Press, 1981.

Babb, Ellen J. "Women and War: St. Petersberg Women during World War II." *Florida Historical Quarterly* 73 (1994): 43–61.

Bailey, Beth, and David Farber. "Hotel Street: Prostitution and the Politics of War." *Radical History Review* 52 (1992): 54–77.

Blicksilver, Edith. "The Japanese-American Woman, the Second World War, and the Relocation Camp Experience." *Women's Studies International Forum* 5 (1982): 351–53.

Campbell, D'Ann. *Women at War with America: Private Lives in a Patriotic Era.* Cambridge: Harvard University Press, 1984.

Campbell, Julie A. "Madres y Esposas: Tucson's Spanish-American Mothers and Wives Association." *Journal of Arizona History* 31 (1990): 161–82.

Capshew, James H., and Alejandra C. Laszlo. "'We Would Not Take No for an Answer': Women Psychologists and Gender Politics during World War II." *Journal of Social Issues* 42 (1986): 157–80.

Chafe, William H. "American Women during World War II." *European Contributions to American Studies* 18 (1990): 183–93.

Danker, Anita. "Government Policy and Women in the Workplace through Depression and War." *New England Journal of History* 45 (1988): 16–38.

Diamond, Jared. "War Babies: What Happens When Mothers-to-be Become Victims of Starvation?" *Discover* 11 (1990): 70–76.

Enloe, Cynthia. *Does Khaki Become You?: The Militarization of Women's Lives.* Boston: South End Press, 1983.

Forestell, Diane G. "The Necessity of Sacrifice for the Nation at War: Women's Labor Force Participation, 1939–1946." *Social History* 22 (1989): 333–48.

Fox-Genovese, Elizabeth. "Mixed Messages: Women and the Impact of World War II." *Southern Humanities Review* 27 (1993): 235–45.

Frank, Miriam. *The Life and Times of Rosie the Riveter: The Story of Three Million Working Women during World War II*. Emeryville, CA: Clarity Education Productions, 1982.

————, Marilyn Ziebarth, and Connie Field. "Rosie the Riveter." *Society* 21 (1984): 75–78.

Gabin, Nancy Felice. *Feminism in the Labor Movement: Women and the United Auto Workers. 1935–1975*. Ithaca: Cornell University Press, 1990.

————. "Women and the United Automobile Workers in the 1940s and 1950s: Reconstructing Their Story." *Labor's Heritage* 1 (1989): 56–67.

Gluck, Sherna Berger. *Rosie the Riveter Revisited: Women, the War, and Social Change*. Boston: Twayne, 1987; New York: New American Library, 1988.

————. "What Did 'Rosie' Really Think? Continuity, Change and Subjective Experience: Lessons from Oral History." *Southwest Economy & Society Newsletter* 6 (1983): 56–68.

Goldin, Claudia D. "The Role of World War II in the Rise of Women's Employment." *American Economic Review* 81 (1991): 741–56.

Harris, Jonathan, Franklin D. Mitchell, and Steven J. Schechter. "Rosie the Riveter Remembers." *American Heritage* 35 (1984): 94–103.

Harrison, Patricia G. "Riveters, Volunteers and WACs: Women in Mobile during World War II." *Gulf Coast Historical Review* 1 (1986): 33–54.

Hartmann, Susan M. *The Home Front and Beyond: American Women in the 1940's*. Boston: Twayne, 1982.

Heacock, Nan. *Battle Stations!: The Homefront World War II*. Ames: Iowa State University Press, 1992.

Higgonet, Margaret Randolph, Jane Jenson, Sonya Michel, and Margaret Collins Weitz, eds. *Behind the Lines: Gender and the Two World Wars*. New Haven, CT: Yale University Press, 1987.

Honey, Maureen. *Creating Rosie the Riveter: Class, Gender, and Propaganda during World War II*. Amherst: University of Massachusetts Press, 1984.

————. "New Rules for Women and the Feminine Mystique: Popular Fiction of the 1940s." *Journal of American Studies* 24 (1983): 37–51.

————. "The Working Class Woman and Recruitment Propaganda during World War II: Class Differences in the Portrayal of War Work." *Signs* 8 (1983): 672–87.

Huron, Amanda. "A Temporary Glory: Women's Involvement in the Second World War." *Concord Review* 2 (1990): 1–12.

Kesselman, Amy V. *Fleeting Opportunities: Women Shipyard Workers in Portland and Vancouver during World War II and Reconversion*. Albany: State University of New York Press, 1990.

————, Tina Tau, and Karen Wickre. "Good Work Sister! The Making of an Oral History Production." *Frontiers* 7 (1983): 64–70.

Kessler-Harris, Alice. "Rosie the Riveter: Who Was She?" *Labor History* 24 (1983): 249–53.

Kochendoerfer, Violet A. *One Woman's World War II.* Lexington: University of Kentucky Press, 1994.

Koehler, Pat. "Reminiscence: The Women Shipbuilders of World War II." *Oregon Historical Quarterly* 91 (1990): 285–91.

Kossoudji, Sherrie A., and Laura J. Dresser. "The End of a Riveting Experience: Occupational Shifts at Ford after World War II." *American Economic Review* 82 (1992): 519–25.

———. "Working Class Rosies: Women Industrial Workers during World War II." *Journal of Economic History* 52 (1992): 431–36.

Litoff, Judy Barrett, and David C. Smith, eds. *"Dear Boys": World War II Letters from a Woman Back Home.* Jackson: University Press of Mississippi, 1991.

———. "'I Wish That I Could Hide inside This Letter': World War II Correspondence." *Prologue* 24 (1992): 103–14.

———. *"Since You Went Away": World War II Letters from American Women on the Home Front.* New York: Oxford University Press, 1991.

———. "'To the Rescue of the Crops': The Women's Land Army during World War II." *Prologue* 25 (1993): 347–62.

———. "'Will He Get My Letter?' Popular Portrayals of Mail and Morale during World War II." *Journal of Popular Culture* 23 (1990): 21–43.

———. "'Writing Is Fighting Too': The World War II Correspondence of Southern Women." *Georgia Historical Quarterly* 76 (1992): 436–57.

Manley, Kathleen E. B. "Women of Los Alamos during World War II: Some of Their Views." *New Mexico Historical Review* 65 (1990): 251–66.

Matsumoto, Valerie. "Japanese American Women during World War." *Frontiers* 8 (1984): 6–14.

May, Elaine Tyler. "Rosie the Riveter Gets Married." *Mid-America* 75 (1993): 269–82.

McArthur, Judith N. "From Rosie the Riveter to the Feminine Mystique: An Historiographical Survey of American Women and World War II." *Bulletin of Bibliography* 44 (1987): 10–18.

Meyer, Leisa D. "Creating G. I. Jane: The Regulation of Sexuality and Sexual Behavior in the Women's Army Corps during World War II." *Feminist Studies* 18 (1992): 581–601.

Milkman, Ruth. *Gender at Work: The Dynamics of Job Segregation by Sex during World War II.* Urbana: University of Illinois Press, 1987.

Miller, Marc. "Working Women and WWII." *New England Quarterly* 53 (1980): 42–61.

Nash, Michael. "Women and the Pennsylvania Railroad: The World War II Years." *Labor History* 30 (1989): 608–21.

Noble, Antonette Chambers. "Utah's Rosies: Women in the Utah War Industries during World War II." *Utah Historical Quarterly* 59 (1991): 123–45.

Noggle, Anne. "Return of the WASPS." *Air and Space/Smithsonian* 5 (1990): 82–87.

Obermayr, Lorna. "I Was a Welder in World War II." *Rendezvous* 22 (1987): 83–85.

Ohmer, Susan. "Female Spectatorship and Women's Magazines: Hollywood, *Good Housekeeping* and World War II." *Velvet Light Trap* 25 (1990): 53–68.

Pederson, Sharon. "Married Women and the Right to Teach in St. Louis, 1941–1948." *Missouri Historical Review* 81 (1987): 141–58.

Pollard, Clarice F. "WAACs in Texas during the Second World War." Southwestern Historical Quarterly 93 (1989): 61–74.

Riley, Susan E. "Caring for Rosie's Children: Federal Child Care Policies in the World War II Era." *Polity* 26 (1994): 655–75.

Santillán, Richard. "Rosita the Riveter: Midwest Mexican-American Women during World War II, 1941–1945." *Perspectives in Mexican American Studies* 2 (1989): 115–47.

Schweik, Susan. "Writing War Poetry like a Woman." *Critical Inquiry* 13 (1987): 532–56.

Scibetta, Barbara, and Elfrieda Shukert. *The War Brides of World War II.* Novato, CA: Presidio Press, 1988.

Sherman, Janann. "'They Either Need These Women or They Do Not': Margaret Chase Smith and the Fight for Regular Status for Women in the Military." *Journal of Military History* 54 (1990): 47–78.

Short, K.R.M. *"That Hamilton Woman (1941)*: Propaganda, Feminism and the Production Code." *Historical Journal of Film, Radio and Television* 11 (1991): 3–19.

Smith, Caron. "The Women's Land Army during World War II." *Kansas History* 14 (1991): 82–88.

Thomas, Mary Martha. "Alabama Women on the Home Front: WWII." *Alabama Heritage* 19 (1991): 2–23.

———. "The Mobile Homefront during the Second World War." *Gulf Coast Historical Quarterly* 1 (1986): 55–75.

———. *Riveting and Rationing in Dixie: Alabama Women and the Second World War.* Tuscaloosa: University of Alabama Press, 1987.

Wagner, Lilya. *Women War Correspondents of World War II.* New York: Greenwood Press, 1989.

Walsh, Andrea S. *Women's Films and Female Experience: 1940–1950.* New York: Praeger, 1984.

Wasserstein, Bernard. "Women Psychologists and Gender Politics during World War II." *Journal of Social Issues* 42 (1986): 157–89.

Weatherford, Doris. *American Women and World War II.* New York: Facts on File, 1990.

Wilson, Jane S., and Charlotte Serber, eds. *Standing By, and Making Do: Women of Wartime Los Alamos.* Los Alamos, NM: Los Alamos Historical Society, 1988.

Index

About the Editors and Contributors

William C. Beyer teaches American Studies and serves as Coordinator of the Premajor Advising Service at the University of Minnesota. He is the author of numerous articles on Louis Adamic and midwestern literary culture in the early twentieth century.

Roger Daniels is the Charles Phelps Taft Professor of History at the University of Cincinnati. He is among the nation's foremost historians of immigration and was one of the first scholars to examine carefully the history of the Japanese-American internment during the war. His most recent work on that subject is *Prisoners Without Trial*.

Nancy Felice Gabin is an Associate Professor at Purdue University where she also directs the graduate program in history. In the past decade, she has published articles that focus on various aspects of the experiences of modern America's working women. In 1991, *The Politics of Gender* was published by Cornell University Press.

Maureen Honey is Professor of American Studies at the University of Nebraska, Lincoln. She has published widely on women in twentieth century America, including her ground-breaking book, *Creating Rosie the Riveter*. Her most recent study is *Breaking the Ties that Bind*.

Clayton R. Koppes has held the Irvin E. Houck Professorship in the Humanities at Oberlin College since 1986. He has published extensively on modern American culture and society, with interests ranging from Hollywood to environmental history. In 1988, he co-authored *Hollywood Goes to War*.

John Modell is Professor of History at Carnegie-Mellon University. Professor Modell has published an extensive number of articles and books about modern American society, with his subjects ranging from men in the military to Japanese

American small businesses. Among his most recent works is *Into One's Own*, a study of youth in modern America.

Kenneth Paul O'Brien is Associate Professor of History at SUNY, College at Brockport. He has also served as Monroe County Historian since 1989, and in 1992, he supervised the production of the exhibit, "The War Comes Home: Monroe County and the Second World War." Currently, he and a co-author are working on an article on women and work in Monroe County during the war.

Lynn Hudson Parsons is Professor of History at SUNY, College at Brockport. Although a scholar of early nineteenth century American political culture, particularly the career of John Quincy Adams, he turned his interests to more recent decades and served as Project Director of "Lest We Forget," the NEH-funded Public Humanities Program from which the articles in this collection were produced.

Richard Polenberg is the Goldwin Smith Professor of American History at Cornell University. Author of *War and Society*, he is recognized as one of the leading historians of the modern government and law. His book, *Fighting Faiths*, won the Silver Gavel Award from the American Bar Association.

George E. Pozzetta was Professor of History at the University of Florida, Gainesville. A prolific and insightful scholar of America's immigrant communities, Professor Pozzetta died unexpectedly in 1994.

Janann Sherman is Assistant Professor of History at Memphis University. Author of several recently published articles on the early career of Margaret Chase Smith, she is now completing a book-length biography of that distinctive Senator from Maine, which should be published next year.

ISBN 0-313-29211-6

9 780313 292118

HARDCOVER BAR CODE